CONFLICT ZONE, COMFORT ZONE

STUDIES IN CONFLICT, JUSTICE, AND SOCIAL CHANGE
Series Editors: Susan F. Hirsch and Agnieszka Paczyńska

This series is funded in part through the generous support of the
School for Conflict Analysis and Resolution at George Mason University.

Susan F. Hirsch and E. Franklin Dukes, *Mountaintop Mining in Appalachia: Understanding Stakeholders and Change in Environmental Conflict*

David Rawson, *Prelude to Genocide: Arusha, Rwanda, and the Failure of Diplomacy*

Agnieszka Paczyńska and Susan F. Hirsch, eds., *Conflict Zone, Comfort Zone: Ethics, Pedagogy, and Effecting Change in Field-Based Courses*

CONFLICT ZONE, COMFORT ZONE

Ethics, Pedagogy, and Effecting Change
in Field-Based Courses

EDITED BY AGNIESZKA PACZYŃSKA AND SUSAN F. HIRSCH

OHIO UNIVERSITY PRESS, ATHENS

Ohio University Press, Athens, Ohio 45701
ohioswallow.com
© 2019 by Ohio University Press
All rights reserved

Front cover images:
(*top*) Olive Tree Initiative student trip to the Middle East
Photo by Daniel Wehrenfennig

(*bottom*) Students walking the disputed property boundary
during GMU field-based course in Liberia
Photo by Agnieszka Paczyńska

To obtain permission to quote, reprint, or otherwise reproduce or distribute material from Ohio University Press publications, please contact our rights and permissions department at (740) 593-1154 or (740) 593-4536 (fax).

Printed in the United States of America
Ohio University Press books are printed on acid-free paper ♾ ™

29 28 27 26 25 24 23 22 21 20 19   5 4 3 2 1

HARDCOVER ISBN · 978-0-8214-2344-8
PAPERBACK ISBN · 978-0-8214-2345-5
ELECTRONIC ISBN · 978-0-8214-4652-2

Library of Congress Cataloging-in-Publication Data available upon request.

CONTENTS

Acknowledgments   vii

Introduction
    The Benefits and Challenges of Field-Based Courses in Conflict Zones
    Agnieszka Paczyńska and Susan F. Hirsch   1

PART ONE: CONSIDERING ETHICS

one   Ethics and Field-Based Courses
       How to Prepare Students for the Challenges of Practice
       Susan F. Hirsch and Agnieszka Paczyńska   21

two   Framing "Experience" in International Field-Based Learning
       Leslie Dwyer and Alison Castel   41

three   Field-Based Courses as Transformative Education
       The Role of Practical Ethics as a Framework
       Pushpa Iyer   64

PART TWO: IMPROVING PEDAGOGY

four   Developing Leaders through Innovative Education
       The Olive Tree Initiative's Experiential Learning Approach to Teaching about Intractable Conflicts
       Daniel R. Brunstetter and Daniel Wehrenfennig   85

five   Windows and Mirrors in the Wall
       Experiential Learning in Northern Ireland
       Jennifer M. Ramos   104

Contents

six The Use of Service Learning in Teaching about Conflict
   Allyson M. Lowe and Sandi DiMola   119

seven Field-Based Service Learning Pedagogy and Its Effects
   Patricia A. Maulden and Lisa Elaine Shaw   138

PART THREE: EFFECTING CHANGE

eight Making Change Makers
   Integrating Service Learning into NGO Management Courses
   Maryam Z. Deloffre   159

nine When Context and Pretext Collide
   Reflective Practice as an Ethical Framework for Field-Based Learning
   Gina M. Cerasani and rj nickels   180

ten Cultivating Transformation in Field-Based Courses
   Alexander Cromwell   199

eleven To Hell and Back with Good Intentions
   Global Service Learning in the Shadow of Ivan Illich
   Anthony C. Ogden and Eric Hartman   221

Conclusion
   Best Practices and Next Directions
   Susan F. Hirsch and Agnieszka Paczyńska   242

References   257
Contributors   271
Index   277

ACKNOWLEDGMENTS

In 2010, we were thrilled to receive generous financial support from the US Department of Education's Fund for Improvement of Post-Secondary Education (FIPSE) to pursue a research project on experiential learning in the conflict field, which we called Linking Theory to Practice. Our project also benefited from funding through the Point of View Academic Committee of the School for Conflict Analysis and Resolution (S-CAR) at George Mason University.

This volume is one of the products of what became a multifaceted initiative that, over eight years, involved dozens of people to whom we are grateful. We would like to thank our colleagues and friends at George Mason University, especially S-CAR dean Kevin Avruch (and Dean Andrea Bartoli before him), for their support, and Patricia Maulden, Lisa Shaw, and Mara Schoeny, who were with us every step of the way, contributing in multiple ways to the project. Arthur Romano and Leslie Dwyer brought their significant experience with field-based courses to the project at crucial moments. Ned Lazarus and Andria Wisler were, respectively, the inside and outside experts on evaluation for the project. Associate Dean Julie Shedd has provided welcome advice at many junctures.

We want to thank the many former and current undergraduate and graduate students who worked on the project: Rochelle Arms, Alison Castel, Erica Brosnihan, Gina Cerasani, Alexander Cromwell, William David, Habtamu T. Dugo, Ethan Finley, Philip Gamaghelyan, Thanos Gatsias, Kwaw G. de Graft-Johnson, Matthew Graville, Shinae Hong, Samuel W.

Acknowledgments

Johnson, Vandy Kanyako, Linda Keuntje, Mariam Kurtz, Nathaneal Lash, Montserrat Lopez, Amani Mansour, Gul Mescioglu Gur, Mindy Matthews, Julie Minde, Kristin Moriarty, Yasmina Mrabet, Martha Mutisi, Dhirendra Nalbo, Cynthia Nassif, Sixte Vigny Nimuraba, Erika Roberts, Mery Rodriguez, Sarah Rose-Jensen, Alexandra Schaerrer, Lori-Ann Stephenson, Molly Tepper, and Ted Thompson.

Our project would not have succeeded without the efforts of our school's staff. We are grateful to Brydin Banning, Barbara Breckenridge, Jay Moon, Sigrid Nuckolls, Jeremy Peizer, Paul Snodgrass, and Elizabeth A. Thompson.

We thank Terrence Lyons and Michael Sullivan for supporting the project in many ways over the years.

We would like to thank the contributors to this volume. Your willingness to engage with us in workshops, conferences, discussions, and the long process of writing and editing is much appreciated. The book is richer for the range of perspectives that you represent. We thank Michael English for creating a superb index.

We would also like to thank everyone at Ohio University Press and especially Gillian Berchowitz and Rick Huard for their enthusiasm for this project and guidance through the editing and publication process. And many thanks to Nancy Basmajian and Don McKeon for the help with final preparation of the manuscript for publication.

Finally, we thank each other; it has been great fun to work together on the project and on this book.

Introduction

The Benefits and Challenges of Field-Based Courses in Conflict Zones

AGNIESZKA PACZYŃSKA AND SUSAN F. HIRSCH

This edited volume showcases new approaches to field-based learning in the most difficult of places: conflict zones in the United States and abroad. Increasingly, and for good reason, postsecondary education incorporates experiential learning options, such as service learning, study-abroad, and other field-based courses. Whether in domestic or international contexts, such courses engage students more directly in comparison to classroom-based learning, as they offer the opportunity to apply theory to practice in real-life settings. Instructors appreciate the educational value of experiential courses yet acknowledge that certain requirements for teaching in field settings—for example, using innovative pedagogy and addressing ethical predicaments—pose challenges to even the most seasoned instructor.

For both instructors and students, the challenges deepen when "the field" for a field-based course is a site of active or recent conflict. The chapters in this volume illustrate how the challenges of field-based classes are magnified in conflict and postconflict contexts, where students can experience the complexity of conflict, and the dilemmas faced by those seeking to resolve it, in ways not possible in the classroom. Such conflict zones can be found in a variety of settings: in community meetings in Pittsburgh where working-class, long-term residents of German and Eastern European descent experience strained relationships with newly arrived Somali refugees; in West Virginia mining towns where tensions run high as residents debate the effects of mountaintop mining on employment and the environment; in the streets of Jerusalem and Bil'in in the West Bank where Israelis and Palestinians contest over land, political power, and historical narratives; and in Tubmanburg, Liberia, where relatives fight over the demarcation of boundaries between their farms. Field-based courses in such settings allow students to encounter the dynamics of conflict in ways that are difficult, if not impossible, to replicate in the traditional classroom. By engaging students both intellectually and emotionally, they provide unique opportunities for linking theory to practice and also for self-reflection and thus give students a deeper understanding of the complexities of conflict and the challenges of working with people who are experiencing conflict.

By taking students out of their comfort zone, field-based courses have the potential to be learning experiences that some might call "transformative"—learning that changes a student's outlook or aims as much as it adds to their knowledge base. What do we mean by "comfort zone"? We are all familiar with the glib use of the phrase to demarcate the experiences with which one feels comfortable as compared with those one finds disturbing. Asserting that some practice or experience is out of one's comfort zone conveys a self-protective urge to keep unfamiliar experiences at bay or at least under control, and such assertions are increasingly common. Yet, at the same time, protecting the boundaries of one's comfort is an agentive act that many people across the world lack the power and position to undertake. People living in conflict zones have daily experiences of the violation of their comfort to the extent that the notion of a comfort zone may have become nonexistent for them. For many students, the desire to disrupt their own comfort zones is an aspect of the decision to enroll in a field-based course. What they seek is a challenging experience. In this volume, we examine the link between transporting students out of their comfort zones and guiding them toward deep, meaningful learning. We do so mindful of the many ethical questions raised by choosing to teach and learn outside our comfort zones, even when we consent to have our comfort disrupted. As the chapters demonstrate, instructors, too, must leave the comfort zone of traditional pedagogy and of their own lifestyles to meet the challenges of field-based education, especially when it takes place in conflict zones. Does the learning achieved justify the risk of operating outside one's comfort zone and thus encountering thorny logistical and ethical challenges? We argue that it does but that instructors and students need explicit, careful preparation to ensure that they can meet the challenges and, in some instances, turn them into learning opportunities.

The volume offers an analysis and critique of key issues in field-based learning in conflict zones along with detailed descriptions of this type of learning in action. Taken together, the chapters are intended to (1) emphasize the value of field-based courses for conflict studies and related fields, (2) highlight rich, case-based examples of field-based learning in and about conflict zones, (3) describe and analyze the challenges of such courses, especially when they take place in conflict zones, (4) identify best practices that will assist aspiring instructors in developing successful field-based courses for delivery in conflict zones, and (5) stimulate scholarly conversations about field-based learning in conflict zones, especially among instructors in the conflict studies and related fields to whom the book series is directed.

In the section that follows, we acknowledge the growth in experiential learning options in higher education and highlight our own efforts to help foster attention to experiential learning for the conflict field specifically. Our discussion considers the question of why faculty might undertake field-based courses in and about conflict zones and, consequently, what their needs might be. The next three sections then address the three interrelated themes that serve as the organizational framework for the volume: considering ethics, improving pedagogy, and effecting change. We end this introductory chapter by highlighting several best practices for field-based courses in conflict zones.

The Rising Interest in Field-Based Courses

In the last decade, US experts who focus on reforming higher education have embraced "high-impact" forms of learning and teaching. Often requiring labor-intensive instruction, these experiences can include inquiry- and project-based activities, service learning, and global learning (Kuh 2008; see also Brownell and Swaner 2010). One or two high-impact experiences can improve a student's likelihood of finishing a degree and doing so successfully (Kuh 2008). Whether as part of a reform initiative or as a response to student demand, field-based courses are on the rise in American higher education, especially study-abroad options. The benefits associated with field-based courses provide a wide range of reasons for their proliferation. Increasing globalization has made study-abroad options more relevant to a student's future career, more affordable, and more logistically viable (Altbach and Knight 2007). Service learning is similarly viewed as contributing positively to future career prospects. Depending on where it is sited, service learning projects can help blur the town/gown lines that can threaten to isolate institutions of learning or can offer students an experience in a very different context. These types of experiential learning options—highly valued because students develop learning skills outside the classroom—become part of the "package" that students evaluate when they select a school and are thus developed in part to achieve an advantage in a competitive market (see Dwyer and Castel, this volume). We acknowledge that courses are prime selling points in the increasing tendency to commodify all aspects of student learning, yet they also offer some admirable opportunities to students who learn to think on their feet, to apply theoretical knowledge to real-life endeavors, and to wrestle with the ethical dilemmas of acting in a complex world.

The many varieties of field-based education are linked to the broader pedagogical approach called experiential learning, which also takes a very wide range of forms. Without getting into a discussion of how to define experiential learning, over which there is some contestation, we use the phrase broadly. Our definition captures classic approaches, such as internships and study abroad, at the same time as it recognizes classroom simulations and most exercises—in and out of class—that emphasize actively applying theory to practice. Educators have endorsed the value of experiential learning, especially in higher education and with adult learners.

Experiential learning has always been of interest in the conflict field, where the pedagogy has included simulations and role plays used to acquaint students with the dynamics of conflict resolution practice. A few years back, our experiences teaching in the conflict resolution program at George Mason University led us to the conclusion that experiential learning has special value for the conflict field. Many of our colleagues used experiential activities in their classes, which, according to anecdotal reports, students greatly enjoyed. Field-based courses were also popular among both students and faculty. At the same time, we noticed some shortcomings, such as the dearth of materials to use in class. Students sometimes complained that they did the same simulation or experiential activity in more than one course. Also, pedagogical guidance for developing and implementing experiential activities was lacking. Finally, the limited attention to pedagogy meant that it was difficult to know whether any particular experiential activity or field-based course resulted in student learning. Given the extraordinary efforts needed to mount field-based courses and even simulations held in a classroom setting (not to mention the risks involved), we wanted to understand more fully how, whether, and why these kinds of educational experiences worked. Believing that quality experiential learning was not only possible but perhaps integral to understanding conflict, we endeavored to create the best examples.

In 2010, we were awarded a US Department of Education grant through the Fund for the Improvement of Post-Secondary Education for the Linking Theory to Practice project. Our grant focused on improving undergraduates' ability to apply theory to practice. Toward that end, we developed ten Experiential Learning Activities (ELAs) for use in a variety of classroom settings.[1] We also created a model for field-based courses called Service Learning Intensives (SLIs), which were run in Liberia, Colombia, and West Virginia. Research conducted on all these forms of experiential learning was a key initiative of the grant, given the limited scholarship on experiential pedagogy in the conflict field. Our research findings confirmed the speculation, based on anecdote, that student engagement increases when the ELAs are used in class. In addition, certain substantive knowledge also increases. The type of learning fostered through the ELAs helps students to comprehend difficult concepts and theories, such as global complexity, at the same time as it improves their understanding of their own role as budding practitioners (Romano, Hirsch, and Paczyńska 2016). Other exercises provide students with the opportunity to practice skills that they might need for conducting research, whether academic or toward informed conflict intervention. For instance, one exercise engages students in planning and running a focus group about conflict (Hirsch et al. 2013). Two other exercises ask students to conduct a conflict assessment in a community and to design an intervention, drawing on the findings of that assessment (Paczyńska 2015). Our experiences related to experiential learning in the classroom convinced us of the value of expanding the conversation about experiential pedagogy, particularly for instructors teaching about conflict.

We also conducted research on the SLIs created through our project. Here too students' understanding of conflicts, their ability to apply theory to practice, and their capacity to use conflict resolution and research skills all improved through participation in the SLIs. Our assessment of the SLIs also revealed multiple challenges associated with field-based courses mounted in conflict zones with respect to managing logistics, securing local partners, and handling ethical questions. Attention to these concerns could sometimes result in reducing the focus on the content and delivery of the course itself. Moreover, heavy expectations are placed on these courses. Everyone involved—students, teachers, and administrators—believes that students should have a significant "transformative" experience through a field-based course, and course marketing often says as much. We wondered what "transformative learning" actually means in practice and found ourselves hesitant to use the term to describe what we were trying to achieve. Also, student perceptions of their own learning can vary depending on when they are measured. Appreciation of the depth of the learning might not come until months or years after the experience (see Lazarus 2011). During our work with instructors on the project, we focused concertedly on processes that could be used to deepen student learning, such as pre-trip preparation, reflection, and debriefing.

Our work on the Linking Practice to Theory project convinced us that field-based courses could have dramatic effects on students and that more could be learned about how to improve their experiences and the courses overall. At multiple conferences and several workshops, we brought together instructors of field-based courses in conflict zones to discuss how this might be done. These gatherings highlighted the multiple approaches taken by faculty and the wide range of results achieved. Our aim then, and now, is not to prescribe a particular approach to experiential learning generally or to field-based courses specifically but to bring together a variety of well-considered examples from which we can learn. Our openness is evident in the lack of narrow definitions for many of the concepts. For instance, "experience" is used in multiple ways by our authors, including with skepticism. The same is true for "transformative learning" and "service learning." Even the term "conflict zone" is questionable, as situations of systemic or structural violence might be called conflict zones by some scholars and practitioners but not by others. Rather than resolve what are long-standing, important debates over terminology, we welcome the range of approaches.

Although many themes run throughout the volume, the following sections of this introduction will highlight the key questions addressed by the authors of the chapters: What ethical challenges do these courses pose? How do we go about teaching these courses, and what is different about them in comparison to other types of study-abroad or service learning programs? What pedagogical approaches have been used, and how effective have they been? By taking students and instructors out of their comfort zones, do these courses produce significant changes in how students learn or how much they learn? How are students, instructors, and field communities affected by this form of education? And a final, big question: Do these courses result in constructive interventions into ongoing conflict?

Considering Ethics

We decided to begin the volume with chapters that focus primarily on ethics to highlight an aspect of field-based courses that tends to be given less attention than the subject matter of a course or the logistical challenges of teaching in a conflict zone. It is clear that these kinds of courses can be used to teach differently about how to confront ethical challenges. In the classroom setting it is possible to read about ethical dilemmas that emerge in practice and to discuss the various options that practitioners might face in addressing them; however, it is quite a different experience to see an ethical dilemma emerge in the context of a field-based course and to wrestle with how to address it. Examples of such dilemmas are described in the chapters on ethics. For instance, what should students do when faced with requests to help a community financially or to provide a quick solution to a complex problem? When such questions arise, they open the possibility of learning by doing. They also provide an opportunity, reinforced through debriefings and assignments, for students to explore a wide range of ethical challenges that practitioners encounter. Students thus gain practice assessing and responding to ethical dilemmas in real time.

One of the conclusions that emerges from these chapters is that running field-based courses in conflict zones presents particular ethical challenges that are distinct from those encountered in other types of courses, including other courses mounted in the field. These challenges reflect the particular vulnerabilities and traumas that people in conflict settings experience. The imperative to "do no harm"—a bedrock of conflict resolution practice and social science ethics codes—underlies the design of most field-based courses. Nonetheless, interacting with residents of such settings can be as overwhelming as it can be profound and can pose dilemmas for students. Without a sense of how to frame the encounter, students might fall into identity traps such as "savior" or "helper" and thereby miss the opportunity to collaborate with residents as partners in strengthening conflict resolution processes. However, these kinds of courses raise a whole set of ethical issues that go well beyond the ethical dilemmas of practice.

Among the questions raised by these chapters are: How can we prepare students and instructors for the ethical challenges of such courses? What are some of the best practices? What happens when things go wrong? With respect to how we might prepare students to face ethical dilemmas, the literature on field-based courses, taken together with the literature on field-based research, suggests that students need to learn about the following ethical commitments related to practice prior to undertaking these kinds of courses. Ideally, students should be primed to

1. feel a moral responsibility for their interventions that foregrounds doing no harm;

2. recognize that they are poised to do harm by infringing the security, privacy, and well-being of people with whom they are working;

3. be mindful that their own good intentions cannot guard against negative consequences;

4. understand the frame, limits, and dynamics of their engagement with others, including their own positionality; and

5. prepare as fully as possible and remain reflective and flexible during the experience.

Presenting students with these aspirations during the preparatory phases prior to a field course, and even engaging them in activities that provide the opportunity for them to discuss expectations, might not ensure that students fully appreciate the range of ethical challenges they might face and the centrality of ethics to field-based courses in general. Examples from the chapters illustrate that serious ethical entailments that arise can be those that are often completely unanticipated. Yet other ethical challenges are more predictable, and, given the likelihood that they will emerge, trip preparation can target them directly.

Our concern over the difficulty of preparing students for ethical challenges led us to write a chapter on ethics, which opens the volume's first part. Early sections of the chapter describe several specific ethical concerns that have emerged in field-based courses, including situations where students can be led to overpromise to partners and strangers, to simplify complex situations, or to increase the vulnerability of our partners. More concertedly preparing students can help, and we argue that including classroom-based experiential learning across the conflict curriculum can improve students' capacity to respond to ethical challenges in the field.

How a field-based course is organized and advertised, who goes on it and with what intentions, and how the students understand the "real-world experience" that they can expect to have while in the field are treated as fundamental to the ethical concerns raised by field-based courses in the chapter by Leslie Dwyer and Alison Castel. Centered on the key theme of experience and critical of how this term has been used to endorse and promote field-based learning with little acknowledgment of the power dynamics involved, the authors highlight their efforts to develop more collaborative approaches to field-based learning in Indonesia and Colombia. Their aim is to confront directly the tendency to commodify experience for the benefit of the US students who often pursue such trips for their personal academic empowerment. The chapter highlights particular ethical dilemmas encountered by the authors, even as they have sought to teach in ways that expose the power dynamics of field-based courses and that encourage students to reflect on their own assumptions and positioning.

Mindful of both the broader power dynamics that frame field-based courses and the many on-the-ground challenges that can emerge when students are in the field, some instructors include considerable attention to ethics as part of the course curriculum (see the chapters by Patricia A. Maulden and Lisa Elaine Shaw and by Gina M. Cerasani and rj nickels). In chapter 3, Pushpa Iyer describes her use of "practical ethics" to anchor how she and her students approach issues that arise during courses that she leads in Cambodia, Sierra Leone, Nepal, India, and the Philippines. Students study practical ethics, which also emphasizes the ethical entailments of their own privileged positioning, and they practice using this perspective to make decisions before and during the field component of the course. Notwithstanding her emphasis on ethics, Iyer makes the important point that it "is hard to be prepared for all possible ethical challenges." Rather than viewing this uncertain ethical terrain as a negative feature of field-based courses, she asserts that transformative learning can emerge in precisely those spaces that are ethically challenging in unanticipated ways.

Even with preparation beforehand, a strong ethical frame, and repeated efforts to reflect, unexpected challenges can emerge in conflict and postconflict settings, and these challenges demand constructive and reflective responses. A later section of the introduction addresses this issue.

Improving Pedagogy

The chapters in part 2 introduce examples from the wide variety of pedagogical models for field-based courses mounted internationally and domestically. Field-based courses vary with respect to many factors, including the length of time students are in the field, the number and type of conflict and postconflict communities visited, the nature of the encounters with local residents, the knowledge and skills that they are expected to acquire or deploy, and the range of assignments used to assess their learning. Perhaps most importantly, such courses are characterized by pedagogy that emphasizes learning through engagement, most notably engagement with people living or working in the field sites. In contrast to lecture/discussion pedagogy common in classroom settings, students in field-based courses generally learn through experiences that take many forms, such as meeting local residents and visiting organizations, volunteering and providing labor or another service, holding classes or trainings with local residents, and engaging in social activities in the local context. How they reflect on these experiences and what they ultimately learn from them depend as much on the instructor and the pedagogical models employed as they do on the motivation of the student. The authors of chapters in this part of the volume make the case that the intentional use of sophisticated pedagogical models can help ensure that students learn effectively in conflict and postconflict field settings. At the same time, the chapter authors describe many teaching techniques that could be adapted to other contexts and also identify barriers to learning.

The nature of the conflict itself is a key factor in shaping pedagogy. Not surprisingly, the approach to teaching and learning is different where a conflict is long-standing and intractable, as compared with situations where conflict is emergent or the subject of historical study. In designing a course, indeed an entire project called The Olive Tree Initiative, focused on the ongoing conflict in Israel/Palestine, Daniel R. Brunstetter and Daniel Wehrenfennig emphasized learning from multiple perspectives and avoided the pitfall of privileging one perspective or narrative over others. Thus, in the field students learn from many different people and are exposed to many different contexts and viewpoints. Preparation for the course includes significant attention to developing the skills needed to engage in dialogue and reflection. During the course students draw on these skills in their encounters with people in the conflict context and also when discussing the experience among themselves. As the authors point out, in The Olive Tree Initiative, learning the skills that will be needed during the field portion of the course happens prior to departure so that students have time to practice them before entering a conflict zone. The emphasis is on practicing particular skills related to conflict resolution, such as dialogue facilitation, debriefing and reflection, and culturally sensitive interviewing. Such preparation is a feature of many of the courses discussed throughout the volume.

As discussed in chapter 5, Jennifer M. Ramos's decision to take students to Northern Ireland, where there was "no war, no peace," also shaped the pedagogy she employed. The course was focused on building research skills while learning about the history of the conflict, including the violence experienced in the past. The students were trained to conduct and analyze interviews with people who had lived through the Troubles. The relatively short field-based portion of the course was embedded within a broader semester-length class. With this model, Ramos solves two problems. First, the class meetings before and after ensure that the trip will result in deeper learning than might be expected from nine days of residence in a new context. Second, students who are unable to enroll in a study-abroad course that would require a semester of living abroad are able to participate in a field experience.

Looking across the chapters, the trips that take students away from campus vary widely in their length. Even when the time away is very short, all of the instructors have to consider how to prepare before the trip and what kind of follow-up is needed. Ramos highlights her own thinking about these aspects of field-based learning and a wide array of other issues, as she takes the reader through her decision process in setting up the course. Her discussion offers a blueprint for much of what needs to happen to mount a successful field-based course, such as gaining the buy-in of administrators, setting up logistics, defining learning goals, and connecting with partners, and could thus be very useful for anyone who has never planned a course away from campus, be it abroad or in the United States.

A frequent criticism of field-based learning—including internships and service learning—is that the experience is not well integrated into the broader curriculum. The concern is that what students are learning, as well as how they are learning it, differs so much from their other courses that it feels like a one-off occurrence. In designing two different domestic service learning experiences, Allyson M. Lowe and Sandi DiMola were intent on using the field experiences to augment what students of political science were learning about conflict. Their courses were carefully designed to involve students in deliberative democracy and community conflict resolution and to connect these experiences directly to theory and case studies on the topic. At the same time, the service aspect of the courses reflects the commitment of the universities to civic engagement and community service understood through both secular and religious lenses, depending on the institution. In that sense, the learning experience was explicitly framed holistically as part of a student's university experience rather than a disconnected, extramural activity. It might be the case that the integration of field-based courses into the curriculum and the university's values is easier when they take place closer to home. However, the volume includes many pedagogical strategies for achieving the desired level of integration in courses mounted internationally.

Maulden and Shaw try to ensure student success by adapting well-known formal models of pedagogy for use in the field. Underlying this course as well as many other courses described in this volume is Kolb's approach to experiential learning, which emphasizes the dynamic and cyclical nature of learning and places particular importance on the interaction between action and reflection and between experience and abstract theoretical concepts (Kolb and Kolb 2005). Maulden and Shaw build out this model emphasizing the pre-trip field-experience preparation, which includes not only familiarizing students with the conflict context and community dynamics in Liberia and training in conflict theory, assessment, and resolution skills but also exploration and self-reflection of students' individual strengths, weaknesses, and expectations as well as uncertainties regarding the field-based course. They also place particular importance on the reciprocal nature of learning that students and faculty engage in with local partner organizations. Maulden and Shaw examine the pedagogical impact of encouraging students throughout the course to interrogate their positionality and power relations vis-à-vis those local partners. At the core of the model is the underlying assumption that prior knowledge and experience will be continuously challenged while students are in the field and that it is this very process of dealing with these challenges where learning takes place. As a result, turning an experience into deep learning puts reflection and debriefing at the center of course activities before, during, and after activities in the field. In their chapter and across the volume, a wide array of strategies to achieve the aims of the formal model emerge, such as daily debriefings, journaling and blogging, and self-reflection papers.

More broadly in the volume, multiple questions about pedagogy arise: What is the balance between innovative approaches and ones that work in other, nonconflict or non-field-based settings? How do particular contexts determine or shape the pedagogy used? What can be learned from and with local residents, and how can they be involved more directly in the learning process, such that it becomes colearning? Throughout the volume, chapter authors also reflect on how they assess learning in field-based courses and whether measureable learning is the primary goal in all instances.

Effecting Change

The chapters in this part explore how field-based courses in conflict and postconflict zones can serve as sites for effecting change of several sorts. Students often use terms such as "transformative" and "life-changing" to describe the experience of a field-based course, which suggests that profound individual change can be the result of participation. Instructors might be pleased to receive such accolades at the same time as they wonder what students mean by these terms and whether other goals, such as individual learning or even broader social change, are being accomplished. Moreover, instructors themselves experience shifts in their own beliefs and understandings as a result of participating in a field-based course. In educational contexts change is often measured and thus made more concrete through evaluation and assessment. This part discusses those techniques, as they apply to participants' engagement, learning, and roles, as well as the course as a whole. The authors are able to identify best practices in course delivery by measuring the extent of learning and other aims of the course experience. At the same time, the authors' healthy skepticism prompts the question: Can all the change effected during a course be measured? In addition to directing attention to assessment and evaluation, the chapters in this part also focus on processes of reflection during and after fieldwork, debriefing, and assignments, as reflecting on the experience can help shape and deepen its significance. Through reflection, instructors can guide students in connecting their sense of transformation to individual development and also to broader processes of social change. As field-based courses come to play a more central role in the higher-education curriculum and their potential to effect change of various types grows, the imperative to appreciate the implications of such courses becomes more urgent. Thus, the chapters in this final part ask pointed questions about the enterprise of field-based education in conflict and postconflict zones and offer some examples of the difference it can make in a highly conflictual world.

In chapter 8, Maryam Z. Deloffre explores how to effectively incorporate the development of applied, technical skills and training that will facilitate the transformation of students of conflict analysis and resolution into practitioners able to enter the job market following the completion of their studies. She does so by examining the experience of integrating a service learning component into a course on nongovernmental organization (NGO) management. Students complete various projects with the American Friends Service Committee, a Quaker organization committed to social justice and peace. The experience, Deloffre underscores, allows students to make connections between the theoretical concepts discussed during lectures and the programs and operations of an NGO. She guides students through this process by utilizing multiple forms of interaction, including Skype calls, site visits, and reflective journaling, with both structured prompts and opportunities for unstructured reflections by students. Deloffre incorporated assessment of the learning experience into the course evaluations and found that the service learning component of the course enriched students' understanding of NGO operations and enabled them to grow professionally, gain confidence in their ability to navigate through unfamiliar terrain, and improve their capacity to deal with change and ambiguity, as well as develop critical-thinking and leadership skills.

In the following chapter, Cerasani and nickels discuss the process of facilitating the development of students' practice skills and their capacity to make ethical decisions as practitioners through two forms of field-based education: a service learning course (in Charleston, West Virginia) and an academic project (in Prince William County, Virginia). These two forms of education tend to differ. Whereas service learning courses tend to be short (usually from one to four weeks), academic projects can take up to a year, thus giving students additional opportunity for deep immersion in a community as well as for design and implementation of interventions. Cerasani and nickels explore the role that instructors play in guiding students through this process, noting that, very often, they must be willing to find an uncomfortable balance between supporting students as they engage in practice and allowing them, on occasion, to fail as they learn and try out new practices. Similar to other authors in this volume (Maulden, Shaw, and Iyer), they emphasize that the reflective-practice approach effectively facilitates this learning. Additionally, they point out that by encouraging practitioners to make explicit the assumptions underlying their work, to think about the values and priorities that underpin the theories they rely on, and to anticipate consequences of their intervention, reflective practice also provides students and instructors with a powerful ethical tool (Warfield 2002).

In chapter 10, Alexander Cromwell focuses on how transformative learning can be achieved in field-based courses. Specifically, he investigates two transformations that occur for students engaged in a field-based course in a context affected by conflict: learning to reflect critically on their roles as interveners in conflict and gaining motivation to engage in conflict resolution. As Cromwell argues, to facilitate such transformative learning, field-based courses should include three crucial elements: meaningful contact with local people, space and flexibility for interactions between students and local people, and, finally, reflective practice as a learning strategy. Cromwell brings to this discussion the perspective of someone who participated in field-based courses in conflict zones (Israel/Palestine, Syria, Serbia, and Croatia) as a student, and he explores how encountering people engaged in conflicts awakens powerful emotions that deepen the process of reflective practice, which in turn contributes to the transformative nature of the learning process. What is needed going forward is to more systematically examine the medium- and long-term effects of such programs to gauge whether the insights from transformational learning experiences persist and if so for how long and in what form.

In the volume's last chapter, Eric Hartman and Anthony C. Ogden take a historical perspective on global service learning, noting the growth of interest in these courses over the past half century. They ask whether such courses are founded on ethical principles or whether they rely simply on the good intentions of participants—that is, the desire to help or do good. The authors worry that without explicit attention to the ethics of engagement in global service learning, students can end up with an overblown sense of their ability to transform local communities. As a counterpoint to their discussion of ethically flawed approaches, particularly a service learning project mounted in Ethiopia, they profile Fair Trade Learning, a type of global service learning built on strong ethical foundations that emphasizes reciprocal learning and mutual benefit between students and local partners. Fair Trade Learning foregrounds ethical socioeconomic transformation as a goal of service learning that depends on giving equal weight to engaging in service and undertaking serious intellectual work. Hartman and Ogden draw attention to the key role played by administrators in developing valuable and sustainable field-based courses and thus highlight the need to consider how field-based courses fit into the university context and the broader context of higher education in the United States.

The chapter by Hartman and Ogden invites us to think about the big picture of field-based learning in conflict zones. Why is it that we go on these trips? If the aim is to make some kind of difference, how can a course be organized in an optimal way ethically, pedagogically, and logistically? Effecting change of multiple sorts is an aim of all the courses discussed throughout the volume, and among the best practices that emerge are several that relate to this commitment to transformation. For one, although anyone interested in designing a field course should dare to dream big, he or she will need to manage expectations, particularly of students and partners whose varied interests in transformation might be difficult to meet. As a second best practice, frequent reflection on the experience is invaluable for tracking and assessing the changes achieved through learning, practice, and engagement with partners. Finally, instructors need to be mindful that an educational experience in a conflict zone always comes with some discomfort. Expect that you and your students will be taken out of your comfort zones, and treat it as an avenue toward constructive change.

Note

1. See "Experiential Learning Activities," School for Conflict Analysis and Resolution, http://scar.gmu.edu/experientiallearningproject/11613.

ONE

Considering Ethics

ONE

Ethics and Field-Based Courses

How to Prepare Students for the Challenges of Practice

SUSAN F. HIRSCH AND AGNIESZKA PACZYŃSKA

For instructors in conflict studies and related fields with an applied or practice component, a serious question remains largely unanswered: What are the best ways to prepare students to become ethical practitioners? The practice of conflict analysis and resolution (CAR) differs from other applied fields, such as medicine, with long-standing pedagogical traditions of shadowing established practitioners. As an example, medical interns literally look over the shoulder of a more experienced physician. Shadowing a conflict practitioner is rarely possible for confidentiality reasons, as the presence of multiple third-party practitioners risks changing the fundamental dynamics of the interaction, be it a negotiation, dialogue, or some other activity. With little or no opportunity to observe practitioners in real time, CAR students miss out on learning through experience and observation how practitioners engage in forms of third-party intervention. A subtle but key aspect of this hard-to-achieve learning are practitioners' approaches to the ethical dilemmas—big and small—that arise during conflict resolution practice. Most CAR instructors are aware that students, as budding practitioners, need to develop an ethics that will underpin their practice, yet the pedagogical tools for shaping the ethical thinking of CAR students are underdeveloped and infrequently discussed.

In this chapter we describe our efforts to develop new pedagogical approaches to teaching CAR students ethical practice. From 2010 to 2014, we directed the Undergraduate Experiential Learning Project (UELP) based at George Mason University.[1] Funded by the US Department of Education, UELP was a large research project focused on experiential learning in the conflict field. It had three components: creating Service Learning Intensives (SLIs) that would allow students to hone their skills in conflict resolution practice in field-based intensive courses, developing Experiential Learning Activities (ELAs) for use in traditional classroom settings, and, finally, pursuing research and outreach activities to enhance the quality and profile of experiential learning in the conflict field generally.

The aim of the SLIs was to challenge students to experience the sorts of logistical, conceptual, and ethical dilemmas faced by practitioners in the conflict field. The discussion in this chapter explores key insights and challenges that emerged from our experience in developing and running SLI courses in Liberia, Colombia, and West Virginia. In particular, we focus our attention on the ethical challenges that students and instructors encounter in the field and explore how best to prepare both students and instructors to engage in ethically informed teaching and learning in these complex settings, which are characterized by a variety of conflicts.

Mounted in both domestic and international contexts, the SLIs are short courses (three to six weeks) that involve students in applying theory to practice through service activities focused on conflict and its resolution. Thus, the SLIs are field-based opportunities for students to engage in conflict resolution practice. Although each SLI course is unique, they share common characteristics. For instance, all SLIs are based on the principle that students and instructors work *with* community partners and that the learning is a reciprocal experience for community partners, students, and instructors (see chapters 2 and 7). Learning takes place in both formal and informal ways, and ethical engagement and reflective practice are at the center of this learning. The following incident, which occurred on an SLI to Liberia where students partnered with a local nongovernmental organization (NGO), highlights the centrality of ethical dilemmas to the learning experienced on an SLI:

On a visit to a small village where our local partner sought to learn from villagers about their experiences with returning home after the war had ended, the students from our university were shocked to see the poor state of the local school. The teacher told them that the educators had not been receiving a regular salary and the kids did not have school books. Our students decided that they needed to do something and told the community that upon returning to the United States they would organize a fund-raiser and send the proceeds back so that the school could be improved.

A key part of the course was daily reflection about what had taken place during the day. That evening, the reflection centered around the proposed fund-raiser. By that point the students were sensing that what had happened in the village was problematic. After all, following the visit to that community, they had stopped by other villages and heard about other schools in dire straits. By the evening it was quite clear that the community school they had visited was not something out of the norm. Rather, most Liberian schools faced such challenges. They wondered aloud how they could justify helping one school but not another. They also began to wonder if they were in fact going to help the one to which they had made promises. Would they actually organize a fund-raiser? After all, some of them would be graduating and moving away. Others would be busy with the new semester's coursework.

The more students reflected, the clearer it became that the probability of organizing a fund-raiser was fairly low. Yet the community had taken their promise seriously. The students had to admit that, by raising expectations, they had failed to abide by the essential principle of intervention emphasized during the trip orientation, namely "Do no harm."

The students learned a difficult and significant lesson that also exposed the insufficient preparation prior to the trip. From the beginning of the UELP, it was clear to us that preparing students for ethical practice in field-based courses in conflict zones was both crucial to the success of the learning experience but very difficult. Yet, as instructors and project directors, we had not fully appreciated how students would react to the challenging environments in which they would be working. In particular, we had not fully anticipated how students' strong desire to "do good" in the world would create situations in which they might harm the very people they were trying to help by, for instance, raising their expectations unrealistically. As the UELP continued, we devoted increasing amounts of attention to students' preparation prior to field-based courses. Our experience with the UELP reinforced our initial belief that preparation is absolutely essential when sending students to do hands-on practice in challenging environments. Moreover, we gained additional insights into why it is essential and how to accomplish it more effectively.

As the following section shows, the literature on the ethical difficulties of conducting field-based research and practice in conflict zones confirms our experience that courses mounted in such contexts are fraught with ethical dilemmas that risk creating harm. We then dig deeper into the particular ethical challenges that emerged in our SLIs and identify three examples of ethically problematic approaches that students are susceptible to taking: overpromising, simplifying complex problems, and inadvertently increasing the vulnerability of those with whom they engage. These are serious issues with complex ethical dimensions, and our actual experience of encountering them while running the field-based courses reinforced the importance of preparing the students and faculty more intentionally with respect to ethical dilemmas. Accordingly, in later sections we discuss techniques for better preparation to deal with ethical challenges prior to the field-based portion of these courses.

We conclude our chapter by advocating that teaching students how to handle the ethical challenges of practice needs to be accomplished throughout the curriculum so that both those students who decide to go on field-based courses and those students who choose not to or cannot participate in them are better equipped to deal with ethical challenges that they may encounter as they engage in field-based research and practice once they complete their education. Challenges will inevitably arise for those students whose careers take them into the conflict field and many other fields. As we argue, one way to allow students to explore the ethical challenges of practice, without risking harmful consequences, is through the ELAs developed for traditional classroom settings through our work on the UELP. Classroom activities with an experiential component, such as small-group problem solving and role play, can support students' preparation for field-based courses in a relatively controlled setting. The discussion also includes attention to cocurricular activities, such as peer mediation and facilitating campus dialogues, that allow students to engage in practice in contexts that mimic "real-life" situations where the stress level is lower and the context is more familiar and controlled.

Our overall conclusion is that attention to ethical practice in prior coursework helps ensure that students will understand the complexity of the ethical issues that they will undoubtedly confront in field-based courses. Moreover, they will have acquired skills that allow them to avoid significant blunders in field-based courses and in professional practice should their careers take them in that direction.

The Challenges of Field-Based Conflict Courses

Conducting field-based research and teaching field-based courses necessarily involve some degree of resituating researchers, students, and instructors outside their comfort zones. Undertaking these activities in conflict-affected environments intensifies the experience and presents unique challenges. As Elizabeth Wood, who has conducted extensive ethnographic research in El Salvador, notes, "Ethical imperatives of research (e.g., do no harm) are intensified in conflict zones by the general unpredictability of events, and the traumatization through violence" of people living in these zones (Wood 2006, 373). Instructors and students participating in field-based courses focused on conflict intervention of some type face similar challenges. At the very least, anyone engaging in such endeavors must recognize the particular ways in which their intervention, or their very presence, might do harm by infringing the security, privacy, and well-being of people with whom they are working.

"Do no harm" is a broad maxim that emphasizes the caution required in undertaking field-based courses. At its simplest, to adhere to "do no harm" means not placing others in danger as a consequence of one's actions and thus carefully weighing which activities are appropriate to pursue and how these might be justified in relation to the potential for harm. Although preparation before going to the field is necessary regardless of where the activities will take place, the "do no harm" imperative is heightened in conflict-affected settings. Quite simply, the complexity and precarity of conflict and postconflict contexts means that conventional reasoning about what causes harm may be insufficient. An ethical approach means that the imperative to "do no harm" must include being mindful that one's actions may inadvertently put others at risk and thus require additional scrutiny. When a field situation includes many vulnerable people, such as individuals who have lived through civil war or experienced traumatizing events, any forms of intervention or engagement that might render them more vulnerable present especially troubling ethical dilemmas that require considerable forethought.

Encountering a conflict zone takes researchers and students out of their comfort zones, challenging both their intellect and emotions. As Jonathan Darling notes, "Entering 'the field' can be a daunting, demanding and at times bewildering experience, with researchers negotiating a myriad of assumptions, expectations and motivations" (Darling 2014, 201). Understanding the context, including the history of the conflict—its political, social, cultural, and economic consequences, and the current implications for the future—is essential to enable researchers, instructors, and students to better anticipate and therefore prepare for potential ethical dilemmas that might be encountered and to respond to such dilemmas. Furthermore, a recent survey of conflict-zone researchers found that in particular the importance of appreciating local conflict dynamics and relations were critical to good ethical practice (Thomson n.d.).

Similar to scholars conducting field research, instructors and students who participate in field-based courses need to anticipate and negotiate often difficult ethical dilemmas in real time with real people. They need to be mindful not to engage in exploitative relationships with the people whom they work with and encounter while in the field (see, for instance, Drole 2014). As Audra Mitchell cautions, when designing and leading field courses in conflict zones, instructors need to ensure that even in the interest of exposing students to learning and practicing in these contexts, they do not create a situation "in which 'experiences'—the internal states, trauma and memories—of some of the world's most vulnerable people are framed as resources for the personal development of some of the world's most privileged people" (Mitchell 2013, 1256). Understanding their own position in a broad global political economy and appreciating how that positioning leads them to a context framed by multiple forms of global and local power can help students become conscious of their situated subject positions in relation to those whom they encounter in a field-based course. This insight might require that students understand more fully various aspects of globalization and their positioning in the global political economy (see Romano, Hirsch, and Paczyńska 2017).

When in a field setting, one of the challenges students face is that they are working with real people who face real problems and conflicts in their lives. For instance, in the courses created through our project, students engage in mediating land disputes among family members, conducting conflict assessments of an educational institution, and designing and delivering conflict resolution training to community leaders, among other activities, and must therefore be mindful that their actions, responses, and verbal comments can have an immediate impact on those with whom they are working. Yet these activities are being undertaken in a context with which students are unfamiliar, one that takes them out of their comfort zones, induces stress, and asks them to make judgment calls about how to respond to unexpected developments in real time, which can require lightning-quick action. These stresses, in turn, generate challenges for ensuring that students (and faculty) do not reproduce hierarchical relationships between the students and the communities in which they are working.

Elsewhere in this volume (e.g., in chapters 7 and 9), authors explore how incorporating ongoing reflective practice, dialoguing, and journaling are essential components of running successful field-based courses. These pedagogical practices facilitate students' critical self-assessments, including the exploration of their positionality within the context in which they are engaging in practice, and thus serve as ongoing opportunities for students to develop the ethical dimension of their practice. In the introduction to this volume, we present a list of ethical commitments that can be used in preparing students for field-based engagement. Whether intentionally or unintentionally, each of these commitments was addressed in some way in pre-trip preparations for the SLIs associated with our project. Yet, as the next section describes, once the students were in the field tricky situations emerged, testing their knowledge and understanding of these commitments.

Experiences with Ethical Practice in the SLI Courses

One of the challenges that students in CAR face when engaging in field-based learning is that the overwhelming majority of these students come to the CAR field because they want to work toward resolving conflicts and because they care about social justice and peace. Yet this desire to "do good" can present particular challenges during students' first encounters with practice and working in the field. For instance, they can readily make promises they cannot keep, as illustrated by the initial anecdote about holding a fund-raiser. In that instance and others, students' sense of the strength of their commitment to do good can obscure the limitations of their ability to effect change. Relatedly, instructors face the challenge of how to balance the need to encourage students to trust in their abilities and overcome the inevitable fears about engaging in field-based practice and yet to make the students aware and self-reflective about the limits of what their interventions can achieve. This delicate balance has to be cultivated and managed with patience and over time.

However, another challenge that students and instructors face when participating in field-based courses is that ethical dilemmas emerge out of nowhere and require immediate response. Dilemmas, such as how to respond to a request for assistance and whether to intervene in an emerging dispute, can be especially acute in contexts of insecurity that often characterize the places where field-based conflict courses take place. They are not unlike the dilemmas that practitioners of conflict resolution and peacebuilding face when they engage in a variety of professional activities in the field, such as organizing dialogues, mediating conflict, and allying with local organizations. Yet when students engage in these courses, their inexperience can heighten the seriousness of the ethical challenge and put pressure on instructors striving to support both experiential learning and ethical practice.

This section explores several examples that demonstrate particular ways in which students might encounter choices that challenge their ethical approach. Specifically, the examples illustrate how ethical practice can be compromised through overpromising (albeit with good intentions), simplifying the context and the conflict, and rendering the vulnerable more vulnerable. The field-based experiences developed by the UELP included an intensive course focused on peacebuilding in Liberia, during which the students and instructors partnered with Don Bosco Homes, a local NGO that worked with communities on family reunification and conflict resolution. In Colombia, the SLI course focused on transitional justice. Students from George Mason University and Javeriana University in Bogotá partnered with a local NGO in the city of Soacha. Finally, the West Virginia SLI course focused on collaborative skills-building with community-based organizations and partnered with the Charleston Job Corps Center. As the project leaders, we had the opportunity to observe all three courses. Although the political and social context and the content differed across the three courses, some overall lessons learned emerged. Specifically, in each course, students confronted ethical dilemmas that they struggled to address. Here we will focus our discussion in particular on the Liberia and West Virginia courses.

OVERPROMISING AND SIMPLIFYING ON THE LIBERIA SLI

The peacebuilding course in Liberia was a four-week course that was mounted three times. On one of those trips the twelve students partnered with Don Bosco Homes. Students were divided into three groups of four and worked on a variety of projects both in the capital city of Monrovia and other parts of the country. The students conducted conflict assessments, developed and delivered conflict resolution trainings to high school students and NGO staff, facilitated land and youth-elder dispute cases,

Figure 1.1. Students walking the disputed property boundary in Liberia. *Agnieszka Paczyńska.*

facilitated family reunifications, and participated in outreach activities to encourage homeless children to come to the rehabilitation and family reunification center run by Don Bosco Homes.

The work performed by the students was often not only complex but also mentally and emotionally difficult, even draining. Students were directly engaging people who were struggling with very hard problems and who themselves had complex, often opaque (to the students) interests, goals, and needs. Of course, students deal with such complexity in their everyday lives as well as in the classroom. Here, however, they were strangers, freshly arrived in these communities, and the nuances that they may have been expert at discerning back home could quite easily escape them. Their unfamiliarity with the situation may have contributed to the instance of overpromising described in the opening vignette.

Students coped with the stress they experienced in a variety of ways. However, one of the responses, one that turned out to present serious ethical challenges, was their urge to simplify the complex in order to make the unwieldy and hard-to-understand social interactions among local community members more manageable. This simplification was sometimes accompanied by an effort to quickly "fix" the problem or conflict they were encountering. These tendencies became especially clear during one of the land-dispute meetings that the SLI students were asked to facilitate.

The land dispute had deeply divided an extended family in a rural community. The boundary between two properties belonging to two different family members was unclear, and there were contested versions of which trees formed the demarcation line. The conflict had lasted for a number of years and resulted in many family members severing ties. The longevity and severity of this dispute was also beginning to impact the broader community as the family was a prominent one in the village. A local government administrator reached out to Don Bosco Homes for help. Don Bosco staff in turn asked the students to facilitate a meeting among members of this fractured family. The students decided to first gather more information. They spoke to the different family members, they walked along the disputed demarcation line, and then they strategized about how they were going to facilitate the actual meeting among the estranged family members. The preparations went well, and the students were pleased with the results of their efforts. Then the day of the facilitated discussion came and with it a very different, deeper level of engagement with the conflict and a higher level of stress.

The meeting took place in a very small room in a local government building. Close to twenty people filed in and sat in a tight circle. The students explained the ground rules of the meeting and encouraged different participants to share their stories about the dispute with the intent of laying out the various narratives about what had been dividing the family. The plan had looked good the night before, when the students were preparing the facilitation. The actual meeting, however, quickly took an unexpected turn. Rather than taking turns in laying out their narratives, the various family members became irate at the first few that were shared. Voices became tense. The volume of the exchanges rose. Then, to the students' consternation, as tempers began to flare further, people abandoned English and switched to a local language. The students were stumped and fast losing control of the meeting. Literally unable to understand, they were pushed by this experience with practice very far out of their comfort zones. One of the students abruptly got up and told everyone to be quiet. Startled, everyone quieted to listen to him. Energized by this response, the student began to explain that he knew what needed to be done. Agnieszka Paczyńska, who was evaluating the course, instinctively tried to step in and motioned to the student to stop what he was doing. He did not listen. Instead he continued, saying he knew how to resolve the dispute and proceeded to explain the solution. Not surprisingly, rather than calming things down, this inflamed tempers even more. People stood up, and some began to shout. The other students were clearly worried by this turn of events. Realizing that the situation was getting out of control, Paczyńska told the student who had asserted that he knew how to resolve the dispute to "sit down and be quiet." He stormed out of the room. It took some time for the rest of the students to get the participants back into a less adversarial discussion. By the end of the day, while the land dispute had not been resolved, everyone felt that progress toward a resolution had been made. Most importantly perhaps, the estranged family members had agreed to meet on a regular basis to continue the conversation.

Paczyńska then took on the long task of calming the student whom she had reprimanded. He was angry with her and with his fellow classmates.

They were frustrated with his intervention, even as they were pleased with the result of the meeting. Paczyńska, too, was frustrated. While she was convinced that her intervention had been necessary to stop the situation from deteriorating, she regretted that she was forced to silence the student so abruptly and publicly. She was also frustrated, seeing quite clearly that the students were not adequately prepared to deal with the stress that would come with the kind of practice they were engaged in, especially the ethical aspect of that practice. That evening, during the daily reflection meeting, the students began to realize that the challenging moment during the facilitation was, at least in part, the result of the one student trying to reduce stress by simplifying a complex situation and rendering it familiar. "I grew up in a village," the student who attempted to resolve the conflict explained. "It was in another part of the world, but I thought I knew what to do."

What makes these situations all the more challenging is that there are no opportunities for a "do-over." Because students are working on real disputes, unlike during a role play in the traditional classroom setting, instructors might need to step in when things are not going well. This, too, poses an ethical dilemma: how to best ensure that no harm will be done to community members while allowing students to learn an extraordinary amount from actual practice for which they may not have sufficient preparation or familiarity?

The experience underscored how important preparation for such field courses needs to be. Although students may have had significant theoretical preparation in doing conflict assessment or facilitation and may well have practiced these skills in class, in a field-based course they need to recognize and be mindful that what they will be doing is not just a practice run and that there is a lot at stake. Students need to be mindful of the local social context and local power dynamics. They need to also be sensitive to the fact that, as outsiders who are new to the community and the conflicts that community faces, they are likely to have only a partial understanding at best of the conflict dynamics, the relationships between the various actors that are party to the conflict, the history of these relationships, and the broader social, political, and economic context of the conflict at hand. By being sensitive to the limitations of their knowledge, they should be self-reflective when engaging with community members and not offer expertise that they do not yet possess.

INCREASING VULNERABILITY ON THE CHARLESTON SLI

Working with partners at the Charleston Job Corps Center (CJCC) brought both similar and different ethical concerns to the fore. Job Corps is a federally funded residential educational program for young people from low-income backgrounds with hundreds of sites nationwide. As a result of preliminary discussions with CJCC staff, we decided that our students would provide conflict resolution trainings for a group of residents who were in leadership positions. Although mindful of many logistical challenges, we all expressed the hope that the initial "one-off" trainings could grow into a more comprehensive partnership. CJCC staff members hoped that our activities would "change the culture" at Job Corps, which, for them, meant helping residents to adopt more positive attitudes about the institution and one another. We cautioned that changing institutional culture was a more difficult task than a student/faculty team could accomplish but promised to work on assessing the level and types of conflict at the CJCC and making a report that could help guide future activities.

Although the CJCC is an American institution and is located only a day's drive from our university, it was an unfamiliar context for the students. For one, the institution is very hierarchical, and the teenage and twenty-something residents, with whom our students tried to identify, were on the bottom of that hierarchy. Relatedly, as a "secure" institution, freedom of movement was not possible for the residents or guests, including our team. As they passed through security, put on badges, and followed an escort, students began to appreciate that Job Corps residents live under many rules and regulations. We learned from our first encounters with staff that, from their perspective, rule violation is at the center of conflicts at Jobs Corps.

As students prepared to engage residents in a focus-group discussion of conflict at Job Corps and then a training session based on the focus-group findings, they had to take seriously the particularities of the context, especially the power dynamics. They were well aware that following the rules at Job Corps had significant consequences for residents' daily lives and for their ultimate success in the institution and perhaps beyond. At the same time, they wanted to encourage Job Corps residents to speak out about how rules themselves, especially those that appeared irrational, arbitrary, or unclear (of which there were several), might be a source of conflict. For our students, they took for granted that they were able to voice criticism or concerns about rules and other power dynamics. Moreover, they embraced conflict resolution approaches that link empowerment and "voice" to constructive social change.

As our team planned the activities at Job Corps, we became more conscious of ethical concerns. For instance, the fact that a staff member was required to be present—though was not always attentive—during all our activities made us aware that engaging in a discussion of conflict could alter relationships between residents and staff. Our students expressed concern that their work with the Job Corps residents could have serious ramifications. In encouraging Job Corps residents to open up, they might be asking them to reveal information that could be used against them later by other residents or by staff members who were observing. Perhaps simply speaking out about rules they disagreed with could be viewed by staff as insubordination.

The focus-group discussions and other interactions with the residents generally went well. Residents were careful about what they revealed of themselves, although they made veiled and overt criticisms of the institution in relating their perspectives on conflict at Job Corps. Students focused on learning enough so that they could create relevant conflict resolution trainings, which they delivered on a subsequent day. With the guidance of instructors, they held back from pushing students to reveal more than they needed to under the circumstances, even though they were curious and empathetic.

Through this aspect of the SLI experience, our students learned a valuable lesson about the vulnerability of those with whom we work in conflict resolution practice. They practiced some initial approaches to navigating institutional power and thus learned some initial lessons about how to avoid increasing the vulnerability of the least powerful members of our partner organization. In subsequent years of running this activity, course instructors determined that lack of experience among the students required a different approach. In some instances, instructors led the focus-group discussion while the students learned through watching. On another occasion, when a resident broached a personally painful topic, instructors took over the facilitation.

Concerned about the constraints of working at Job Corps, course instructors and project team members had many long discussions about the ethics of our activities and assessed whether working in a secure, hierarchical institution where rule-breaking had significant consequences for residents could be understood as a partnership. At times there were divergent perspectives among students, instructors, and project leaders and disagreement over whether we were engaging in ethical practice. We struggled, for instance, over how much to reveal to Job Corps staff about the dissatisfaction of the residents. Such dilemmas were learning experiences for instructors and students and experiments in how to address conflict in a hierarchical institution without rendering the least powerful more vulnerable. Moreover, it was equally important to manage students' perceptions of their own power in the situation. We all had to understand the limits of our engagement: we could neither "change the culture" of Job Corps nor fully protect its residents. However, within its limits we could try to minimize conflict and offer residents tools to think about the context.

LESSONS LEARNED

From our experiences with the SLIs, we learned that students need preparation in ethical practice not only prior to going into the field but also during the course. After all, one of the challenging aspects of ethical practice is that it is impossible to prepare anyone for all the possible contingencies that may arise in the field, especially how to deal with circumstances in which all available options for action appear suboptimal. Instructors also need to determine how and when they will step in if they feel that students are on the brink of committing an ethical breach when engaged in field-based practice, including when they are unaware that such a breach is about to occur. We also learned that it is crucial to help students conceptualize the frame for their engagement with a partner: that they are not there to help or to save or to rescue or to enlighten or to judge. The frame of the partnership remains something that they need to experience and reflect on throughout the course itself and beyond. Our experiences with the SLIs led us to ask: How can we respond to the partner's request that the students "do something" and yet counsel the students that they need to be humble about their capabilities? How can they gain the confidence that it takes to be a practitioner and yet not get an inflated idea of their power? In the next section we describe what we have tried to do to prepare students.

Preparing Students for the Ethical Challenges in Field-Based Courses

PRE-TRIP PREPARATION

Our conversations about ethics multiplied and deepened over the three years of our project. Initially, the talented instructors of the field-based courses were drawing on sophisticated approaches to reflection and learning that stemmed from their own ethical commitments and appeared to engage students in learning from ethical dilemmas that emerged while in the field. However, as we encountered the kinds of situations described in the previous section, we worried that a good deal of learning about ethics might be happening "on the fly" in the field, with insufficient preparation and reinforcement, and that such learning, while powerful, carried significant risks. We redoubled our efforts to prepare students more intentionally to engage in field-based courses in ways that would allow them to gain experiences around ethics and practice that would serve them well in their future work and put our partners and other interlocutors at less risk.

The typical way that students are prepared for field-based courses is through pre-trip training and orientation, which include a variety of activities. Our growing interest in preparing students more intentionally for ethical practice led to the development of a code of conduct for field-based trips.

1. Respect confidentiality.
2. Respect the security needs of those around you.
3. Respect cultural differences.
4. Recognize power dynamics, and don't exploit your own position.
5. Don't overpromise.
6. Don't be a "knight in shining armor."
7. Be humble and open to new ideas.

These kinds of checklists and the related pre-trip discussions of them are important for getting students and instructors on the same page with respect to ethics. Even the list itself can be a touchstone that students revisit when they find themselves facing an ethical dilemma in the field. But checklist options can be easily lost amid the flurry of information provided to students during a field-course orientation. The items on the list can seem simplistic or mundane when lumped in with advice about what clothes to pack. The inherent inadequacy of addressing ethics primarily through pre-trip information sessions led us to think about how to build preparation for the dilemmas of ethical practice into students' prior coursework and their other experiences as students studying conflict. Given our project on conflict resolution pedagogy, we had the opportunity to explore how classroom-based experiential learning could contribute to preparation for field-based courses.

PREPARATION THROUGH CLASSROOM-BASED EXPERIENTIAL LEARNING

As we discuss in the introduction to this volume, we became convinced during the UELP initiative that ELAs conducted in the classroom also offer opportunities to provide students some of the skills needed to succeed in field-based courses. This preparation can also expose students to ethical dilemmas that practitioners can expect to encounter when in the field. For instance, one of our activities, Community at Odds in Voinjama, Liberia: An Introduction to Conflict Intervention, asks students to play the roles of four organizations that take on developing intervention strategies to facilitate community conflict resolution following violent clashes that had left four people dead and many buildings destroyed. The groups are an international conflict resolution NGO, an international service-oriented organization focusing primarily on educational and health issues, a local interfaith group, and a government of Liberia–supported committee that works on issues of human rights and reconciliation. The ELA has a number of objectives, including helping students to better understand how to link the diagnosis of conflict dynamics with intervention strategies and to consider how third-party goals for intervention align, or do not, with local community goals. The students work in groups developing their intervention strategies, report them to the whole group, and then engage in a facilitated discussion about their experience.

During Community at Odds, students have the opportunity to explore some of the ethical questions that third-party interveners often face.

The questions students grapple with include: How do you ensure that the intervention you are designing does not make the conflict worse rather than facilitate its resolution? What kind of ground knowledge would you need to design an effective intervention? How would you go about ensuring that what the community wanted and saw as desirable was what you provided? How would you determine what outcomes parties want out of the intervention? How do you recognize the limits of what you can achieve through your intervention, and how do you communicate those limits to your community partners? When we ran this exercise, we found that students came to appreciate the complexity of conflicts and their multidimensional nature and how challenging therefore is the task that interveners face. They also came to appreciate how essential it is to listen to diverse voices within the community as they design their intervention.

In 2014, we expanded the exercise to include the Ebola epidemic, which had thrown the region into turmoil. Halfway through the exercise the students were told that two of the groups (the international ones) were being pulled out because of the epidemic and that a new group was arriving to provide the needed medical care. Students were asked to grapple with the implications of international groups leaving during a crisis situation, what it did to their programming and their relationships with their local partners. We found that introduction of this development provided an especially fruitful opportunity to explore the ethical implications of interventions. The students' reactions to the evacuation order were often quite dramatic. Some students assigned to the international groups simply refused to go, arguing that they had made promises and commitments to the community and therefore leaving when that community faced such a profound crisis was deeply unethical. Many students who had taken on the roles of local organizations expressed shock and dismay and often a profound sense of betrayal, thus allowing the whole class to explore ethical dilemmas that interveners face when working in zones of conflict.

In general, role plays are a significant form of classroom experiential learning that can be used to build the skills and understandings that students will need in the service learning setting. Any well-crafted role play has some general characteristics that are useful preparation for field-based courses: they force students to view conflicts from multiple, specific positions. Such experiments in perspective-taking get students outside of themselves and push them toward recognizing that their own view might not be paramount in a practice situation. They must also adjust quickly yet thoughtfully as the dynamics of the situation change and they are compelled to respond to other participants. Thus, they experience how relationships are intersubjective and negotiated. If proper reflection on the exercise takes place, students are provided with a good base for understanding their influence on others. In the role-play exercise described above, multiple characters could take a leadership role in addressing the conflict. The role plays we have created invite students to try to move toward some kind of constructive change, yet we try to encourage them not to simplify in order to resolve the conflict in an unrealistic way. Role plays can also acquaint students with the experience of missing the chance for a do-over, because once the activity is over, the grade is determined. Although a grade is quite a different kind of consequence than what students face in the field, the need to rise to the occasion is still prominent and important.

Our experience with the UELP convinced us that field-based courses are extraordinary forms of learning. But pulling them off requires direct and sustained attention to ethical practice and reflective practice in the broader curriculum. Building experiential exercises into the curriculum so that they have an effect on the students can require a concerted effort. Other course topics and pedagogical approaches can also improve students' ability to succeed in field-based courses. For instance, students need to be aware of history—including, in some cases, the history of colonization, marginalization, exploitation, displacement, and so forth—in the areas in which they will travel. Students need to understand better the context into which they will be going and to reflect upon their own privilege and how they may be perceived by those with whom they will work and interact when in the field. This preparation could entail a wide range of activities, such as reading poetry or novels, perhaps in addition to history; seeing films or a play might supplement other classroom work based on more conventional conflict literature. We recognize that such curricular innovations can be difficult to pull off. Faculty often do not share a common approach to curriculum, and departments and schools seldom set aside time to consider such issues comprehensively. Discussions of pedagogy can be a struggle for overworked faculty focused on their own research or handling their many other duties. Likewise, faculty may have only limited time to engage in cocurricular activities with students. Despite these limitations and challenges, however, faculty can draw on the resources that a growing number of journals provide through the publication of articles that focus on pedagogical innovation and best practices, such as *Conflict Resolution Quarterly*, the *Journal of Peace Education*, *Peace and Change*, and *International Studies Quarterly*. Sharing experiences of field-based education in a wide range of venues will spark improvements in course delivery and help instructors anticipate and prepare for the ethical challenges that they and their students might encounter.

Note

1. The project was funded by a grant from the US Department of Education Fund for Improvement of Post-Secondary Education. The overarching framework of the project was "linking theory to practice." The project had multiple goals related to improving student learning in the interdisciplinary field of CAR. In particular, three overarching objectives guided our work: curricular innovation, challenging students to connect theory to practice, and teaching critical thinking, perspective-taking, and problem-solving to students.

TWO

Framing "Experience" in International Field-Based Learning

LESLIE DWYER AND ALISON CASTEL

> I had never wanted to surrender the conviction that one could teach without reinforcing existing systems of domination.
>
> —bell hooks (1994, 304)

What do we mean when we invoke "experience" in our calls to expand students' opportunities for learning? And how do our ideas and assumptions about experience—what it is, how it operates, and how to value it—shape possibilities for transformative learning in contexts marked by social conflict and human suffering? To address these questions, we draw in this chapter on our own involvement in designing and teaching field-based study-abroad courses for students of conflict analysis and resolution. We critically reflect on how framings of experience as a commodity form, as a direct encounter with "the real," and as a site for self-actualization in an era of neoliberal personhood shape and constrain the potential of field-based learning. We conclude by offering some practical models and suggestions for curricular design and pedagogical strategies, stressing the importance of sustained reflection on the ethics and politics of fieldwork, as well as open dialogue with students on their positioning, the pressures they face, and the narrative storylines they use to make meaning of their work.[1]

At the universities where we teach, experiential learning is often described as "hands-on" learning, a pedagogical innovation that "connects the classroom to the world" (School of Integrative Studies n.d.), or a "process through which students develop knowledge, skills, and values from direct experiences outside a traditional academic setting."[2] Faculty are encouraged to incorporate experiential elements into their pedagogy, both to benefit students and to "make teaching more exciting and rewarding" (Stearns Center for Teaching and Faculty Excellence n.d.). The Association of American Colleges and Universities (AACU) describes experiential learning in similar terms, classifying it as a "high impact educational practice," one that can "give students direct experience with issues they are studying" and help them "apply what they are learning in real-world settings" (AACU n.d.). Yet what is sometimes missing from these calls to ground learning in experience is a reflection on the category of experience itself and the ethical challenges it raises (see chapter 1, this volume). Experience is often positioned as strangely self-evident: through some mysterious alchemy of self and world, learning happens when we loosen the ties binding us to the traditional classroom, engaging "real-world" others in ways that are imagined, explicitly or implicitly, to be authentic and universally relevant.

We suggest, however, that more consideration of the category of experience and how it is envisioned and enacted in pedagogy is vital for designing truly transformative learning. Of course, we are far from the first to call for such theorizing of experience. Karl Marx famously stated that people "make their own history, but they do not make it just as they please; they do not make it under circumstances chosen by themselves, but under circumstances directly encountered, given and transmitted from the past" (Marx 1974, 146). In the experiential learning context, this means that when students and faculty experience, they do so in relation to past experiences, expectations for what would constitute an "exciting and rewarding" experience, and, in field-based study-abroad experiential learning programs, in relation to the experiences of the others they encounter, who may have long histories of being subject to the interest and aid of scholars, tourists, or even military or colonial regimes (see chapter 3). Feminist scholars have also been profound critics of the undigested notions of experience that were common to first-wave feminist attempts to render the slogan "the personal is political" into grounds for scholarship and activism. These thinkers advocated for deeper engagement with people's everyday gendered struggles, challenging ivory-tower pretensions to theorize at a distance, just as those of us who advocate for field-based learning recognize the extraordinary value of student engagement with the complexities of people's lives and contexts. Yet these feminist scholars reminded us that experience itself is never unmediated; instead, it emerges out of discursive fields structured by power.[3] The experiencing subject, whether that experience is of gender oppression or a university trip to a conflict zone, does not exist in a priori relation to experience; she does not simply "have" an experience or "take" a course. Instead, her voice, agency, and meaning-making practices—the languages she uses to challenge power or to engage with another's hopes and history—are manifested through frameworks that structure the possibilities for how she apprehends her own and others' experiences. Experience is thus not always transformative in a predictable way. Indeed, the force of the frames that shape it may provoke misidentifications or mistranslations, as when victims blame themselves rather than oppressive structures or when students filter the sights and sounds and events of study abroad through prefigured screens.

Theorists of narrative have also opened up the black box of experience to critical light. Narrative theory emphasizes how we apprehend the world through stories about its meaning (Bruner 1990), including those we tell ourselves about the past and our imaginations of the future, about what we think we know of others, and what we anticipate our interactions with them will be like. These narratives are constantly changing, their life histories evolving as they encounter others' stories. Experience, in such a view, is never simply "direct"; it is fundamentally mediated by the social, by the forms and practices of the languages we are given to use, at the same time as these are open to creative agency. In field-based learning, students may arrive in another context with hopes of engagement with difference but with their habitual narrative frames intact (Winslade 2009). Without intentional pedagogical work to make these frames first visible and then porous, students may wrench others' words to fit their own structures of meaning, a risk that becomes all the more prevalent when study abroad is viewed primarily as an opportunity to gain "expertise" in others' conflicts or to speak sensibly on behalf of others in the terms most familiar to professors or policymakers at home.

Using a narrative lens to consider the dynamics of experience can also be helpful in making transparent the politics of speaking about experiences in the field itself. In a narrative landscape, personal and community stories are inflected by master narratives that operate to constrain, elaborate, or contain experiences (Cobb 2013). These master narratives, which are not always apparent to us even as we deploy them, provide the conditions that make certain actions possible: they influence which stories can be told, which stories may be silenced (Nelson 2001), and, in the context of study abroad, which stories are considered appropriate, safe, or suitable for students and researchers to access. Understanding our positions as speakers and listeners within these narrative landscapes is crucial (Harre and Slocum 2003): it helps us to avoid the assumption of a flattened narrative terrain in which all voices carry equally, as well as to resist the notion that others' stories are commodities that have been purchased along with course credits, a temptation that we suggest is a real one in an era of "eating the other"—bell hooks's description of the drive to consume difference (hooks 1992)—and of education itself as a consumer good rather than a challenge.

In this chapter, we build upon these critical insights to consider how we, as university faculty members and administrators, understand, teach, and, indeed, sometimes market experience. Specifically, we are interested in how powerful discursive frames shape the "experience of experience" in field-based study-abroad programs for students of conflict analysis and resolution, an academic arena that has seen a radically increased commitment to providing students with the field experience deemed necessary to prepare them for careers in peacebuilding work (Carstarphen et al. 2010). We consider field-based experiential education not simply as an opportunity to expand the geographic scope of learning—as it is so often framed in calls to move students beyond the walls of the classroom to engage in the "real world"—but as a pedagogical project that participates in powerful narrative frames, some of which may in fact diminish social imaginations and interactions. We discuss how shifting demands for professional competencies impact students' expectations of experiential study-abroad programs, arguing that a framing of experience as something to be acquired—and, quite often, acquired in a form that can be neatly encapsulated on a résumé—can mold experience into a commodity, a material object to be consumed or transacted. Here we draw upon narrative theories that highlight the workings of constraint, which thins the kinds of meaning that participants can make of their experiences, as well as scholarship on education in an age of neoliberal profit and personhood.

The reflections we share in this chapter emerged out of our own participation in experiential learning projects as faculty designing and leading field-based study-abroad programs, both separately and collaboratively. Both of us have taught field-based courses for over a decade, Dwyer in Indonesia and Castel in Colombia, Rwanda, West Virginia, and Israel/Palestine. In 2005, we worked together to create a program that would bring US undergraduate, and later master's and PhD, students to Indonesia to teach them ethnographic field methods in collaboration with local community organizations and in direct partnership with Indonesian counterpart students. In designing these varied programs, we have sought intentionally to transgress canonical study-abroad practices that position non-US students and scholars primarily as resources to enable the experiences, and academic empowerment, of US participants. Instead, we have implemented models that emphasize collaboration and mutual benefit among US students, local students, and local community organizations. We share illustrations of our own programs not to evaluate their successes and failures—although there certainly have been both—but to offer ethnographic insight into key themes that we suspect shape similar programs organized around the pursuit of experience. We conclude by drawing upon both theory and ethnography to suggest how instructors might address some of the challenges we have identified.

Scene 1, Dwyer: Was It Worth It?
The Consumption of "Experience" in Study Abroad

> "Wow, that was amazing! It was so worth going there," Anna (not her real name) exclaimed as the van transporting our study-abroad group wound its way down a narrow Balinese street on the way back from an evening meeting with a

group of women activists. As the instructor of a two-week-long intensive experiential learning course on gender and conflict in Indonesia, I had organized a meeting with local gender rights advocates, imagining a forum where US students and Indonesian activists could learn from each other about the issues facing their communities. Four Indonesian women had just shared stories of challenging violence and social marginalization to fight for gender equality in their communities.

The formal discussion had been lively and moving, but I had grown frustrated with my students who, after seeming so alert and engaged as we sat together in a circle, retreated to a corner of the open-air courtyard for the postdiscussion refreshments, huddling together to chat about their social-media posts and upcoming course selections, ignoring the women who had just shared their stories with such passion. Looking around the segregated space, it was easy for me to imagine that our meeting had done little to challenge global divides between feminist movements or to upend colonial histories of privileged Westerners visiting places such as Bali, viewing the Balinese themselves as merely an exotic backdrop for their touristic entertainment.

With these thoughts racing, I spoke to my students more harshly than I intended, telling them that these women, part of a community with whom I had long-standing personal and professional ties, had come there that night with their own desires to engage, to learn alongside students devoted to working against gender inequality in the United States, a country they considered to have achieved milestones in gender equality. As I recalled the young single mother who had just shared a heartbreaking story of a husband who had infected her and her unborn child with HIV before passing away, leaving her stigmatized in her society but determined to work for social change, I grew more upset. "They're not here because they're being employed to teach," I said. "They're here because they're interested in your reactions and experiences, in what they can also learn from meeting you. Can you get out of your American corner and show them more respect?"

The students immediately dispersed and engaged their Indonesian hosts in deeper conversations. The Indonesian women thanked us for our visit, although I left with an uneasy feeling that they had given far more than they received. It was only later, in the van after Anna commented on the "worth" of the experience, that I was able to more clearly and critically reflect on what had just happened. I knew from long days of conversation with these students that Anna and several of her classmates had needed to take student loans to participate in the program and the prospect of debt, combined with a competitive job market, weighed heavily on their minds. Anna had shared stories of how she had sent out hundreds of job applications, hoping to find a position in the international development field after graduation but still had not seen success. Employers were looking for "field experience." While my students were *genuinely interested in how gender and conflict issues took shape in Indonesia, they were also keen to gain an experience that could be read by others as a competency, as the ability to speak with expertise on behalf of suffering others. It was perhaps no surprise, I realized, that they had a heightened consciousness of the commodity aspects of experience—of whether or not it was "worth it." Consciously or not, perhaps after they had acquired what substance there was to consume from the conversation, they had turned off their attention, positioning the women they met as "content providers" whose job was done.*

I had also, I realized, failed them as a teacher, assuming they would be not only eager but prepared to engage, to step out of the scripted format of the university classroom to interact openly and informally with those they were meeting. I hadn't made clear my vision of experience as give-and-take rather than a passive acquisition of knowledge. I underestimated the breadth of the divide that made it so difficult for students to speak with those who had suffered injustices they had, in many cases, only read about. I hadn't fully explained the thirst I knew the Balinese women were bringing to our meeting, their hopes that they could also learn something from US experiences with gendered oppression. Confused at what I saw as my students' reluctance to engage, I hadn't considered that maybe they simply didn't know how, that their prior educational experiences hadn't taught them to identify and break down the consumer model of knowledge acquisition they had been socialized into. And in my framing of the meeting as a dialogue, as an opportunity for mutual sharing, I failed my Balinese colleagues, not realizing they would be treated as visiting lecturers, not anticipating that I should in fact have paid them as such. For all of us, there were missed opportunities to move past our prefigured frames.

Field-based experiential learning in conflict and postconflict contexts tends, more often than not, to bring Euro-American students into encounters laden with power. By this we do not simply mean that our study-abroad students have more material resources than those they meet—often they do, and sometimes they do not. Nor do we mean that local conflict survivors, activists, and students lack agency to challenge the positions they are given to occupy, either by pedagogical designs or global political economy. (The number of times our students have been asked by Indonesians or Colombians about police violence, racism, or warmongering in the United States bears witness to this). We do suggest, however, that it is important to recognize that our students are entering into sociopolitical fields that are typically marked by long histories of complex and often violent contact. Despite the language of direct experience that frequently accompanies experiential learning, our students step into arenas that are highly mediated by past and present inequalities and abuse. It is difficult, for example, for anyone visiting Indonesia to escape the fact that cross-cultural encounters there have been shaped by centuries of exoticizing tourism, exploitative colonialism, and the appropriation of local resources and labor for the pleasure and profit of Northern elites. We do not meet on equal historical ground, and we do not meet simply as humans unencumbered by past stereotypes of each other or ongoing complicity in global disparities. Even when our students position themselves in critical relation to power—or when we fairly compensate local teachers for their time—field-based courses may become little more than "infotainment" or a more exclusive form of tourism in which local lives become objects for consumption. When course structures discourage us from raising critical questions about who benefits from students' presence in the field or how social encounters can resist the unequal positions historical precedent has set for us, we fail to optimize the benefits of field-based learning not only for individual students but also for solidarity and peacebuilding writ large.

In raising these issues of power, we are not claiming that international experiential education programs are inherently exploitative or that they work simply to reinforce domination. Certainly some have made such claims. Talya Zemach-Bersin is one such strident critic, warning that "the discourse of study abroad appropriates the global to service the interests of the U.S. by re-naming imperialist and nationalistic projects with the rhetoric of 'global understanding,' 'international education,' and 'global citizenship.' The 'globe' is something to be consumed, a commodity that the privileged American student has the unchallenged and unquestioned right to obtain as an entitled citizen of the world" (Zemach-Bersin 2007, 26). Study abroad, according to this critique, becomes an extractive industry in which the fortunate few consume the spectacle of others' experience on demand or, in the case of field-based conflict resolution programs, others' suffering. And indeed it is important to recognize the privilege of being able not only to travel and witness but also to experience conflict without living it, without being vulnerable to the harms it causes, to exit the field site and return to the relative safety of the US university, as mentioned in the introductory chapter of this volume. For students asked to analyze and represent their experiences through course papers and journals, there is an additional privilege inherent to being assigned the role of the cosmopolitan analyst who arranges the raw "data" of others' lives and words into an academic product typically of primary—or sole—benefit to the student herself. The risk, of course, from such a critique is that we abandon projects that bring people together across borders and barriers at a time when, perhaps more than ever, we need to attach a human face to difference, along with a deep and complex understanding of how conflict is lived and resisted. We believe that too much of the knowledge that is produced about conflict is generated from afar, through "experience-distant" methodologies or from the comfortable confines of international development consultants' air-conditioned itineraries. Field-based study-abroad programs that push students off the worn tracks of their intellectual or political assumptions and that force them to engage with the messy and often ambiguous contours of conflicts can play a role in challenging these dynamics, but it is crucial not to assume that this will inevitably happen without sustained pedagogical attention to the process of experiencing.

At the same time, to understand fully the frames that shape our students' "experiences of experience," it is also important to acknowledge their own vulnerabilities within contemporary systems of power, especially the political economic structures that shape higher education. With few exceptions, our US students have been socialized from their early years into educational cultures that position them primarily as consumers of knowledge, and they face a postgraduation marketplace that assigns value to their experiences to the extent that they can be easily translated into professional competencies. Students now have the opportunity to pay thousands of dollars for short-term travel to conflict zones in order to become socially legible as "experts," ideally equipped to advance their careers or fill more boxes on their job applications. On university campuses, the market for international study-abroad programs has expanded to meet growing demand, and global studies offices, international service learning programs, and short-term field courses play an increasing role in students' educational programs. Declining state support for higher education means that those who take advantage of these field experiences often go substantially into debt, an anxious state that can be relieved by its reframing as an "investment."

Much has been written challenging the increasing marketization of education, from Paulo Freire's (2008) formative critique of the "banking" model of learning, in which expert teachers "deposit" knowledge into students' passive minds, to more recent rebukes of the neoliberal university in which audit cultures and their rhetorics of performance, accountability, and outcomes, along with bureaucratic oversight and quantitative metrics, work to recast teaching and learning as market correlates.[4] And while field-based study-abroad programs, with their intentional efforts to innovate and expand the domain of learning, might seem well positioned to flout these trends, they are not just embedded in the same political-economic field—they also often work to produce and amplify the kinds of personhood that emerge through neoliberal "technologies of self" (Michel Foucault, as cited in Shore and Wright 1999) in which empowerment and self-actualization are achieved by framing one's subjectivity as "a collection of assets that must be continually invested in, nurtured, managed, and developed" (Martin 2000, 582). Writing of neoliberal personhood, Ilana Gershon states that "a neoliberal perspective assumes that the actors who create and are created by the most ideal social order are those who reflexively and flexibly manage themselves as one owns and manages a business, tending to one's own qualities and traits as owned and even improvable assets" (Gershon 2011, 542). For study-abroad students, this often means directing keen attention to the transformation of debt into potential, to the market value of knowledge and its valuation as skill, and to the relative "worth" of experiences.

In the conflict resolution field, which has long struggled to be recognized as a professional discipline, such discourses of personhood are perhaps even more weighted; certainly they are able to be easily recast in the legitimizing light of altruism, or what social entrepreneurship and corporate social-responsibility discourse calls "doing well to do good." These forms of personhood have extraordinary influence on the practice of field-based teaching and learning, from the kinds of evaluations and metrics that we use to measure the effectiveness of instruction to the everyday encounters students have with those they meet while abroad. Yet it is rare that we intentionally highlight their operation as part of our pedagogical strategies. Instead, our focus has traditionally been on content rather than process, on "the field" as a stable context students enter into and exit from, an "out there" in which one gains fluency or mastery, on experience as acquisitive.

Scene 2, Castel: Artisanal Swag—Narrative and Commodification

Our field-study course brought us to the largely unvisited Montes de María region on the Caribbean coast of Colombia to meet and spend time with victims, victims' advocates, nongovernmental organizations, human rights defenders, peacebuilders, military, government officials, and former combatants of the country's long-standing conflict. The students had been anxiously awaiting our scheduled meeting with an Afro-Colombian community, eager to explore how race, class, faith, and victimhood intersected for people reweaving their social fabric in the aftermath of violence. The community members we were to visit had gained a significant amount of national and international renown, both for their participation in the successful judicial sentencing of the paramilitary organizers of their forced displacement fifteen years earlier and for a quilting project in which local evangelical women gathered to heal from the trauma of violence by sewing and embroidering while sharing hopes and memories together.

During the two-hour ride in an air-conditioned van, one student blared hip-hop music from her iPhone, while others chatted or slept. Upon arriving, as we exited the vehicle off of the main road and entered the community, we passed local vendors selling fruits and vegetables and preparing a traditional soup to sell to peasant farmers returning from their fields for lunch. We were guided down an unpaved road lined by homes that had been upgraded with funds from reparations the community had recently received, eventually arriving at the home of one of the community leaders, whom I'll call Graciela. Graciela had initiated the women's quilting project, and she stored the materials as well as the finished products in her home. Upon entering Graciela's house, the students immediately gravitated to a pile of quilted items casually placed on a table by the window in the front room. Without acknowledging the community members who were gathered around to welcome us, the students huddled, anxiously discussing their Colombian cash flow while trying on quilted shirts and taking "selfies," hoping they could pool enough funds together to make their purchases. As the group rummaged through the "local artisanal swag" produced by the women's quilting circle, two students hung back, visibly uncomfortable. One of them turned to me and said that he would like to write his final paper for the course on what he characterized as the "spectacle" of that moment, which was defined by the capitalistic *exchange of goods. It was obvious that Graciela was not anticipating the clamor for the products; however, she actively participated in the moment, exhibiting pride as a Muslim student of African descent posed with her artistry. One of the students exclaimed, "You should be on the flyer for next year's field-study course!" Eventually, Graciela organized the chaos, and once the negotiations for purchasing the various items were settled, we were able to begin to meet the community members, and listen to their stories.*

I watched these interactions unfold with a healthy dose of discomfort as I considered the ethics and politics of the material exchange. Did the students' swift consumption of goods undermine the history of the women and their quilting process because it was not linked to an acknowledgment of their experiences of violence or to any articulation of the meaning of the products? In retrospect, I wondered if I had missed a teachable moment, an opportunity to tease out the complexity of the interaction. On the one hand, these women were accustomed to sharing their tapestry work with other communities and to selling small quilts to family members of foreign volunteers. They were also managing to create an income stream that could contribute to more stable livelihoods for themselves and their families. On the other hand, an exchange of goods on this scale with strangers was new to the community, raising important ethical questions about the potential that moments like these have for encouraging relational dynamics between community members and visitors that privilege what can be consumed with money over a politics of solidarity.

Once again, it is important to understand the frames that lead students to "experience the experience" through the logic of the commodity form. As instructors, we have sometimes been tempted to interpret events such as souvenir-buying and selfie-taking as idiosyncratic expressions of individual behaviors that could be controlled by setting firmer ground rules (e.g., "make sure you greet people first" or "ask people before taking pictures"). However, we also want to analyze this in terms of broader global relations of exchange. There are many transactions that take place during field-based study abroad, from the exchange of tuition fees for travel, teaching, and access to instructors' networks of communities and organizations to the compensation of translators, drivers, guides, and vendors. At any of these transactional moments, students' experience may thicken or thin as opportunities for learning are taken up or missed.

When students engage in field-based programs as consumers of an experience-as-product delivered in order to satisfy a relationship of exchange, they may miss a broader political economy of experience in which they become often unwitting participants. When students parachute into particular contexts in order to hear "real" stories "on the ground" and when the acquisition of such narratives is viewed as a key component of developing students' expertise, pressure is placed on communities affected by violence and marginalization to voice their experiences of harm and/or recovery. Of course, study-abroad participants are not the only ones soliciting such stories; academic researchers, activists, journalists, and formal postconflict mechanisms (e.g., truth and reconciliation commissions) all attempt to elicit narratives from survivors of traumatic experiences in order to make sense of conflict. In many contexts, however, survivors of violence are increasingly cognizant of how these narrative flows are all-too-often unidirectional, involving minimal vulnerability on the part of foreign listeners while accruing uneven benefits. Christopher J. Colvin's research with the Khulumani of South Africa is telling in this regard, describing local efforts to charge researchers for their stories, with communities staking their claims through a language of intellectual property rights. Within what Colvin characterizes as a "global political economy of traumatic storytelling," where neoliberal economic frameworks cast narratives of suffering within frames of value, student encounters with others' experiences may be shaped by mutual expectations of benefit whose logics may be illegible or misunderstood by the parties to these transactions (Colvin 2006).

Indeed, Graciela's neighbors were no strangers to the commodification of experience. In the aftermath of violence, their community had been incorporated into frameworks of neoliberal peacebuilding, which privilege free-market economic structures and development strategies as remedies for conflict. (For a critical overview of liberal peacebuilding approaches, see Richmond 2011). As the women's quilts gained increasing visibility through their circulation in other forcefully displaced communities and, eventually, in an exhibit at the National Museum in Bogotá, their stories took on new meanings, weaving into master narratives of entrepreneurship as a remedy for conflict. As their stories of suffering, represented through the vivid colors and patterns of their quilts, found appreciative buyers, they became linked to material profit. Originally a space for women to spend time together, quilting their traumatic stories and engaging in dialogue about violence and women's marginalization, the once-private quilting circle had shifted to become a small business. Eventually the quilts themselves changed, with those sold to the students depicting not experiences of violence but images of a "healed" and "flourishing" community, including scenes of children swimming in flowing rivers framed by a mountainous backdrop. This imagery, so appealing to tourist buyers, was not wholly untrue, but it did obscure the history of violence in the community and its continued role in the complex reality of everyday life.

In telling the story of the students' quilt purchases, it is easy and comforting to nestle into the moment of connection when Graciela, an Afro-Colombian, encountered her first Muslim of African descent and embraced her in a photograph, a medium for connecting two people who do not share a common spoken language. Yet simply to focus on this moment, without attention to the complex histories that made it possible, is to miss an important opportunity for questioning. Who is the audience for these quilts? How did these representations of a flourishing Colombia become desirable, both to the artists and their buyers? What are the social and political implications of this commodification of representations of postconflict Colombia, as an intracommunity healing process becomes a business endeavor, beholden to the aesthetic judgment of outsiders? And how do students studying conflict become positioned not simply as consumers of community stories but as part of their circulation as well? As their selfies move across the Internet, as they reminisce and represent their experiences to friends, family, and colleagues, and as they display their souvenirs brought home from conflict zones, they also help shape what is possible—and impossible—to know about others' lives and struggles. How are students prepared to narrate their experiences and take responsibility for their portrayals of others? What might they say, not just in their academic papers but also in conversation with a friend about a quilt hanging on an apartment wall?

To raise these questions here, and to raise them in conversation with students, is not to criticize either Graciela or the student she embraced for seeking human connection across culture, religion, and class. As illustrated in the vignette above, Graciela appeared happy to pose for a photograph and to sell the women's work. Nor is it to suggest that students should not contribute to local economies through the purchasing of artisans' goods, that colorful selfies of others' lives and livelihoods are necessarily reductionist, or that the bonds they form with others, no matter how momentary, are not meaningful or genuine. Certainly, by purchasing the women's quilts, the students were making much-welcome contributions to local livelihoods. It is, though, to urge that moments like these not be overlooked as rich points of learning, where the complexity and context of such engagements can become visible. Rather than remain silent about the positionality created through such commodified, material exchanges, it is possible to imagine more ethical engagements that support relational exchanges and the creation of new social relationships through dialogic processes that acknowledge the tensions in the framing of "experience."

Scene 3, Castel: The Uncomfortable Adventure— Authenticity and Entitlement

During our field study in Colombia, we visited members of communities who had been victimized by violent conflict and were working to make themselves visible to the state, which had neglected them for years. For many communities, especially in rural areas, having visitors come and share a meal and learn about ongoing local struggles for recognition and rights is considered a rare relational opportunity that comes with the potential to increase community visibility. In the effort to spread this opportunity more widely, our Colombian colleagues requested that our study-abroad group visit a distant community in the High Mountain Region. Having my own knowledge about the harsh terrain in that area, I agreed reluctantly, wanting to be responsive to my colleagues' wishes but also concerned about how the students would react to the inevitable discomfort.

Climbing a mountain for almost two hours while packed into open-air, all-wheel-drive vehicles worn from too many journeys on barely passable, uneven ground, proved to be as challenging as I had anticipated. As the line of vehicles slowly careened up the mountain, I could feel every bump and crack in the dirt road. I gripped the dashboard tightly to give my Colombian colleague as much space as possible on our shared seat, but still she had to fight to keep her body inside the vehicle. In the back seat, local peasant farmers sang songs about the mountain and conversed with relative ease as I contemplated the backlash I was convinced I would receive from the students who were in the vehicle ahead of us. I turned to my colleague during a moment of calm, commenting that we should reconsider this excursion for next year's field course. Her back arched uncomfortably as we traversed the next bump, and she agreed.

When we finally reached our destination, one student immediately rushed out of the vehicle to the nearby bushes to vomit. The rest of the students gathered around in a celebratory mood as they shared their reactions to the "crazy authentic ride" and the triumph of reaching the top. A few students groaned, while others whined loudly about their pain and suffering during the ride. One student teased the group, saying, "You've all been abroad [in the developing world] before. Seriously, you should be able to handle this!"

As we approached the gates to the local school, community leaders welcomed us and gave us a tour of the grounds. They explained that sometimes the school's two teachers have difficulty getting to work because of the roads. This meant that students could not always attend classes in the event of rain. They also shared that the community's inaccessibility by road meant that it only had access to health care every other week when a doctor came to visit. The US students were awestruck as the community leaders described their system for transporting people to the hospital during an emergency. Because the vehicle journey was so harrowing for a pregnant woman in labor or an ailing elder, community members would gather at the road in response to a neighbor's shout for help and carry the patient on a hand-made stretcher down the mountain to the nearest municipality. Sprinting down the mountain between communities, they would hail a new set of stretcher-bearers to take over the next relay as they descended. In this fashion, they could reach the hospital in about forty minutes.

Hearing these stories about a road they had just hailed as a thrilling authentic experience raised a host of concerns and emotions for the students. They were impressed to hear of the community's initiative and angry to learn about its challenges accessing health care and education. But most of all, they were able to engage in serious conversation and reflection about the fact that the journey along the bone-shattering road was not an optional "experience" for people living there but a daily reality. Yet the following year, when the road was finally paved, the next group of US students expressed disappointment that they were not able to experience the infamous "authentic" journey they had heard so much about from their peers.

In many field-based conflict courses, including the ones we have designed, students are given access to activities and understandings that lie off the typical tourist path. Faculty may draw on their personal and professional connections to provide students with access to marginalized communities and narratives and to places and practices that are underrepresented in either travel brochures or scholarly literatures. There is a privilege inherent to such access as well as an ethical risk, which is intensified by discourses of authenticity, a concept that weighs the relative value of one's own and others' experience against an implicit standard of difference. The idea of authenticity is often central, either implicitly or explicitly, to field studies, especially those that navigate roads less traveled. It often characterizes our observational judgments of our interlocutors or serves as a goal in our interviews, where we work to elicit stories of "real-life" events and emotions. Yet when students operate with an expectation of entitlement to other's narratives and evaluate their worth in terms of their level of cultural difference or the weight of trauma they bear, there are real risks of exploitation. These discourses of authenticity position victims, communities, geographic locations, or unpaved roads as landscapes for mining authentic experiences for the edification of outsiders. Often it is meetings in poor, rural areas or contexts that are maximally different from where students originate that take on the luster of authenticity. As instructors, however, we need to be mindful that these characterizations of "the poor" or "the less developed" as maximally authentic risk romanticizing hardship in ways that can be dangerous for those who live with, and challenge, such realities, diminishing the value of their struggles.

In discussing authenticity, Arthur W. Frank argues that the concept falls prey to neoliberal frameworks that disconnect experience from history, politics, and ethics, writing that "people can move from experience to politics only when their experience is narratable to themselves and others, and thus made legible" (Frank 2002, 8). In the context of field-based study, this politics of legibility incorporates both students and those they encounter. When students travel to study conflict, they may privilege stories of violence and suffering as reflecting an ultimate reality, legitimizing a particular articulation of communities in relation to themselves, other communities, and the state. The irony of this is that, in many cases, including that of Colombia, we frame our conversations with individuals and communities such that they address a particular experience of violence, which risks losing the point that the experience itself is not something that can be abstracted from everyday life. Violence has a history, politics, and a legacy that results in ongoing daily struggles in its aftermath, making the focus on the event of violence partial. It is crucial not to undermine the need to understand how history and politics created the conditions for certain people to be differentially vulnerable to violence not only in the particular moment but also in their everyday lives. Again, we believe that by leading our students through processes of critical questioning we can help them understand broader and deeper contexts. Moreover, this approach entails considering authenticity as dialogic, part of interactional dynamics that also require students to become vulnerable to shifts in their perceptions and understandings. We can help them ask: How do some communities of victims gain the legibility and legitimacy to have an audience of students and scholars to hear their stories? Does one need to be a victim to speak authentically of conflict? How do our assumptions of authenticity shape which stories are heard and how they circulate locally and globally?

These frames of authenticity do, however, sometimes fracture in the field, working to expose dynamics of difference and privilege, which in turn can lead to powerful learning opportunities when these productive conflicts are opened to dialogue. For example, in Indonesia, our students regularly spent time in homestays with local families, an experience that, for most students, is a welcome opportunity to gain greater insight into ordinary people's lives. However, tensions have arisen when such opportunities push students out of their comfort zones, away from more desirable forms of authenticity toward experiences that feel like constraint. Few of our students have complained about eating local foods or listening to local music. They have, however, expressed dismay at homestay curfews that require students to be in by ten o'clock or at bathrooms that fail to meet Western standards of cleanliness. The latter, in fact, have often provoked fascinating conversations. When one US student of privileged social status took photographs of her grimy squat toilet to share her "authentic" experience abroad on her Instagram account, other students criticized her for "exoticizing" and "demeaning" Indonesian practices. Yet even as this student boasted online about her sacrifice for the sake of "going native," a fellow student from an elite socioeconomic class in a Middle Eastern country expressed reluctance to use such bathrooms, as they offended her sensibilities.

Other tensions emerged when a student traveling abroad for the first time criticized her classmates on her blog, claiming they were "unethical" and "unserious" for spending time writing and relaxing in a guesthouse near the ocean while she was in an "authentic" and impoverished rural area, where her homestay family had moved her to tears by sharing fruit from their backyard tree. After learning of this public defamation, the students whom she criticized, some of whom had been engaged in human rights and social justice work for some time, took offense at the judgment, attributing it to a first-time traveler's "righteousness" and lack of knowledge about "how things really work."

These incidents were often difficult for the students involved. Yet, when framed in discussions as something more than "problematic behavior" or individual preferences or idiosyncrasies, they led to valuable reflection. By asking students to consider how our assumptions about authenticity are shaped and what impacts they have on others, we can break open the concept of "authenticity" as a frame for understanding how students characterize their own experiences, the experiences of others, and the relationships they engage in across cultural divides and sociopolitical landscapes. By opening the idea of "authentic experience" to critical questioning, students can more easily grasp how it operates as a narrative trope that makes certain stories legible over others and certain people or practices seemingly more legitimate than others.

Toward a Transformation of Experience in Field-Based Pedagogy

In our discussion above, we explore how "experience" is shaped in field-based study-abroad programs and how it links to other powerful frames of professionalization, commodification, privilege, and authenticity. But how do we move beyond the constraints of these frames when they are so dominant in today's globalized economy of international study abroad? What kind of pedagogy can create openings for questioning the production of experience, the commodification of others' stories, the politics of authenticity, and the power relationships between researcher and researched? Can we leverage our critical insights to better design field-based curricula, evaluate our programs, and identify opportunities for transformative learning?

First, we believe it vital for these conversations about experience to occupy a more central place in field-based learning. Helping students develop insight into the shaping of their experiences by often unseen, taken-for-granted assumptions is crucial to this effort. Dominant frameworks of experience create grooves in our narratives about ourselves and the world that block us from creating new meanings and understandings and require intentional efforts to dislodge. For John Winslade (2009), these grooves, or "lines of force," reflect the power relations inevitably at play both in conflict settings and in our practices of engaging across difference. By opening these meaning-making practices to shared critical reflection, we have an opportunity to collaboratively investigate power and its complex articulation with structures and subjectivities.

Critical reflective practice is a model we have found enriching in designing dialogues with students in the field. According to Donald A. Schön (1987), as we foray into unfamiliar learning environments, we ask our students let go of their prior conceptions of know-how, which destabilizes their senses of control and confidence. In turn, they may experience confusion and puzzlement and are left to trust in processes created by their instructors. This "submission of self" may be accompanied by feelings of vulnerability that increase the likelihood of defensive responses and behaviors. Schön calls this a "learning bind" that risks reproducing power relationships and narrow perspectives and ultimately undermines the purpose of getting students out of the formal classroom setting. When the stakes and emotions are so high, as is often the case when students are brought into contexts marked by conflict, there is an important distinction to be made between reflection as a space for students to share their feelings and responses and a reflection-in-action that opens up space for analysis, one that helps move the dialogue toward a deeper understanding of not only self but also of self in context and of the context in and of itself. The purpose of such processes is not to create new generalizations—"Oh, so that's why that happened, because Colombians are X!"—but to provide generative tools for new forms of making meaning. Some of the ways we opened such critical reflective conversations in our own teaching are simple. For example, we have asked students to reflect on their own complicity within tourism economies in Indonesia, questioned them about whether they felt comfortable with continuing relationships of solidarity after their grades are submitted, called attention to the narratives that circulate as a result of their selfies, and prompted them to think about how they might narrate the meaning of a locally crafted quilt that will hang on their apartment wall. This kind of critical reflective questioning helps students to gain a deeper understanding not only of their own positioning but also of how their actions and representations help shape the conflict context.

These kinds of dialogues can also help challenge assumptions about authenticity and encourage students to move past the commodification of experience toward a more nuanced understanding of what they are encountering. Not only can we engage with the dominant frames that choreograph students' understandings of themselves in interaction—we can also guide them toward deeper reflection on how experience is produced for those with whom they engage. In our dialogues with students about our interactions with host communities, we encourage students to attend to what they have seen and heard through questions that emphasize narrative context, including: What stories about people and situations did we just hear? Who supports those stories and tells them freely? Who might disagree with or be uncomfortable with these kinds of stories? Whose voices did we not hear? Who is silenced, and who is legitimized? By viewing the encounters they have in the field in terms of these narrative dynamics, students move past simplistic assumptions about a homogeneous, authentic "local," at the same time as they deepen their understanding of the narrative dimensions of conflict itself.

In addition, we have found it crucial to emphasize repeatedly the ethical dimensions of study abroad and the efforts needed to help make our field-study programs beneficial to all of those involved. Fairly compensating those who serve as teachers to our students is important, but it is far from enough. Emphasizing the importance of mutual learning opportunities is crucial when students have been socialized into learning cultures that position them to be passive consumers of others' experiences. Here we have found it helpful to hold conversations with our students about the need to show sensitivity and appreciation, especially when engaging with other people's traumas in contexts where their stories have been historically marginalized. We have also sought out opportunities for more formal mutual learning, for example by designing collaborative program elements where local students join our classes or where our students pair with local students or activists to interview each other about their experiences. These kinds of exercises, which encourage students to work across divides of privilege and to become vulnerable to other's questioning, help shift relational dynamics toward a greater mutuality.

Finally, another arena ripe for rethinking is our evaluation of experiential education programs. Traditional study-abroad models position students as "entering into" and "exiting from" their cross-cultural experiences, as if the contexts in which these experiences take place are fixed and the boundaries between the two well defined. Program evaluations generally focus on measuring students' satisfaction and are typically performed immediately upon conclusion of a program. For example, the National Association for Study Abroad offers a sample evaluation form that includes questions such as "What was your best experience while abroad?," "What was your worst experience while abroad?," and "What did you think of the food?" (NAFSA n.d.). These questions have some benefit, as programs, of course, have a serious responsibility to keep students safe and healthy. However, such metrics fail to generate insight into the often intentionally uncomfortable transformations that well-designed experiential programs seek to engender. Questions that could assess the degree to which students are guided to exceed their comfort zones, to engage with unfamiliar ideas or narratives, or to reflect on their own changing positions throughout the program would ideally generate far more useful data for evaluation.

In addition, in field-based courses that engage with local communities, evaluation should not reinforce the students-as-consumers versus communities-as-content-providers binary. Asking communities to reflect on their own experiences hosting visiting students and making these insights available to students in order to help them see field-based programs as two-way exchanges can be helpful practices. In addition, evaluation practices can better account for the fact that, more often than not, the insights gained from field-based learning unfold over a length of time that exceeds the frame of the course. We have regularly found that students return to us weeks, months, and even years after their field-based courses to explain that it was only later that they understood just how much they had learned, once they had sufficient time to process what in the moment felt simply like discomfort or unease. Evaluations conducted both at the close of a program and at intervals thereafter would be far better positioned to gauge the long-term and often nonlinear effects of field-based learning.

In conclusion, field-based study-abroad programs, especially in conflict zones, generate challenges that require us to rethink our pedagogy and the category of experience itself. We believe that there are powerful opportunities for bringing conversations about experience into our teaching in ways that benefit students, faculty, and host communities alike. In order to do this, we need to expose and understand the dominant narratives that frame our students' understandings of their experiences, the experiences of those whom we encounter during our field studies, and our own experiences as instructors. This critical reflection opens up the space to creatively explore complex dynamics in our interactions, as we move beyond our comfort zones into challenging conflict environments.

Notes

1. The authors would like to thank Susan Hirsch and Agnieszka Paczyńska for the opportunity to share our reflections in this volume. In Indonesia, thanks are due to Elizabeth Rhoads, Sani Widowati, Ngurah Termana, and Ika Ilvania. In Colombia, deep appreciation is owed to Ricardo Esquívia, Lillian Hall, Larisa Zehr, the *equipo* at Sembrandopaz, and the communities of Mampujan, Pichilín, and Alta Montaña who hosted our visit. At George Mason University, Lisa Shaw has been instrumental in supporting our field experience courses with generosity and cheer.

2. "What Is Experiential Learning?," University of Colorado, accessed September 2, 2016, http://www.ucdenver.edu/life/services/ExperientialLearning/about/Pages/WhatisExperientialLearning.aspx.

3. For classic feminist critiques of the category of experience, see Scott (1991) and Mohanty (1992). For a recent compelling discussion of feminist ideas of experience, see Oksala (2016).

4. For discussion of neoliberalism and the university, see Giroux (2014) and Shore and Wright (1999). Pat O'Connor (2014, 38) succinctly describes the key characteristics of the neoliberal shift in university cultures as "a differential evaluation of various kinds of knowledge; a commodification of teaching and research; a focus on commercialization; an audit culture characterized by an increased stress on accountability procedures and budgetary control; a decline in the perceived trustworthiness of professionals; a strengthening of executive decision making and a reliance on appointment rather than election of decision makers."

THREE

Field-Based Courses as Transformative Education

The Role of Practical Ethics as a Framework

PUSHPA IYER

We, a group of US-based graduate students and I as their faculty leader, were watching a cultural dance performance put on for us by our local hosts in Sierra Leone. In the middle of the performance, a male leader of a nongovernmental organization (NGO), whispered in my ear, "You are watching an initiation dance." I was stunned; I had never considered that I could be watching a rite of passage without making an explicit request. Becoming very quickly aware of my ignorance and the questions I had failed to ask, I whispered the news to my students. Our ears perked up; we began viewing the dance, the music, and the dancers differently. Therein began our interest in the practice of female genital mutilation (FGM) in Sierra Leone and the desire to include it in our broader academic research goals for that particular field course.

We were in Sierra Leone to study the challenges to building peace after war. We were meeting various actors from the NGO sector, the government, and civil society. Studying the cultural practice of FGM fitted well with the other issues we had started exploring in the country. We began asking questions about it everywhere we went and quickly realized that we were stepping on a minefield. We met with opposition and reluctance, but, being field researchers, we persisted in trying to educate ourselves on the various perspectives about this practice present in the country. We ended up meeting with many people who wanted to tell the story, wanted to share their views, and wanted to detail their work related to the practice—either its maintenance as an important practice or its eradication as an oppressive one. We took it all in as researchers.

On our very last day, a few of us who were scheduled to fly home the next morning were at dinner when, by pure chance, we met a female anti-FGM activist who shared with us her personal stories and her determination to eradicate the practice in her country. Also present at this conversation were a couple of male NGO workers, including one from our host organization. The female anti-FGM activist had no reservations sharing with us some of her thoughts and experiences, most of which she revealed unprompted but some in response to our questions. Our Sierra Leonean male colleagues (and maybe even some of our male students) did feel uncomfortable with the detailed nature of our conversations on sexual satisfaction and relations. However, the women around the table, led primarily by the anti-FGM activist, continued the discussion.

At one point, the discomforted male Sierra Leonean colleague turned around and asked my students, "How do you derive sexual pleasure?" The students sat in stunned silence, not knowing how to respond, and I quickly told them that they did not need to answer the question. To which, I was directly challenged by our local host: "How is that you come and ask personal questions of our women while you won't answer personal questions?" I responded that while the question was fair, the facts were that we were the ones who had traveled to Sierra Leone to conduct research and that we had acquired permission of the people and our local host NGO. Besides, it was our host organization (of which he, the questioner, was a member) that had assisted us in finding individuals with whom to talk. Moreover, the anti-FGM activist had come forward of her own accord to speak to us. We had not known her or invited her. I also reasoned in my head that I did not want the conversation to reveal the sexual orientation of some of the students in the group, which could have led to security concerns. The anti-FGM activist was silent briefly during our exchange but soon jumped back into her agenda—which was to highlight the negative aspects of the practice. She also gave us her contact information and promised to continue the discussions by email. She begged us to tell her story and talk about her work when we returned to California.

To me, the most important questions as we left the country were: Had I made an ethical decision to ask my students not to respond when we were asked a challenging question? Did we have the right to go to another country and ask them those questions if we were unwilling to be questioned ourselves? How ethical was it for our local host to use his discomfort to discredit our role as researchers? Had we not described our purpose when we initially sought permission months earlier? Had we not stayed true to the role all through the previous two weeks? Finally, a related question: How did we deal with our feelings as a group in response to his question?

I found the answer to the last question soon after our return. The group was torn between guilt and outrage. For me, there had been an ethical dilemma that necessitated me making a quick decision on behalf of the entire group: the desire to give our interviewees the same rights that we had as researchers versus the need to ensure the security of my students and to protect them. For some of my students, the ethical dilemma was how to respect their professor's decision not to answer the question while wanting and being willing to be as open as their interviewee. For others, the ethical dilemma was their desire to be honest versus their fear for the safety of their peers or their unwillingness to be open about sexual practices. There was also another ethical dilemma for some: the guilt about being the outsiders (often "white") who went to "research" others in what could be an exploitative relationship versus the goal of being a researcher for social change. Basically we were all grappling with our ethical dilemmas and coming to different conclusions about the course of action we took.

How do we prepare ourselves for dealing with such ethical dilemmas in the field? Mainly, how do we as a group agree on best practices? Using the framework of practical ethics, I detail the methodology I use when leading field courses. My approach is to prepare the group for ethical challenges while also accepting that it is hard to be prepared for all possible ethical challenges, which makes for many life-changing or transformative learning experiences.

My Field Courses

My field course to Sierra Leone was part of one of my immersive-learning series titled "Challenges to Peacebuilding." Challenges to Peacebuilding is an academic research course that I lead, in which students are introduced to the theory and practice of peacebuilding through the study of a postwar country.[1] The two-week field component of this course is organized during the winter term. Challenges to Peacebuilding has two goals. The first is to supplement and complement conflict resolution theories and concepts learned in the classroom with "real-world" examples of the nature of conflict, its impact on people, peacebuilding initiatives, and the kinds of actors involved in rebuilding and bringing peace to a country. The second goal of this course is to have students learn to deal with the complexities of conducting field research, develop data-collection instruments, and summarize data through qualitative analysis.

In 2009, Challenges to Peacebuilding went to Cambodia; in 2010, the course traveled to Sierra Leone; in 2012, to Nepal; in 2013 to Gujarat, India; and in 2015, Mindanao, the Philippines. Preparations for the field component of the course include predeparture workshops (fall semester) in which students learn about the conflict's history and background. Experts are brought in; students watch documentaries and read scholarly and journalistic articles. Upon return, a debriefing workshop (spring semester) helps students reflect on their experiences, analyze their findings, and present them in a variety of forums.

The two weeks of research in the field is a very structured experience. Visits are planned, meetings organized, and interactions arranged with interviewees ranging from government and military officials to members of NGOs and community organizations. Students get to conduct group interviews, although they each might individually focus on just one aspect of peacebuilding. The learning experiences from the five courses I led as part of Challenges to Peacebuilding lay the foundations for this chapter.[2]

Ethics and Fieldwork

In his 1991 article, Tony Rees quotes Aristotlen J. Barnes (1979, 141), who argues that ethical problems are "those that arise when we try to decide between one course of action and another not in terms of expediency and efficiency but by reference to standards of what is morally right or wrong." This definition is straightforward, but it captures the trickiness when dealing with ethical dilemmas as a group: what happens if the group does not share the same moral values?

Here is another definition that allows a group to deal with ethical challenges more effectively. Feminist scholars Marcia Hill, Kristin Glaser, and Judy Harden (1995) argue that "ethical dilemmas are problems for which no course of action seems satisfactory; these are situations in which there is no 'right' decision, only a decision that is thoughtfully made and perhaps 'more right' than the alternatives" (141). This definition implies that a group that is well prepared—they know and trust one another, and they have anticipated challenging situations—may be better equipped to handle ethical dilemmas. In the example presented at the beginning of the chapter, we spent a lot of time preparing as a group and getting to know one another. However, tension around researching FGM was unanticipated and thereby divided the team.

Fieldwork involves ethical dilemmas at every step because we in the social sciences step into the lives of other humans.[3] Interactions with humans always require us to be sensitive about our behavior, which invariably will affect another person. It is therefore essential that we prepare ourselves to become better at taking ethical decisions. As a first step, it is vital that we know how to recognize an ethical dilemma. John C. King (2009, 8) cautions that if researchers are not trained to recognize and respond to these ethical issues and dilemmas, especially when in conflict zones, they can "at a minimum threaten the validity of one's data and at the maximum threaten the personal security and well-being" of themselves, their team, their interviewees, and their families. Without a doubt, then, the ethical aspect of fieldwork is a crucial element; it is something to be taught and something to be trained in, for one to become a reputable, effective, and ethical fieldworker.

There is yet another reason to include training in ethics before beginning fieldwork. Although, as King (2009, 8) points out, we often leave researchers to their own "innate sensibilities, talents and skills" to deal with ethical and other challenges in the field, what researchers often do has legal ramifications. Consequently, ethical decision-making requires taking into consideration existing laws. This legal aspect of ethical decision-making has influenced the rise and need for institutional review boards in educational institutions. Educational institutions, therefore, have placed more pressure on faculty leaders to prepare students to better deal and resolve ethical dilemmas. However, as Rees (1991, 141) reminds us, there are also dangers that come from overpreparation and too much focus on potential ethical dilemmas and argues that "the more one emphasizes the 'normality' of the ethical problems in social research, the more difficult they become to spot and to sort out unambiguously." With this caution in mind, we turn in the next section to examining the usefulness of the practical ethics framework as a tool for preparing a group to conduct fieldwork.

Understanding Practical Ethics

Ethics has become an important area of study beyond the discipline of philosophy. Applied ethics focuses on applying generalized ethical theory when dealing with moral issues in public and private life, and professional ethics focuses on having a common moral code that is shared by members of a profession. The shortcomings of these approaches gave rise to what Peter Singer (1993) calls "practical ethics." Practical ethics are a form of applied ethics, but they are also about working with a problem in a given context.

Singer argues that practical ethics are the application of ethics or morality (he uses the terms interchangeably) to practical social issues. Ethics, he believes, should not be about an ideal system or a set of rules that has no value in practice. According to him, practical ethics is not having society dictate what is moral or ethical but about judgments and decisions made by individuals when faced with ethical problems. Practical ethics would therefore say subjectivity is okay—that is, we are all entitled to believe and act in accordance with completely different ethical values as long as those judgments are made from a universal point of view that goes beyond self-interest. Thus, practical ethics suggest utilitarianism (greater good of all) with a twist. It should result in the best consequence for an affected population. In the example from Sierra Leone, the decision I made was one, I would argue, that was the best for our group in that given context. I could very well have made a different decision if I had been on my own, had been in the company of only women, or if we had been in a country with more tolerant views on sexual orientation.

The reason I believe practical ethics is the most useful framework for a field-based course such as Challenges to Peacebuilding is that it keeps the focus on the context and it helps us understand why in a context where conflict exists ethical decisions might be different for those who belong to more privileged groups and for those from marginalized communities. However, this also suggests that our context as US-based group visiting a conflict zone means that our decisions in the face of ethical challenges will be different from the choices of the people who live in those conflict zones. Practical ethics can then be a tool for the group to understand their own decisions in a foreign country and also to communicate the moral reasoning behind their decision to others in the group. For example, as it often happens, stomach problems or dietary requirements may lead us to choose to eat a snack we brought along and gently refuse what has been offered by the community. Instead of doing what we think is the polite thing to do, we can articulate our decision to go against culture, using the reasoning of practical ethics. Finally, practical ethics also helps us navigate issues of identity and self-representation (how we present ourselves and want to be known) to other members of the community from whom we are trying to gather information. In the sections below, I explore how I facilitate awareness of practical ethics when I prepare students for their fieldwork experiences and what challenges I continue to experience when leading students on a field course.

Transformative Education through an Ethical Experiential Learning Process

A field course is an experiential course, which then by default is transformative education. I make this statement by drawing on David A. Kolb (1984), who argues that in experiential courses, learning is a process and that knowledge is created or acquired through a personal transformation that comes from that experience. This transformation happens through four stages: concrete experience, reflective observation, abstract conceptualization, and active experimentation.

Kolb's most important point is that for real learning to take place, a person must go through all four stages. Each stage is connected; it does not matter where one starts, but it is only when one goes through all four stages that effective learning takes place. The circular route of learning with clear feedback loops makes transformative education possible. While Kolb's framework applies to learning in general, it can also inform a framework for reflecting about ethics in fieldwork.

Kolb's framework reflects a circular process of learning, but the stages of learning happen during three (linear) components (predeparture, during fieldwork, and postfieldwork) of a field course. In Challenges to Peacebuilding, my pedagogical approach builds on Kolb's idea that learning through experience can be transformational if the stages of experimentation—concrete experience and reflections—are well managed both at the conceptualization stage and also during each of the three periods of a field course. My pedagogy is to encourage the use of the practical-ethics framework to interpret ethical dilemmas during the experience and active experimentation stages. The practical ethics framework not only helps manage the experiences to the greater benefit of those who are affected by a challenge, but it also helps us to refine repeatedly our ethical decisions and thus contributes to a more transformative learning experience. Every ethical decision reflected upon feeds into a loop of changing behavior and attitudes.

My approach of transformative education through a practical ethics framework focuses on two processes in particular:

a. Developing greater humility when in conflict zones through a negotiation of identity. Identity is in flux, especially in conflict zones, and knowing that the experience in the field will see our identities morph means our preidentified identities will be challenged. When identities are challenged, we begin negotiating, and successful negotiation requires a degree of humility because holding on to aspects of identity or imposing identities on others will lead to conflict and be detrimental to the goals of field research. Practical ethics will help provide the tools for successful negotiation.

b. Challenging structures that hold and disseminate knowledge. Knowledge is power, and power is intertwined with knowledge. How knowledge is allowed to be disseminated, who provides the knowledge, and who challenges the knowledge are all integral questions for any field researcher. Further, knowledge is embedded in imbalanced structures, and it is up to the field researcher to reach every level of the structure to gain knowledge. Field courses are my pedagogical strategy to gather knowledge from a variety of sources that dwell in various structural levels. Practical ethics provides the tools to challenge and question knowledge structures.

The following sections deal with how these two aspects of transformative education are addressed in my courses by incorporating practical ethics framework into every component, including predeparture, the trip itself, and the post-trip period.

Negotiating Identity and Challenging Knowledge Structures

When training volunteers, expatriates, and scholars who will spend time in an environment different from their own, the relevance of predeparture training is well recognized. Authors such as Xiaoli Jiang (2016) stress that the predeparture stage is probably the most important stage in a field course and has a direct impact on learning outcomes. In teaching Challenges to Peacebuilding, I devote a considerable amount of time to predeparture training, which takes place over the fall semester when we put in fifteen to twenty hours of time together as a group.

One of the first activities during predeparture training is answering the question "Why are we doing this?" Sharing personal goals for participation in the course sharpens one's reasoning for what one hopes to accomplish through this course. The element of ethical framework applied to this activity leads to conversations around questions such as "What if my goals do not match those of others in the group?" and "What if my goals do not fit with broader goals of the course?" Further, if your goal does not fit the meta goal, then how do you, the student researcher, justify group membership? Practical ethics will demand that the students not only reevaluate personal goals but also apply their ethical reasoning to how they feel about others with goals dissimilar to their own.

Our next set of activities answers the question "Who are we?" to further build on our identity as field researchers. In these activities, students share aspects of their identity that they will carry with them on the trip and evaluate how they will work with the identities of the other group members. Potential identity clashes are reflected upon, and strategies are developed for dealing with conflicts. For example, when I led a course to my hometown in Gujarat, India, I was very up front with the students, telling them that they should see me both as a member of that community (and therefore treat me at times as an interviewee) and as their faculty leader. I spoke with them about the fact that I had strong opinions about the conflict, that I was inevitably biased, but that I also intended to play the role of the course leader to the best of my abilities.

In reflecting on their identities, students are asked to share with the group the personal challenges they anticipate when in the field: What might be some of the assumptions tied to those identities, and how do they anticipate handling such challenging situations? A common one that often comes up is how the "white and American" identities correlate with an assumption that the person has a lot of money. Therefore, if in the field the students are asked for money either for a charitable cause or as compensation for participating in the research activity, how would we as a group, come up with an ethical response? Even if the assumption were completely wrong, we would in most situations have more money than the people to whom we were speaking. Through this discussion, we also identify our views and responses to being asked for cash, which might differ. While I usually insist on a uniform group response when being asked for money (only because money is not unlimited in a field course), discussing our different answers helps us to avoid spending time providing reasons for our predetermined ethical decision. During this activity, I encourage participants to consider the identities that unite us as a group; usually, they are identities of student, researcher, and learner. As much as I firmly believe in this process of knowing yourself and communicating your identity so that others might acknowledge you for who you are, I do think that once we step into the field, our confidence is to some degree challenged both within our group and in the communities in which we spend time.

Recently, I have begun using the framework of Helping, Fixing, Serving developed by Rachel N. Remen (1999) to tie individual and group identities to individual and group goals. For Remen, the framework represents three different ways of seeing life: "When you help, you see life as weak. When you fix, you see life as broken. When you serve, you see life as whole.

Fixing and helping may be the work of the ego, and service the work of the soul. We cannot serve at a distance. We can only serve that to which we are profoundly connected" (Remen 1999, 1).

Remen's framework helps me connect these two activities centered around identity: *Who am I?* and *What am I going to do here?* The two activities lead us to the acknowledgment that, irrespective of our identities, we, as researchers, learners, and students are in the communities to serve. Serving is the work of the soul, and thereby it teaches us humility, dedication, and commitment. There should be no place for arrogance as Western-educated students because ego would mean we were either trying to fix or help.

During predeparture training I also focus on developing humility. This goal comes from my experience in the classroom, where I am often obliged to remind my students that we simply should not be stepping into another country for two weeks and teaching its citizens how to solve their problems. All we can do is learn. I strongly believe that being humble is the first step in being a good researcher. This often is in tension with the academic environment in many universities, including my school, where we are constantly "telling" students that they are equipped to deal with any of the world's social challenges. My field courses are, then, in some ways designed to challenge education itself, specifically to challenge the structures that hold and disseminate knowledge. What Challenges to Peacebuilding does is force the students to negotiate power over knowledge with the communities in which they conduct research. There can be nothing more humbling than negotiating over what counts as knowledge.

Our next set of activities centers on answering the question "What are we going to do with this?" Once again, Remen's framework is helpful in getting students to process their ethical responsibilities with regard to the data we gathered while in the field. If we are to serve, then how do we serve in the context of conducting research in the field? The answer is in finding ways to give back. When announcing my course, I communicate to students that to be selected as a participant of the course, they should come in with a moral obligation to the people whose stories we hear. We simply cannot return home and forget those stories. We have to be their voice (because often people in conflicts do not have a voice or have very little). I, therefore, include as course outcomes some deliverables that go beyond academic requirements. With every one of my courses, there have been concrete outcomes, such as participation in conferences, publication in journals, magazines, blogs, and a coffee-table book, presentation to the academic community and beyond, and contribution to videos and a documentary. To our interviewees, we make the promise to tell their stories in return for them entrusting us with them.

I am aware that in insisting that students work on projects (the bare minimum) disseminating data we have gathered, I am using my privilege as the course leader to impose my nonnegotiable ethical values on the group. I do, however, give the students the option of joining the optional activities after return from the trip. And this is where they, the students, get to make their ethical decisions as to how much they commit themselves.

The final phase in the predeparture stage involves exploring random ethical dilemmas that we as a group might face on the trip, reflecting on our possible ethical decisions and even negotiating them so that we remain united when in the field.

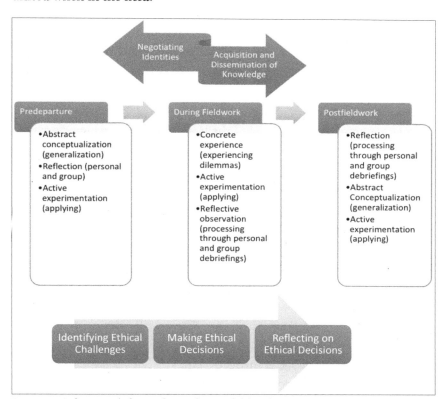

Figure 3.1. A framework for teaching ethics in fieldwork.

To conclude, with predeparture training the group becomes aware that there will be ethical challenges when in the field. To a degree, students are trained to recognize ethical problems, and most importantly they are conscious that the decisions that they make will be ones that must serve the group well. The universality principle in that given context is what makes it all about practical ethics. As mentioned in figure 3.1, all three processes are dealt with: there is reflection in the group, there is some application to real-world case examples, and we end up with some generalized ideas of how we will act in the field.

After our predeparture component, we are mostly prepared to encounter ethical dilemmas in the field, but it does not necessarily mean that the dilemmas we encounter are the ones we thought of or that we make decisions the way we thought we trained ourselves to do. Our capacity to make well-reasoned ethical decisions is diminished by sheer exhaustion from a punishing schedule, by the fact that we are in "foreign" culture, by witnessing and hearing about distressing and traumatic situations, by emotional and psychological stress from being constantly in a conflict area, and by being part of a group for twenty-four hours a day. These experiences result in many tensions within the group and in *conflicts of identity* among group members. For example, one that comes up frequently is whether our behavior is culturally appropriate at all times—for example, when a student who is completely fed up with the heat decides to wear shorts, which may be culturally inappropriate attire. How to deal with the issue of attire, which had been discussed many times during predeparture activities, is often forgotten, and barriers to intergroup communication emerge.

One issue that is becoming more common is the *use of social media* when in the field. Detailing our field activities or posting pictures of the group on social media often exposes our location and members' identities. At times in some countries, security concerns are prominent. The use of social media by some in the group could, in fact, endanger everyone. Of course, we are often a group of twelve to fifteen foreigners—mostly white—who stick out in any context. Social media can dramatically increase the chances of our movements being tracked by those whose attention we might not want. When the use of social media becomes a security issue, our ethical decision is simple: we do not post our plans on social media. On one of my field courses, a student kept posting, and so the group addressed the issue together and conveyed the reasoning behind the group's ethical decision to the offending member. As an instructor, I was thrilled with the way the group handled the ethical dilemma.

Another characteristic of social-media users is the desire to be connected to others. As mentioned above, when our students are in the field, the local community members often quickly find them on social media and connect with them. We all have our opinions on how transparent we should be about who we are when in the field. I believe it is not possible for us to invent a new identity when in the field, but social-media posts are often a considerable giveaway of our lifestyles when back home. Social media is a contemporary problem, and it raises questions about ethical life choices for those engaged not just in fieldwork but also in the field of peace and conflict studies. At the same time, however, we cannot lead our lives in constant worry about how our simple acts of fun in another context may be misinterpreted by local communities. These are some of the things I ask my students to think through in predeparture and while we are in the field.

To overcome the tensions that arise when in the field, we engage in *daily debriefings*. My pedagogy for fieldwork emphasizes the importance of daily debriefings as a way for the group to recollect the happenings of the days, share their feelings, and discuss potential sources of tension. These debriefings never involve local hosts and are meant to be a safe space to discuss our frustrations and challenges openly. Debriefings are semistructured to include reflections on what we heard and what we felt, with an emphasis on what each person found most challenging during the day. It also provides the space for every person in the group to explain his or her individual ethical decisions, because sometimes, when faced with tough ethical challenges on the ground, students revert to personal ethical decisions or decisions that serve only some members of the group. Cliques are quite common during field courses because individual identities are constantly in flux and being negotiated. Some identities in the group naturally come together, while others become outliers to the clique. There is also a tendency to push ethical decision-making responsibility onto the course leader to get out of the responsibility of taking such decisions. I often find myself in such situations where I must make a quick choice, such the one

I made in Sierra Leone. However, as we have established, it is important for the decision-maker—in this case, me as the faculty leader—to be good at communicating ethical decisions. Yet, because the leader is also caught in the same emotional, mental, physical, and psychological stress as the rest of the group, he or she may find it difficult to provide the reasoning for an ethical decision at that very moment. Instead, I was able to explain my choice only upon returning to California. Knowing that we as leaders might also fail in communicating ethical reasoning invokes humility and ends up being transformational education.

We seek to *acquire knowledge* in the field by talking to those who experience conflict and also those who work on conflict. We do this through interactions with some of the most marginalized members of the community we are researching and by witnessing their everyday living conditions. Therefore, in most of my field courses, I include a visit to a village (often a remote one) to learn about the challenges faced by the most marginalized people living in a conflict zone. These experiences are an excellent pedagogical strategy to gain knowledge on what being marginalized means in reality. We share food with the community, visit its members' homes, and learn about the absence of resources and also about their daily struggle to obtain resources. We learn about their culture and the ways that they deal with conflict. These visits help us gain knowledge that often cannot be described or explained even by others in the country, owing to the isolation of these marginalized communities.

It is quite common during these visits for a student or two to *feel guilty* about our visit. Our inability to do anything for these marginalized communities translates into frustration that calls into question our goals for the course. The guilt is also connected to the students' identities of being "wealthy" Westerners witnessing poverty and suffering. Guilt, though, as I tell my students, is a form of narcissism, and the whole point of the visit is not to think about ourselves but about the people we meet and the stories we hear from them. If handled correctly, the visit also encourages students to think about what they are going to do with these stories. If we make ethical choices about reporting and about giving a voice to the voiceless, then the guilt will disappear. Usually, the group comes around to this idea after returning from the field. Over time I have learned to explain the decision to visit a remote community during predeparture training, but it nonetheless still impacts some students in the group.

The feeling of guilt is also tied to the way that we teach international development in our *more progressive* classrooms. For students to be more culturally appropriate and humble and to avoid the savior complex, a few professors encourage them in the classroom to develop programs that respond to the needs as articulated by the communities. Underlying this teaching moment is the emphasis of not going into communities and imposing our ideas of their needs or avoiding initiating programs that are convenient for us but not useful to the communities. Students are taught that pretending or assuming we have the solutions ends up damaging the communities. Although these insights are important and valid, they do not stress the importance of thinking about how we might ask the communities to articulate what they need. The field courses are expected to fill that gap. I teach that spending time with local communities, talking to them, and learning about their realities firsthand is the best way to get them to articulate their needs. Marginalized communities should be able to speak for themselves; if we truly want to challenge the way we tackle structures that control knowledge, we need to trek to that remote village.

Understanding the *team leader's identity vis-à-vis the identities in the student group and vis-à-vis identity of the community* is particularly important if the team leader is a person of color (like me) and is leading white students on a field research trip. In one country, people were incredulous that I could be the leader for a group of white students, while in another my identity as an Indian and as a woman meant that I was discriminated against by most of the male interviewees we met. I expected my students to deal with the ethical dilemma of enjoying the privilege that was naturally handed to them without them having to do anything to gain it; this privilege often gives them access to knowledge. No one stood up for me; I did not have power, and I resented the privilege the students enjoyed. I quickly realized that the students were unable even to notice that they were facing an ethical dilemma. As far as they were concerned, as some explained to me, I was the professor and therefore capable of fighting my own battles. This led me to pose another question that challenged the ethics of the students: How is it that the students, who in a classroom could be so outraged when hearing stories of gender-based violence or discrimination, were incapable of acting when they saw a member of their team (albeit the leader) being discriminated against because of her gender and skin color?

This kind of ethical challenge cannot be resolved in the field. It requires returning to our familiar environment and a period of reflection before we can tackle the ethical dilemmas we encountered. The postfieldwork component involves plenty of self-reflection and group reflection on the ethical decisions the group chose to make or not make and what could have been done differently. This component is often characterized by fatigue, a breakdown in relationships that were sometimes held together artificially to meet the goals of the course, and a general sense of discomfort in revisiting our own ethical decisions. However, this component is probably the most crucial, if we are to apply the lessons learned from this experience to future professional experiences.

It is safe to say that, irrespective of the amount of preparation, there are always unique ethical challenges that emerge during fieldwork. Maybe it would be wrong to expect that we prepared enough to deal effectively with these challenges. Instead, the best thing we can do is to treat them as lessons learned and have better reasoning for our decisions in the future.

Ethical dilemmas are inevitable when in the field. Practical ethics is a useful framework to utilize in identifying and meeting challenges. In a field course, it is important that we think through ethical challenges vis-à-vis identity and knowledge systems while simultaneously understanding the context in which research is being conducted. Being trained in practical ethics gives us the ability to be strategic about our behavior and the fortitude to adjust our behavior with the changing context. Most importantly, practical ethics gives us the ability to communicate our reasons for the decisions we make when facing ethical problems in the field. The practical ethics practice helps the team share values and come across as a unified entity engaged in ethical data collection, analysis, and reporting. As it encourages constant self-reflection, it translates into transformative education given that our decisions are evaluated continuously, modified, and renegotiated. Courses, therefore, must incorporate ethics into every aspect of field-based learning.

Notes

1. I teach at the Middlebury Institute of International Studies at Monterey. The students accompanying me on these courses are all graduate-level students, although I have occasionally taken undergraduate students from Middlebury College, Vermont, and other colleges. I teach conflict resolution courses at the institute, but not all the students who participate in my field courses are conflict resolution students.

2. One other field course that I have led was to Los Angeles in March 2015 to study the varieties in responses made by various governmental and NGOs to direct and structural violence. This field course was part of my series titled "The Praxis of Conflict Transformation" and, although structured similarly to the "Challenges to Peacebuilding" series of courses, is much shorter, lasting one week. In our first Praxis course, we ended up having to navigate identities as well, even though we stayed within the confines of the United States, where we all live or of which we are natives, which created a whole different set of ethical dilemmas that I will not be dealing with in this chapter.

3. Harry F. Wolcott (1995) makes the distinction between being in the field and conducting fieldwork. He says that the former is about physical presence while the latter is about the mind and heart—making sense of your interactions with others and achieving some level of understanding that you then share with others. Challenges to Peacebuilding is a field course that involves fieldwork, because it includes interacting with other humans, it involves making meaning of their statements, stories, and experiences, and it requires the skill to then convey that meaning to the rest of their world but through one's own interpretation.

TWO

Improving Pedagogy

FOUR

Developing Leaders through Innovative Education

The Olive Tree Initiative's Experiential Learning Approach to Teaching about Intractable Conflicts

DANIEL R. BRUNSTETTER AND DANIEL WEHRENFENNIG

Teaching about intractable conflicts such as Israeli-Palestinian or Turkish-Armenian relations is one of the most important, yet challenging, subject areas that potentially bring together students, faculty, and community members.[1] Notwithstanding the global importance of these issues, international events related to such conflicts can have a large impact on campus climate. While reverberations of international events are common in a globalizing world, they can be both inspiring and problematic in the university setting. Activism around such issues at universities is a vital part of the student experience because it marks an expression of the fundamental values of the United States—freedom of speech and the right to assembly. Yet activism can quickly become a battleground dynamic that impedes learning by shutting down alternative or competing perspectives essential to critical thinking. This can lead to divisiveness and the reproduction of misinformation, negative stereotypes, and intolerance among students that can negatively impact campus climate and be detrimental to the broader goals of higher education. The challenge for educators is to harness these issues in a way that promotes learning and an appreciation of difference that reflects the values of democratic society and global citizenship.

In response to tensions on the campus of the University of California (UC), Irvine, related to the Israeli-Palestinian conflict, we developed an innovative model of experiential learning adapted to intractable conflicts that combines rigorous study on campus with a short-term study-abroad component in the conflict region and close mentorship of students that focuses on leadership development. This model is the core of an educational program known as The Olive Tree Initiative (OTI), whose mission is twofold: (1) to promote conflict analysis and resolution through experiential education by providing students with the training and experiences needed to better negotiate and solve conflicts and (2) to develop leaders by training students to bridge the gap between theory and practice by applying the skills and knowledge they acquire to a campus and community setting. Operating since 2008, OTI has become a signature program of the University of California. It has spread to multiple California campuses (including UCLA, UC Berkeley, and Chapman University), as well as internationally at the University of Glasgow.

The main goal of this chapter is to delineate the theoretical underpinnings that inform OTI's innovative educational philosophy and illustrate how theory plays out in practice through examples drawn from our experiences with participating students. In doing so, it can serve, like Jennifer M. Ramos's chapter 5, as a window into the decision-making process, the benefits, and the challenges of organizing such a program. While we do not specifically address the ethical concerns we faced in designing this program, the insights provided by Pushpa Iyer in chapter 3 set the tone for anyone thinking about building a program and offer essential reading for those who must continually reevaluate and seek to improve existing programs. First, we discuss the importance of dialogue as the core component. Then we explain how we combine a narratives approach to teaching about conflict with a short-term study-abroad trip to the conflict region to enhance student learning. Finally, we articulate how the overall experience promotes leadership development. In the conclusion, we highlight the best practices that can be adopted on a broader scale.

Building the Context for Productive Dialogue

OTI's philosophy is grounded in the potentially transformative impact of intergroup dialogue to bridge the differences that define intractable conflicts. From a theoretical basis, the importance of dialogical interaction has been solidly established in major theories on communication and peace and conflict studies. The most influential research on communication and dialogue is the intergroup contact theory (Allport 1954).

According to this theory, interaction over a concentrated period of time between people from different backgrounds (e.g., ethnic, religious, and political) can overcome hostilities and prejudices when the situation fosters close intergroup contact (Williams 1947). This theory spawned a multitude of studies that help clarify the ground rules and conditions that have to be in place for positive attitude-change and prejudice-reduction processes conducive to peace to occur (Abu-Nimer 1999). Miles Hewstone and Rupert Brown (1986) argue, for example, that in order for contact to improve intergroup relations in society, there needs to be a somewhat equal status between the groups and that the groups must be in pursuit of a common or superordinate goal. More recent studies show that dialogue and communication processes are crucial for contact between conflicting groups to be conducive to improving intergroup perceptions. Karen E. Pettigrew (1998) examines the effect of emotional ties of friendship with out-group members on attitudes and found that having an out-group friend was powerfully predictive of lower levels of prejudice. Similarly, Karmela Liebkind and Alfred L. McAlister (1999) conduct field experiments examining the effect of extended intergroup contact, showing that increasing intergroup interactions had a significant positive impact on attitudes.

A significant number of dialogue programs have been developed specifically in the context of the Israeli-Palestinian conflict, with the goal of reducing hostility and increasing understanding and cooperation between Israeli Jews and Palestinians (Adwan and Bar-On 2000; Suleiman 1997). These programs have met with mixed success and inevitably have shortcomings. The most critical concerns raised by scholars include the challenge of creating equality among participants where power differences exist in reality, the tendency of positive effects to decline over the long term as participants return to their communities (Helman 2002; Abu-Nimer 2004; Schimmel 2009), and the limited impact of such experiences when confined to the small number of participants (Bekerman 2007). Despite these shortcomings, such programs nevertheless substantiate the potential impact of dialogue in ameliorating intergroup hostilities (see Maoz 2011 for a review).

OTI's experiential education is grounded in these theoretical findings, with the innovative elements—the study-abroad aspect and leadership focus—designed to address the critical concerns raised by scholars. The first step of the educational process is to foster optimal dialogue conditions. To do so, close attention is paid to four key factors: selecting diverse students, providing a safe intellectual environment, engaging students as partners in the process of achieving common goals, and developing dialogue skills.

OTI members are chosen to represent a multitude of political and religious viewpoints. The goal of student selection is to obtain relative balance in order to have equal representation of students supporting each "side" of the conflict. In addition, we recruit students who self-identify with neither side as well as those who have personal ties to other conflict zones. The former help ensure narrative balance and to promote critical perspective taking, while the latter provide a key comparative element to conversations about victimhood and empathy. These nonpartisan students help reduce the tendency for conversations to break down from dialogue into an "us-versus-them" confrontation by encouraging students to think more generally about the human condition as opposed to specific identities. The nonpartisan students frequently volunteer to be peer facilitators in difficult situations, such as after controversial or emotional speakers. These students can more easily detach themselves from the conflict to carry on conversations about very personal and emotional issues in an inquisitive and nonemotional fashion. For example, on a recent trip after a meeting with Mark Regev—who was at the time spokesperson of the Israeli prime minister—the evening's reflection focused on the question of recognizing Israel as a Jewish state (one of Regev's main talking points). While initially emotions ran high within the group as the affiliated students tended to see things as a zero-sum affair, the nonaffiliated students were able to steer the conversation in such a way that laid out the implications—positive and negative—for various different parties within the region.

Having a plurality of student voices represented is essential to maximize the learning impact, as each student interprets and reacts to the various learning stimuli (a text in class, a speaker in the region) in different ways according to his or her personal biases. The ability to see and hear the reactions of one's peers to the same stimuli is the first step toward perspective-taking and developing empathy for the Other. For example, on one of the Middle East trips, an Arab student remarked to a Jewish peer during the daily reflection, "I still disagree with what you have to say, but this has been the first time I could actually listen to it and understood how you felt."

The next step of the process is developing a safe intellectual and emotional space for students to express themselves. We recognize that embracing the willingness to be emotionally and intellectually vulnerable is essential to learning conflict resolution but very difficult when students' identities are wrapped into the conflict. Students are encouraged to speak their minds and to embrace asking questions and giving personal answers, with the goal of better understanding each other's perspectives (Stone, Patton, and Heen 2010). This openness, however, tends not to develop immediately but rather over time as students learn to trust each other. Following the literature that suggests an optimal dialogue situation is maximized if the parties involved share a common goal (Lederach 1996), OTI is structured in a way that makes students work together toward a shared goal. While the long-term goal of education and leadership development can seem too vague for students to agree to set aside their differences, we find that many students are willing to work together toward preparing the short-term study-abroad experience. As part of the process, students are given the responsibility to organize and run weekly organizational meetings. Working closely with faculty, they formulate an educational timeline to prepare intellectually for the trip, collectively fundraise in the community to pay for it, and choose the speakers and itinerary. Having a diverse group ensures that all relevant narratives are included in the educational sessions that precede the trip and, to the extent possible, on the trip itinerary.

The attempt to find a consensus amid differing opinions is the beginning of a learning process whereby students develop the skills of dialogue. In addition to learning by doing, students take a course on conflict resolution to learn dialogue techniques and familiarize themselves with theories of conflict resolution. They become equipped with the tools needed to carry out a productive dialogue, including how to ask questions, how to be an attentive listener, how to communicate respectively one's own views, and how to engage with those who hold differing viewpoints. In teaching students these skills, role playing and facilitated discussions are the prominent methods. These skills are constantly being put into practice and further honed as students work together planning their trip and, as we will see in the next section, learn together about the conflict.

The Narratives Approach:
Combining Classroom Learning and Travel Abroad

There are many approaches to teaching about intractable conflicts, including focusing on history, social science explanations, or the nature of the actors and their ideas (Caplan et al. 2012). Influenced by literature that illustrates the importance of narratives in shaping identity (Rotberg 2006; Adwan and Bar-On n.d.; Salomon 2004), we privilege a narratives approach that, in the words of Thomas Juneau and Mira Sucharov, "focuses on the experience of political actors in understanding and framing their actions [which] helps to unpack the sometimes elusive concept of identity" that is central to understanding international relations and to engaging in successful dialogue (Juneau and Sucharov 2010, 173).

Narratives are part of the process of constructing identity, because they help create the shared history that produces collective linkages. They contribute to the creation and construction of memories by giving meaning to certain elements of one's past, such as the origin of a people or the trials, tribulations, and triumphs through history, as well as by defining present fears and goals that can affect current and future political actions. Narratives reflect historical events and portray a sense of identity but are not always factually accurate and often contradict other narratives of the same events. They are inevitably selective—whether through the limits of an individual's own experience or by choice through deliberately placing emphasis on certain historical/cultural elements and/or omitting others. There are "master narratives," which project a sense of group identity and are attached to dominant cultural perceptions and institutional actions, such as educational and governmental posturing. These often claim to represent "Truth." There are also individual narratives, which reflect how different people and/or groups perceive events and circumstances, which may sometimes challenge the master narrative. Finally, there is the narrative of the Other, which tends to paint the Other as the enemy while denying the Other a voice to express its own multitude of perspectives. Often in intractable conflicts, the master narrative on each "side" negates the narrative of the Other, which serves to perpetuate negative stereotypes.

A narratives approach seeks to unpack the concepts of identity at the heart of intractable conflicts by exploring a multitude of perspectives in relation to each other, while also giving a voice to the Other. This approach allows the student to better understand the complexities of the conflict, as well as break down monolithic perceptions of self and Other by being exposed to the diverse viewpoints of each side, some of which may provide common ground for positive relations to emerge. In addition, the narratives approach helps students to realize that they enter the dialogue with a specific narrative of their own that privileges certain elements over others and is framed by a specific view of the self and the Other, just and unjust, and so forth. The advantage of this approach is that "focusing on narratives can help students set aside questions of right and wrong . . . and instead focus on the explanatory questions essential to understanding how world politics unfold" (Juneau and Sucharov 2010, 173).

Students in OTI take a specially designed core undergraduate class in narratives of the particular conflict that shows how historical events were interpreted differently by the varying parties to the conflict. In addition, the students work with faculty to establish extracurricular educational sessions. This consists of a thirty-week course for the Israel-Palestine program and twenty-week course for the Turkey-Armenia program. Students meet weekly for sixty to seventy-five minutes to listen to lectures given by trained graduate students, faculty, and expert guest lecturers. These extracurricular courses cover the cultural and religious foundations of the conflict region, closely examine the key historical moments, and explore current debates. Each session consists of a lecture about the required readings, audio files, and/or a movie, followed by an interactive discussion section in which students engage in small or large group discussions. The aim of this preparation course is to teach the students basic knowledge of the conflict from a multinarrative approach while sharpening their critical-thinking and dialogue skills.

One of the key challenges of the narratives approach—and this holds true for dialogue programs as well—is to transmit to students the differences in power that often define a conflict. As Leslie Dwyer and Alison Castel note in chapter 2, it is important to be mindful of power differences on the ground. Exposure to different narratives can sometimes lend the impression that all narratives are equal, which would skew the reality. The narratives approach thus needs to equip students with the skill set to critically reflect on the perspectives they hear to distinguish how each narrative fits into the reality—perceived and actual. While OTI's educational sessions are designed to lead students to grasp the relative strength of a specific narrative within a given society and in the general historical context, and the mixed dialogue-group setting ensures critical reflection on the various perspectives heard, classroom learning has its limitations. Creative techniques such as role-playing and the use of films or graphic novels can enhance the educational experience (Caplan et al. 2012), but the classroom ultimately lacks the visceral experience that renders the power dimensions of the conflict tangible. To overcome this shortcoming, the most innovative part of OTI's educational philosophy combines the advantages of the narratives approach with the educational power of study abroad.

Research shows that study abroad provides students with the opportunity for self-reflection (Younes and Asay 2003), increases resistance to stereotyping, promotes tolerance and respect for peoples of different cultures and values (Carlson and Widaman 1988; Laubscher 1994), and helps students to develop intercultural communication skills through contact with different cultures (Williams 2005). Experiential learning programs that include travel abroad have been found to deliver powerful experiences that enhance student learning in ways that book-based and simulation-based learning cannot, by engaging all of their senses and exposing them to real-world actors (Schnieder and Lonze 2013). The out-of-classroom experience forces students to bridge the gap between theory and practice by balancing the rational and intellectual aspects of classroom learning with the sensorial and emotional experience of visiting the conflict region and meeting people who live there. Inspired by these findings, the OTI curriculum includes a carefully constructed short-term trip (two to three weeks) to the conflict region.

The OTI travel experience also follows the narratives approach. It is designed to be a destabilizing experience that obliges students to perpetually contextualize, problematize, and challenge assertions and assumptions through exposure to the realities outside the comfort zone of their own communities. The itinerary is specifically constructed to engage as many relevant voices as possible by using a speaker matrix to ensure a balanced representation from political, nongovernmental, and grassroots actors across the political spectrum. Students engage leading politicians, chief negotiators, policy experts, members of nongovernmental organizations and citizens movements, religious leaders, community leaders, soldiers,

Figure 4.1. Critical discussion of maps and borders of Jerusalem. *Daniel Wehrenfennig.*

students, and ordinary citizens to develop a deeper understanding of the geopolitical dynamics on the ground. The itinerary constantly challenges students to hear conflicting narratives in order to force them to cross over mental barriers and physical borders almost on a daily basis. During the three-week trip to Israel, the Palestinian territories, and Jordan (a neighboring country added to break down the impression of a binary conflict), students typically engage eighty different speakers in fifteen different cities. On the trip to Turkey and Armenia, students speak with nearly forty speakers in more than ten cities across the region.

Critically, travel to the region exposes students to the power differential between parties to the conflict, shedding light on how this difference affects different people in different ways. An example from a day during the trip to the Middle East illustrates the point. Students visit Bil'in in the West Bank to speak with Palestinians who convene every Friday to protest the construction of a separation barrier, which they assert separates farmers from their land and violates international law. Some of these Friday protests have turned violent, and students hear stories of protesters whose friends and family were killed or injured. Then students cross to the other side of the barrier to speak with Israel Defense Forces soldiers to garner their views, before heading to East Jerusalem where they meet with the Israeli architect of the security barrier, Col. Danny Tirza. On a tour of the barrier, Tirza explains the reasons why the Israeli government tasked him with building it—to prevent suicide bombers from entering Israeli territory during the Second Intifada—and then offers justification as to why the barrier diverges from the Green Line (the 1949 Armistice line of demarcation) in certain places. Immediately after this meeting, the students meet with members of B'Tselem, an Israeli human rights organization critical of the barrier. With the B'Tselem activists, the students embark on another tour of the barrier, hearing arguments that challenge its legality in certain places under international law. The day concludes with a visit to a Jewish cemetery in Haifa where students meet with a father whose daughter was killed in a suicide bombing during the Second Intifada. The varied meetings encompass a range of narratives along with visual and emotional stimulation. Students see the physical separation between Israelis and Palestinians and witness the power differences but also encounter the emotions of grief, sorrow, and bitterness on both sides of the barrier.

Experiences such as these stretch students on emotional, physical, and psychological levels, especially those who have personal connections to the region. While the trip is emotionally charged, the extensive preparation of the group beforehand and the focus on dialogue set the groundwork for turning these experiences into powerful moments in the personal development of students. On the trip the students have ample opportunity to exchange ideas in personal conversations with their fellow travelers, with the speakers, and with random individuals during down time. In addition, as others have noted in this volume (for example, in chapters 2 and 10), we recognize that making the space for structured group reflection is essential to student learning. On OTI trips time is set aside each day for a formal group reflection in which students put into practice and hone the dialogue skills they learned before embarking on the trip. To reflect the equal status of all students, seating is in a circle either in one big group or in small groups, with the role of facilitator changing each day.

The group reflections are a fundamental aspect of OTI's experiential learning module because they provide the forum for students to explore the opinions expressed by speakers during the trip and compare them to what they had learned in the classroom setting. Moreover, in these discussions, students learn what their peers view to be important for their "side" and what others perceive to be propaganda, offensive, or divergent from what previous speakers have said. Students also gain experience listening to others and formulating their own arguments with a more critical eye, while respecting the identity and perceptions of those who hold different views. A good example of this is the discussion following the visit to the Genocide Memorial in Yerevan during the 2013 OTI trip with the Turkey-Armenia branch. Students felt safe and prepared to express their deepest feelings about a place that is powerfully symbolic to Armenian students but troubling to Turkish students. Another example from the same trip is the informative discussion students had after meeting with some representatives of the Armenian Apostolic Church in Istanbul. This discussion introduced the group to the complexity of minority politics in Turkey and brought to the forefront myriad reactions and opinions about broader themes such as the tensions of democracy, identity, and life in the diaspora.

These conversations and other less formal conversations that occur when students have free time contribute to the development of student dialogue skills by exposing flashpoints where dialogue breaks down and revealing common ground where dialogue can be renewed.

Leadership Development: A Holistic Approach to Experiential Education

The shared experience of travel to the region, enhanced by the daily ritual of group reflection, is an important part of breaking down stereotypes, leaving pre-trip preconceptions and prejudices behind, and developing empathy for the Other. The literature, however, suggests that these positive effects tend to diminish once participants return to their own communities and do not continue to engage each other on a regular basis (Abu-Nimer 2004). In order to counteract this tendency, the OTI program is designed to preserve the special bond of learning and respectful interaction between the participants developed before and during the trip through a long-term holistic leadership development approach. This approach combines insights gathered over the last ten years on how students learn, process, retain, and implement three types of knowledge: intellectual, experiential, and emotional.

Despite the changing political situation, student backgrounds, and conflicts, we have identified a learning cycle underlying the leadership development process. Reflecting the need to integrate experiential learning programs into the university curriculum as discussed by Allyson M. Lowe and Sandi DiMola in chapter 6, OTI is divided into three structured segments or phases of learning embedded in the conflict analysis and resolution certificate, which is housed in the international studies program at UC Irvine. After the students are selected from a larger pool of applicants, the first learning phase consists of the intellectual and knowledge development about the respective conflict studied. This initial phase is followed by the experiential learning trip to the region. The post-trip phase back home is designed to provide the context for students to process this experience—what we call finding their own story—and then apply the knowledge and skills they have acquired to their local community and beyond. It is important to note that leadership development occurs throughout the entire educational process, with each phase contributing to the students' development.

To best support the students in all of these learning stages and to further their leadership development, we have developed a number of practices, academic structures, and support networks.

PRE-TRIP LEADERSHIP DEVELOPMENT

The pre-trip leadership development phase is focused on student empowerment. Before the trip, faculty train students to be facilitators of group discussions, to organize on-campus programming, to fundraise, and to cooperate with the faculty in the process of building the itinerary for the trip. Students actively learn to work individually and as part of a team. Part of the process involves students taking responsibility for all the events they organize, which requires working together and thus sharing credit for successful events as well as responsibility for the less successful. We face many of the challenges discussed by Gina M. Cerasani and rj nickels in chapter 9 when it comes to defining the role of faculty and walking the fine line between providing support and allowing for failure. While it is difficult for mentoring faculty to watch events unfold imperfectly, we nevertheless find that students gain valuable lessons from their individual and collective failures. During this preparation phase, students are made aware of their individual and collective strengths and, through individual mentoring from faculty, are challenged to work on their weaknesses. The mentoring role of faculty requires getting to know the students through close observation during pre-trip education and planning and developing a trusting relationship in order to communicate observations and suggestions throughout the program. For example, faculty may need to encourage particular students to speak up more or to hold back, to show more emotional constraint or to engage their emotions more deeply, to take more leadership or let other people shine as well, to manage their time better, to stay motivated through moments of frustration, to lead by example, and to learn to motivate others.

ON-THE-TRIP LEADERSHIP DEVELOPMENT

The main leadership development during the trip comes as a consequence of the group members having to stick with each other over the duration of an emotional and politically charged travel experience, all the while working through their personal and intellectual challenges. Many students have expressed that being in a conflict-laden situation for an extended time was a new experience that forced them to deal with multiple pressures—physical, psychological, emotional, and intellectual—all at the same time. Students cite the fact that they could not simply walk away from these pressures as hugely important in the learning experience. On the trip students have to deal with the physical and mental fatigue of a grueling schedule, process the sometimes tragic or offensive narratives they encounter, grapple with other students "pushing their buttons," and come to terms with continually being confronted with information and experiences that challenge their own frameworks and preconceived notions. This experience of having past knowledge challenged is, as Patricia A. Maulden and Lisa Elaine Shaw argue in chapter 7, a catalyst for considerable learning to take place.

During or, more often than not, after intense conversations with their peers, students have to relearn the skills needed to sustain dialogue and resolve controversial issues (e.g., to agree to disagree). We have noticed that while students try to be very rational in the beginning of the trip—for example during the initial phase of the Middle East trip in Washington, DC, or when students visit key US-based diaspora populations prior to the Turkey-Armenia trip—almost inevitably the intensity grows when the group arrives in the conflict region, resulting in very emotional discussions during the first days in the region. The mood of students tends to change from reserved and reflective to reactive and emotional to angry and entitled. However, over the course of the trip, as each day exposes the students to the on-the-ground complexity, the discussions slowly morph.

By the last days of the trip, reflections have, experience shows, produced some of the most honest, productive, and insightful conversations one can imagine. Knowing this process, we require the students to journal about their experience throughout the study-abroad phase in order to trace their own changes and development and to help them better share their thoughts during in-group reflection, as well as back in their communities upon returning home.

The role of the staff/faculty during this process is to help the vocal and opinionated students become better listeners while inspiring the quiet and more overwhelmed students to share their thoughts and to take a stronger leadership role. This is accomplished during one-on-one discussions with individual students on the bus or on walks in the cities the group visits. For the vocal students, challenging them to compare a speaker they just heard with what was said by a previous speaker, or one of their peers, helps them to grasp nuance while articulating more clearly the broader context. For the shy students, simply asking what they think about a particular speaker and listening without judging helps them to grow in confidence and formulate what they might contribute to the group discussions.

POST-TRIP LEADERSHIP DEVELOPMENT

While the trip itself is the most impactful learning and education moment of the OTI program, the learning process continues well beyond the experience abroad. We have found that the biggest challenge for the growth of personal leadership is continuing student learning after returning to campus. Part of the challenge reflects the observation made by Maryam Z. Deloffre in chapter 8, namely that of assessing whether the learning before and during the trip actually prepares students for the job market in related fields. We find that working systematically with students upon their return helps them to continue processing the experience and, in doing so, to fully realize what they learned, what skills they developed (and what weaknesses they still have), and how they have grown emotionally and intellectually. This self-introspection is key to bridging the gap between the educational experience and tackling real-world problems as a career professional. To this end, we seek to provide a post-trip structure for student engagement with the issues on the campus and in their communities while they continue to improve their personal leadership skills and preserve the trust and relationships developed with their travel companions.

Most conflict resolution programs provoke major changes in participants when they are part of the learning group but cite challenges when it comes to preserving these changes over a longer period of time. Based on our experience, we have identified two main issues that challenge the continuing leadership development. First, there is the "push-back" effect when participants return and try to explain their experiences to their families, friends, and community peers. Returning students often recount that their inner circle is more interested to hear how their preconceived opinions have been confirmed and less interested to hear where they may have been challenged. Some recount that they find their friends and family lack the knowledge or experience to even comprehend their experience in a meaningful way. In addition, sometimes interlocutors try to convince the returning students that their experiences have been incomplete, wrongly interpreted, or even go so far to suggest—as happens to many conflict resolution programs—that students have been brainwashed.

Second, after such an intense experience, students experience a natural "distancing" from the core conflict issues and express the need for space to reflect on their experiences and to acclimate to their normal routines back on campus. For most students this only takes a week or two before they seek occasions to spend time with their traveling companions, but for some it can take longer before they are able or willing to engage again.

Taking into account these challenges, we have developed a multistep approach to help students "find their story" and remain engaged. The first step is to create a "safe" space for students to process their experiences. The safe space can include formal meetings with other students or informal meetings with faculty members or OTI board members. The second step is to prepare a speech illustrating elements of what they have learned during their trip, which they present to their campus peers at the annual welcome-back event. Following the presentation to the campus, students are required to make three presentations in the community at local mosques, temples, churches, high schools, or other community venues. These experiences help students to connect all their experiences with the education they received, while training them to communicate their personal experiences and articulate their individual opinions on key issues to others. By speaking to different communities, including those who might hold alternative opinions, students experience firsthand the challenges of communication across ideological lines. Moreover, public speaking can enhance a student's sense of empowerment. As one undergraduate student observed, giving presentations was a powerful experience. For this student, the opportunity to speak to large audiences of adults, to be listened to, and to engage in conversation afterward stimulated greater self-confidence and was a motivating factor in taking on more active leadership roles.

The third required stage is to turn their speeches into an academic article to be published in a campus journal. This requires students to undertake further research on their chosen topic, thus helping them to develop academic research skills while transforming them from consumers of information into producers of knowledge (cf. Juneau and Sucharov 2010, 180). Through the process, students receive support, critical feedback, and debriefing from their peers and faculty mentors.

The fourth element of the leadership and development process is a post-trip course in scholarship and leadership development taught by a faculty mentor. The focus of the course is on teaching students how to transfer the skills they have acquired—for example, critical thinking, communication, working as a team, and leadership—to their professional and personal development. There are two elements to the class. First, students volunteer with an off-campus organization that is not specifically related to the conflict they studied. Taking a step back from the conflict provides a positive outlet—often a sharp contrast to the resentment and challenges they face when sharing their trip experiences with their own community—in which students can utilize their personal leadership skills. Such a positive outlet provides continuing motivation for students to realize their own potential and to further consolidate the life skills they have developed in the program. Second, students undertake a capstone project related to the conflict. Examples include a photo exhibit, a film festival, mock peace negotiations, roundtable discussions, poster presentations, research projects, and so forth. In undertaking such projects, students revisit the challenges related to organizing events, motivating peers to participate, and communicating complex ideas to diverse audience members but with a more advanced knowledge base and skill set than when they began the program.

The final element of the leadership development phase sees the students personally invest in the educational process. The students who have gone through the program are given the responsibility of recruiting and training the next cohort of students. In addition, students become part of a connected alumni network in which there is continued close mentorship by faculty and ongoing camaraderie among student travelers of multiple cohorts that furthers their intellectual and professional development. Students have the chance to share their frustrations, work through the inevitable push-back, discuss current events, and continue to grow together through a specially designed online forum called Olive-Talk and at biannual student retreats where students from multiple campuses meet. The ultimate goal of the alumni network is to connect OTI students after graduation, thus creating a web of young leaders who, despite their differing political views, share a common educational experience that grounds them in a global outlook based on the view that mutual understanding in the most intractable of conflicts is possible.

OTI is an innovative educational program that has the potential to expose generations of students to the theoretical foundations and real-world challenges of conflict resolution. This chapter described the educational vision of OTI that has allowed it to grow to a system-wide program in the University of California, thus expanding its educational impact well beyond individual classrooms. OTI's educational philosophy is based on an innovative model of experiential learning that provides the educational grounding for students to have informed and constructive discussions related to intractable conflicts, while empowering them in their scholarship and individual leadership development. Having spread to multiple additional California campuses and at the University of Glasgow, OTI can help create a network of future leaders who have a shared understanding of and experience in conflict resolution. The program is designed to train students as future leaders to think about the Middle East and the Caucasus—or any conflict region—in more complex ways by steering clear of falling into easy stereotypes, by thinking critically, and by engaging others with different views in constructive dialogue.

The program is unique because it expands the classroom abroad by leading groups of students on an intense experiential learning trip that exposes them to the raw essence of politics and international relations by providing them unprecedented access to the political actors in the region who influence public policy and decision-making. It does so in a structured environment with close mentoring of students to help them harness this experience for personal and intellectual growth.

Future challenges include evaluating the short-term and long-term successes of the program. We have developed an evaluation protocol that includes pre-trip and post-trip interviews and questionnaires to measure the changes in students over time. Preliminary results point to significant increases in knowledge about the conflict and greater perspective empathy toward the Other, accompanied by decreases in ethnic and religious prejudice.

The continuation of the Israel-Palestine and Turkey-Armenia programs demonstrates that the model is applicable to multiple conflicts. A comparative analysis of the programs may yield important insights into the way in which the model applies to different conflicts, as well as potential shortcomings that would need to be ironed out. In the future, we envision employing the model in additional areas of intractable conflict, including India-Pakistan and Northern Ireland, to empower students to become future leaders with a vision for the future based in the power of dialogue and the importance of engaging with and trying to understand the multiple narratives of one's own community and those of the Other.

Note

1. The authors wish to thank the Carnegie Council for permission to reprint this chapter, whose earlier version appeared as "Teaching about Intractable Conflicts: The Olive Tree Initiative" on their webpage at https://www.carnegiecouncil.org/publications/articles_papers_reports/731. We would also like to thank our community supporters and the School of Social Sciences at UC Irvine for providing encouragement and the academic space for OTI to exist and, of course, the students who have continued to inspire us over the years.

FIVE

Windows and Mirrors in the Wall

Experiential Learning in Northern Ireland

JENNIFER M. RAMOS

As many universities continue to internationalize their curriculums (Battistoni 1997; Fobes 2005; Jacoby and Brown 2009), instructors interested in active-learning experiences for their students also face a growing need to reimagine traditional study-abroad courses.[1] These changes come at a time when instructors seek not only to increase the academic rigor and impact of these programs but also to make these experiences accessible to a broader range of students (Bowman and Jennings 2005). In so doing, a number of programs have sought to structure shorter-term cross-cultural immersions with maximum effect, with the aim of preparing "students with both knowledge and professional skills and networks to help them successfully enter an international career" (Pugh 2013, 791). My course, International Security, reflects these trends by embedding a short-term international immersion experience in a semester-long course. Not all students have the time or money to study abroad for a semester or a summer. Further, integrating the immersion trip over spring break has the advantage of preparing students with a solid academic foundation for eight weeks prior to the trip and then returning after it to analyze and write their research papers based on the original data collected on the trip. Moreover, students also have an extended space to engage in post-trip personal and academic reflection, a critical component that many study-abroad programs lack.

Experiential learning courses, as this immersion course is defined, offer ways to achieve learning outcomes that may otherwise remain elusive when traditional teaching methods are employed. In this chapter, I focus on my experience teaching a course that integrates a short-term immersion experience abroad. I argue that the addition of the international immersion not only facilitates mastery of the course material but also transforms how students see themselves as well as people whose experiences are vastly different from their own. As part of an international security course, students spend nine days in and around Belfast, Northern Ireland, engaged in research on the Northern Ireland peacebuilding process. Through archival research and interviews with a cross-section of community members, such as politicians, peaceworkers, religious leaders, playwrights, and police, students gain a holistic understanding of conflict and reconciliation processes and also acquire a deeper knowledge of the complex relationship between peace and justice. While the experience gives them a window into another world fraught with "peace walls"—physical barriers between Catholic and Protestant communities—it may also act as a mirror of divisions back home.

In the following section, I first provide some background on the Northern Ireland conflict. I then discuss the logistics involved in creating a course with an immersion component. Following this, I give an overview of the course and what it entails. Next, I identify the learning outcomes and how they are attained. This is followed by a discussion of some of the essential features that I believe make the course successful. I conclude with some final thoughts on short-term international immersion experiences.

Background of the Northern Ireland Conflict

After the Good Friday Peace Agreement was signed in 1998 to resolve the decades-long conflict known as the Troubles, many scholars of Northern Ireland turned their attention elsewhere with the understanding that the conflict was fully resolved. Yet one-third of the ninety-plus peace walls in Belfast have been built since the peace agreement, and the tension of an unresolved peace still, though infrequently, boils over into violence. The seeds of conflict date back beyond 1921, when the Republic of Ireland gained independence from Britain and was no longer under colonial rule. The United Kingdom retained sovereignty over the northern part of Ireland, whose population largely identified with the United Kingdom both politically, as Unionists and Loyalists, and religiously, as Protestants. However, the Catholic minority, who identified politically as Nationalists/Republicans seeking to reunite with the Republic, faced structural inequalities that led them to engage in civil rights protests and marches in the 1960s. These efforts led to violent responses from the British government, culminating in the start of the armed conflict in 1969. Fanning the flames of conflict were the paramilitaries on both sides who saw violence as the means to achieving their goal, which was largely to (finally) resolve the political status of Northern Ireland.

In all, over thirty-five hundred people out of a population of 1.6 million died in the violence by the time of the signing of the Good Friday Agreement. Much work remains to be done toward achieving a sustainable peace. For example, besides the physical walls separating communities, over 90 percent of all schools in Northern Ireland are still segregated by religion. With heated (sometimes violently so) political issues still unresolved, today there is neither war nor true peace in Northern Ireland.

Course Development

While I was on my university's London study-abroad program in the spring of 2013, I became more aware of the in-between situation of Northern Ireland. During that time, there were large protests, riots, and violence because of a Belfast City Council decision to severely limit the number of days that the Union flag was flown at City Hall. These events once again ignited sectarian tensions. It became clear that this corner of the world did not yet reflect the peace agreement that had been reached.

With my interest piqued, I connected with my colleague in our School of Education who had been researching Northern Ireland's "shared education" program. She had been studying progress toward integrated schooling and provided me with initial contacts in the community for my first four-day visit. These included scholars, missionaries, peaceworkers, and former combatants. I found a welcoming community, whose members were open to talking about their personal experiences of the conflict and their views of the future. This positive reception can be attributed to several things. First, my colleague was quite well liked. Second, I was an outsider and an American; there was generally a very pro-American stance in Northern Ireland. Third, I came as an educator—a listener with no agenda.

It was only after I returned to London that I realized that Northern Ireland was a microcosm of many of the issues and concepts we were discussing in my international security course that semester. I told the students in my course about the fascinating experience I just had and offered to lead a group there for a long weekend before the semester ended. Eight of my twelve students took advantage of the offer, and I was thus able to pilot the trip to explore the academic possibilities. We were not simply fly-by tourists; I had committed to an authentic, noncommercialized academic experience. We met with the same people I had met with previously and engaged in listening sessions about the locals' experiences and current ways of life. There was something about the interactions of the students and the locals that worked. As Alexander Cromwell asserts in chapter 10, key to transformative learning is meaningful interactions with locals.

Moreover, it seemed that the locals really wanted their voices to be heard and their understanding of the situation to be noted. In addition, they wanted to help the students; the idea that this was an educational endeavor certainly created a positive atmosphere. The students engaged authentically and respectfully, soon recognizing that the conflict was deeply personal and more complex than they had imagined. My students were touched by both the welcome they received and by the willingness of local community members to share deeply personal stories with them. As such, the experience became a journey for both their hearts and their minds; in the language of our university's mission, here was the "education of the whole person" in action.

I received strong support from various community members within Belfast to make this an annual experience. They were willing to coordinate individuals or groups to meet with students again so that students could conduct interviews and more formally integrate what they had learned into their research. Of course, ethics is a key consideration here (for a discussion of ethics in field research, see chapter 1). Students engage in ethical research training prior to the immersion trip, although it is challenging to prepare for every situation.

Part of the locals' motivation for engaging with us is the healing process of the community. They believe that discussing these issues is also useful for their members, as they may never have another outlet to express their feelings or views in this way. This is a "safe" way to begin to articulate their experiences. In addition, our visits act as a reason for cross-community events. While locals from opposing sides may be otherwise reluctant to come to a specific cross-community function, they may be more likely to come when our visit is highlighted and the cross-community aspect is downplayed. In sum, it is important for the community leaders to recognize the mutual benefits of the partnership. (For more on mutual gains of community partners and students, see chapter 11.)

In forming these relationships, it made a difference that there was an understanding that this is a longer-term partnership, that we were investing in each other. We both had a shared commitment to the students and to the community. As these partnerships developed, they led and continue to lead to new relationships. The initial people that I met with offered additional contacts, creating a snowball effect, which had the added benefit of also coming from people whom I had grown to trust. I knew that their connections would likely be very useful. As with the Olive Tree Initiative's emphasis (see chapter 4), one of my goals was to be sure that I was presenting students with a range of views. I thus asked my developing Belfast network if they knew anyone who fit what I was looking for. If not, I would cold-call or email politicians, student clubs, or organizations with some success. It really was a matter of persistence, though the best way to obtain diverse perspectives seemed to be through personal connections.

Coordinating Logistics at Home

Having established the feasibility of the course and being convinced of its value for student learning, I returned to my home university and further modified my international security course to allow for a spring-break immersion experience in Northern Ireland. In order to not reinvent the wheel for some of the logistics, I coordinated with our study-abroad office. While our particular study-abroad office does not arrange airfare and lodging (one of the biggest tasks!), it was helpful in several ways. First, it had a process for risk management and provided liability forms. Second, it had an online orientation for study-abroad students to familiarize them with our university's expectations and policies, as well as a system in place that collected students' emergency contact information and other pertinent travel information (e.g., health and passport information). Overall, it served as a great resource to help me think through the critical, nonacademic pieces of the trip.

The dean's office helped with figuring out how to offer the course administratively and how to secure funding for students who could not afford the trip. Regarding the former, we decided to offer the course plus a "lab fee," which would cover airfare, lodging, and some meals. The class would be smaller than usual, reduced from twenty-five students to twelve, requiring a significant commitment to the course by the dean. Given that only one faculty member was traveling with the group, the sensitive nature of the discussions abroad, and the average size of large vans in Belfast, limiting the course to twelve students was a practical necessity. It is a perfect number in my view; I have not changed it since. Although some professors may choose to interview their students before they can enroll or limit their course to juniors and seniors or by major, I have left the student enrollment up to chance. There are very good reasons for doing this differently, in the ways that I have just mentioned, but I also believe, perhaps in the extreme, in equal opportunity for all. I have never been sure that you can know from a short interview whether or not a student is "right" for a course. Students can and will surprise you. So far, it has worked for me, and I believe part of this is about setting the tone early on and being clear about the workload and expectations.

In terms of garnering funding to make sure that all students have equal access, the dean's office worked to find various ways to support students who qualified for financial aid. Students first enrolled in the course, then indicated if they needed financial aid for the trip. Their applications were vetted through our financial aid office, which indicated to what extent funding was needed. The dean's office then sought to fill those needs for the students. In some cases, students did not qualify for aid on paper but were unable to pay for the trip in reality. In some of these cases, we were able to provide scholarships for the students who met criteria set by our donors. In other words, we tried creative ways to fill the gaps, but guaranteeing equal access for all is never easy. Fortunately, we have been quite successful in financially helping our students one way or another. However, if university resources are not available to help fill the gap, corporate sponsors are increasingly an option (Bowman and Jennings 2005).

The other large logistical piece, airfare and lodging, was initially left up to me. I made the lodging reservations by comparing pricing across various Internet offers, and I worked with a well-known student-travel agency that booked groups. Recently, our dean's office has taken over the airfare reservations, based on my preferences and travel dates. Needless to say, this has helped me concentrate my efforts on other components of the trip that need my individual attention. I still make the lodging arrangements, but I am hopeful that this too will soon be off my plate. This does, however, highlight the point that much of the time investment is borne by the instructor, who is likely balancing other courses alongside research and service obligations. The start-up costs are significant, but over time, as the instructor maintains and continues to build connections with the locals, the costs diminish.

The Course Content

The course is designed to introduce students to enduring and contemporary questions in international security. We explore a number of security challenges to international peace and security, highlighting, in particular, the practical and ethical questions they pose as various actors attempt to address them.

In the first half of the course, we begin to unpack what is meant by "peace" and "security" and consider how those concepts relate to one another and vary across contexts. Students become familiar with international relations theories and concepts (security dilemma, arms race, sovereignty, and so forth) and apply them to current global security challenges issues, such as nuclear proliferation, global terrorism, and climate change. Classes are driven by discussions of readings, simulations, and debates to help students understand the issues from multiple perspectives.

Following this, we move to the state and societal levels of analysis and examine conflict within states through a series of comparative case studies, beginning with Northern Ireland. This section of the course, usually about two weeks long, takes a close look at the historical, economic, political, and psychological aspects of the conflict and the negotiations that led to the Good Friday Peace Agreement. The key is for the students to begin to think critically about the hows and whys of the conflict and its resolution, from multiple perspectives. The spring-break trip then largely picks up where the class leaves off by focusing on the aftermath of the peace agreement.

What happens after the peace agreement is the subject of the students' term research paper, which responds to the following questions: What are the keys to peacebuilding? What are the lessons learned so far? Where are there pockets of possibility? Within these parameters, the students have explored such topics as the role of gender, reconciling victims with aggressors, interfaith movements, and arts and culture as critical to peacebuilding. Prior to the trip, the students will also have a well-developed research proposal in place to conduct in Northern Ireland. Concurrent with their weekly readings and other assignments, the first half of the course is also filled with mentor meetings and regular deadlines concerning research questions, annotated bibliographies, hypotheses, interview questions, certification by the institutional review board, and literature reviews. By the time we are ready to leave on our trip, their in-class work and their projects have aligned with the case of Northern Ireland.

At this point, prior to the trip, it is critical to stress to students the unpredictable nature of research. It is one thing to have a brilliant research design, yet another to implement it. This reality can be difficult and frustrating for students to understand, especially after having put much effort into preparing their ideal project. Once in a while, students encounter unforeseen challenges to their research after we arrive in Belfast, or they acquire new knowledge that requires some retooling of their research plan. When this happens, I work with the student during our downtime to create a revised plan, and the other students are often very helpful in getting a project back up and running. For example, one student was working on a project that looked at the role of television in promoting cross-cultural dialogue. The interviews related to her project got canceled, but we were able to talk with our local contacts about possible other leads. She ended up keeping her project within the realm of arts and entertainment but focused on plays instead. Fortunately, we made wonderful connections to playwrights working on "peace plays" just by asking. It does seem at times that everyone in Belfast knows everyone else.

While in Northern Ireland, students primarily engage in two modes of research: interviews and archival research. Of the former, they meet with people from all different kinds of backgrounds: politicians, peaceworkers, former members of the Irish Republican Army (IRA), former British Army soldiers, religious leaders, educators, doctors, counselors, former prisoners, poets, and playwrights. In terms of the latter, they conduct research at Linen Hall Library, the premier archive related to the Troubles. I arrange with the librarians there ahead of time to have some of the materials available on the days we are planning to be there so that we are assured access. They also let me know if other groups will be visiting the archives as well, since the library space is not that large, and we then have to coordinate schedules a bit more closely.

Upon returning home, we hold several formal debriefing sessions. As Patricia A. Maulden and Lisa E. Shaw (chapter 7) discuss, debriefing is important for deeper learning to occur (just as preparation is). Indeed, we continue to debrief informally throughout the rest of the semester as well. In terms of coursework, we then consider the Northern Ireland case in comparative context to develop a richer understanding of the complexities of securing the peace. We examine other cases of postconflict societies to highlight similarities with and differences from Northern Ireland. At the same time, students continue working on their research papers, processing and analyzing what they have just learned and experienced. Toward the end of the course, they present their papers to the class to get feedback before they turn in the final versions.

Defining and Achieving Learning Outcomes

The engaged-learning experience aims to achieve four learning outcomes. First, students will become familiar with the complexity of defining "security" and "peace." Are these ongoing processes or end goals? Who determines how these are defined and at the expense of whom? Are these terms defined more by what they embody or what they lack? In effect, is peace the absence of war? The answers to these questions have critical policy and societal implications. Second, students will increase their capacity to think critically about the causes of conflict and the challenges of resolving it. Conflict is rarely monocausal but rather is often multilayered and interconnected to other actors and other conflicts, current or historical. Educating our future leaders and engaged citizens demands that they go beyond simplistic understandings of the world, or there will never be any progress on these very crucial issues we care about. Third, students will construct and execute a social science research project, using both primary and secondary sources. Fundamental to their studies is being able to articulate the concepts they have learned in a well-written paper. The engaged-learning experience offers them a unique opportunity to also collect original data so that they feel a real sense of ownership of their projects.

All of the aforementioned learning outcomes are achieved through the research paper. Throughout their paper, but particularly in the literature reviews and in the analyses of the interviews they conducted in Northern Ireland, students cannot help but become frustrated and perplexed that there is no one "right" answer, no "one size fits all" on matters of peace and security. This is what I hope for. While I do expect them to synthesize previous scholarly knowledge and their own experiences into a coherent research paper, I also expect that they come away with more questions than answers.

The fourth learning outcome aims for students to demonstrate cultural sensitivity. It is important for them to value cultural diversity and to respect perspectives that contrast with their own. Putting themselves in the positions of those from different backgrounds enables them to connect with the broader human experience, which can be transformative. In order to assess this outcome, I incorporate reflections into our regular class meetings and trip. Cromwell (chapter 10) asserts that one critical component of transformative learning is reflective practice. Reflections can be done in a number of ways, through journaling online, handwritten notebooks, or even oral discussion. I generally try to vary the prompts, including an option of "free write." Prompts could include a quote, a poem, a video clip, a fill-in-the-blank (e.g., "One thing I learned about myself on this trip is . . ."), or a topic (e.g., "forgiveness"). Creating this habit of reflection should start when the course begins in order to provide for a familiar context for the students when we are immersed in the complexities of the conflict. While in Northern Ireland, students consider how their interactions with locals help them better understand the underlying reasons for conflict and what parallels might be drawn to their own communities back home. They are asked to reflect on how the experience becomes a mirror for the common human condition. This can be very powerful for students. For example, the physical barriers in Belfast are not dissimilar from the (albeit invisible) walls surrounding neighborhoods in Los Angeles. The challenges of societal reintegration for excombatants are parallel to the problems of rehabilitation for former gang members. In recognition of these challenges, Homeboy Industries of Los Angeles, a group of social enterprise businesses that is renowned for its gang intervention and reentry program, has developed a relationship with Belfast's Sandy Row neighborhood, which struggles to find employment for its excombatant community.

Reflecting on Best Practices

In considering what the best practices are for short-term international immersion experiences such as the class research trip that I lead, I consider the following principles. Even though these are geared toward the specific learning goals for the course, they provide food for thought as others consider creating similar courses.

HAVE CLEAR ACADEMIC GOALS

It is important to remember that this is not about taking students on a tour. Tours can be valuable experiences too, but the purpose of this kind of immersion is primarily for them to learn how to do research abroad and more deeply understand the course material in an active-learning environment. Because there are so many things that we *could* do while in Belfast, an easy way to make decisions is to revisit the learning outcomes—often.

It may be tempting to expand these goals with all of the exciting possibilities that arise. However, I am a strong believer in "less is more." Focus on a small set of learning outcomes, and everyone, including the instructor, will be better off in the long run.

BALANCE THE FOCUS BETWEEN PEACE AND CONFLICT

While seeking to better understand conflict in divided societies, I find it important to highlight the activities of the peaceworkers in these areas. For example, our trips have been greatly enriched by playwrights and poets whose work has sought to facilitate cross-sector dialogue. Still others are working on shared remembrance projects, as all sides have suffered painful losses of loved ones. These glimpses of peacebuilding not only add to the substantive knowledge of students but also are an important part of teaching students about the possibilities for resolving conflict in their own lives. It is not that I wish to paint a more rosy picture of the situation itself but rather that I believe students should come away with some sense of the pockets of peace that *do* exist. Moreover, I have been told by the Belfast community members that focusing our attention in this way also reminds *locals* of the progress that has been made.

ENCOURAGE HABITUAL STUDENT REFLECTION

Developing a habit of reflection is critical to knowledge retention and personal development. Once students have created a bond with one another over the first half of the course through shared reflections, their reflections during the intense trip experience flow a bit more easily. Perhaps even more importantly, student reflections should continue after the trip as well. Prior to my use of reflections, my students found it difficult to come back after their transformative experience and resume their lives. They find it problematic to articulate the richness of their experiences to friends and families, and it is within the shared space of group reflections that they are able to give voice to these complex ideas and memories, as well as to further process their experiences. After all, they have just learned firsthand about very personal stories of survival, victimhood, death, persecution, and inequality, with various shades of hope and peace woven in.

Jennifer M. Ramos

FOSTER FACULTY-STUDENT TRIP COLLABORATION

Clearly, the instructor remains a dominant figure in the course, not least of which is because of the grade associated with the course. Yet it may well be worth rethinking the traditional class roles in order to increase student investment and thus the quality of the trip and course overall. Harnessing the students' excitement about the trip, I enlist them to be "cocreators" of the trip itself. As long as the students' learning outcomes serve as the guide, this approach seems to work well. With regard to the immersion experience, students can contribute to suggestions for the itinerary, based on their research of what fits with the course goals. In building the itinerary, one thing that seems to work well is offering students choices from an instructor-approved list. For example, students could choose to meet with the Sandy Row community or the East Belfast Mission, visit City Hall or the Parliament Buildings, or attend a service at Townsend Street Presbyterian or mass at Clonard Church. Having to justify these choices further invests students in the trip, as they debate the merits and significance of each possibility.

AVOID COMMERCIAL VOYEURISM

Conflict, and especially violent conflict, does not need to be sensationalized. Not only can some of the tourist-oriented activities contribute to the reinforcement of the divisions in that society—they can also alienate students from the real experiences of local folks. It is worth the extra effort to research the organizations and companies that offer tours of the area you are visiting to avoid financially contributing to the sensationalism. Ask around. My main resource for tours has been referrals to private citizens from my friends and other local contacts. For example, a church connection knew a local former British soldier who was willing to talk about his experiences in the Troubles; a local playwright had a friend who was a former IRA member. While they appreciated the extra income, my sense was that they really had no other place to express these experiences. Going more local and less commercialized also provides a model for your students for how to travel and learn more deeply about an area and its people. This then better connects them to a more authentic experience that is useful to them both personally and potentially for their research.

INCLUDE MULTIPLE PERSPECTIVES AT MULTIPLE LEVELS

Immersion courses focused on peace and conflict *must* directly provide students with the perspectives of a wide array of people. While the media often portrays conflict as two-sided (or in some way oversimplifies), we all know that this is hardly ever the case. Thus, I seek to arrange the itinerary so that students are exposed to multiple views where they find variation across, for example, political parties, gender, age (most influential may be individuals of their own age), socioeconomic status, and experiences within the conflict and peacebuilding. For example, in Belfast, I make sure that they meet with both Catholics and Protestants, as well as former IRA members and former British soldiers, working-class people and elites, among others. In my case, the precourse trip to Belfast was key to laying the groundwork for locating some of these contacts. In my observations, the more that students became familiar with the personal stories across the community, the more they came to understand the complexities of the conflict and its resolution. Whereas before the trip they thought they knew all the answers ("Why can't they just get along?"), after the trip they come to realize why some conflicts are so intractable.

While I am obviously committed to this course, I would not recommend this type of course in all cases. It all comes back to the learning outcomes and how these might be best achieved. For my course, this works well. Students indicate that this multisensory learning experience helps them to understand not only the conflict in Northern Ireland but also complex course concepts such as peace, justice, and security. Many felt that they had had a transformative experience, emotionally and intellectually. All of them specifically said that they had learned so much more about the conflict and peace process than they ever could have imagined. They concurred that textbooks and articles are simply insufficient; one has to experience and be "in" the culture to begin to understand it. Moreover, when discussing their research projects, students had a light in their eyes when speaking, as if realizing for the first time that they were true scholars. Their pride in their research project and the knowledge that it reflected what they had learned from people they had met gave them a real sense of responsibility to represent the situation accurately and sensitively.

In conclusion, short-term international course immersions offer a unique hands-on approach for instructors seeking to help their students better understand the complexities of peace and conflict resolution. While the logistics can be daunting, the academic and personal benefits to be gained are immense. And the advantages accrue not just to the students but also to the instructor. The course immersion and shared experience enhance the quality of interactions between the students and instructor, the quality of student work, and overall satisfaction in teaching.

Note

1. I would like to thank Dr. Rae Linda Brown for encouraging me to write about my teaching experiences. In addition, I am deeply indebted to the dedicated, hardworking peaceworkers of Belfast and the students who enrich my life more than they know.

SIX

The Use of Service Learning in Teaching about Conflict

ALLYSON M. LOWE AND SANDI DIMOLA

Our study examines the use of service learning to teach political conflict. We chose conflict as the theme for our students' service learning experiences for curricular and practical reasons. First, conflict is inherent to democracy. Conflict has fueled major social movements and, when channeled properly, can empower citizens to effect change. In addition, experience with our students shows that they tend toward being conflict-averse. Our students view conflict as a negative force in their own lives and, generally, have not developed the tools to connect conflict with social change or to see themselves as agents of change (Lowe and DiMola 2012). We wanted to change their perceptions. The second reason involved the ability of the instructors to draw on partnerships with organizations whose work involves issues of community-based conflicts. As we will illustrate, the creation of an effective service learning course has to deliver both a meaningful curricular experience and be sustainable within established departmental and institutional resources (Lowe and DiMola 2012).

The participants in this study were undergraduate students at Carlow University, a Catholic, women-centered, liberal arts university located in Pittsburgh, Pennsylvania. The participants were enrolled in either POL 101-SL: Introduction to American Government or POL 350: The Structure of Conflict: Local to Global. Students in POL 101-SL joined three hundred randomly selected residents of Allegheny County (in which the city of Pittsburgh is located) in a deliberative conversation on the future of county government. Students in POL 350 trained in the techniques of facilitated dialogue and appreciative inquiry and then used this training to work with a local community that was enmeshed in an ethnic conflict.

We draw on both cases to address the challenges of integrating service learning into the teaching of undergraduate courses in conflict studies. In this chapter, the term "conflict studies" is used to describe courses in international and domestic politics whose content addresses the drivers for conflicts. We examine the impact of a community-based learning component on course content, students' learning outcomes, and departmental and faculty resources. A description of the service learning course design is provided together with a discussion of its broader impact on curriculum design within a political science department. The chapter concludes with a reflection on the value of service learning and its connection to the mission of Carlow University.

Service Learning: In the Discipline and in the University

There is a nuanced debate within political science on the role of service learning and its impact on the development of citizen engagement. Carpini and Keeter (2000) point out that political scientists are not in agreement over whether the development of citizen engagement should be part of the discipline's mission. Although there is lack of consensus within the discipline over the issue of citizen engagement, the use of service learning has been explored for many years as a pedagogical strategy in political science (see Barber and Battistoni 1993; Battistoni 2000; Eyler and Giles 1999).

Most of the studies involving the efficacy of service learning were conducted to test the impact of this practice on students' civic participation and attitudes toward civic engagement (David 2009; see also chapter 8, this volume). The results were mixed. Some studies demonstrate a positive correlation between service learning and student civic engagement (Prentice 2007). Other studies, however, find little evidence to indicate that service learning produced a change in students' attitudes about either "democracy or their role as a citizen" (Hunter and Brisbin 2000, 624). In some instances, the value of service learning is critiqued as doing nothing more than "promoting a particular social agenda" (Egger 2008, 183).

Beyond its curricular applications, service learning has become an increasingly popular pedagogical and campus-wide strategy to promote community outreach. The momentum of service learning is evidenced by the growth of Campus Compact, a "national coalition of 1,000+ colleges and universities committed to the public purposes of higher education through civic education and community development" (Campus Compact 2018). The mission statements of almost all Campus Compact member schools include a commitment to service or civic engagement. The creation of university-wide service learning course requirements is one strategy used to institutionalize this mission. For example, since its inception, Carlow University has prominently featured a commitment to service in its mission. Carlow University seeks to "empower individuals . . . to embrace an ethic of service for a just and merciful world" (Carlow University mission statement).[1]

In 2008, Carlow University's faculty assembly approved a service learning course requirement for all traditional undergraduate students. Courses with a service learning designation must include fifteen hours of direct service and a reflective writing assignment that links course content to the field experience. Carlow established the position of "service learning coordinator" to support the execution of this initiative. The service learning coordinator provides resources for faculty in course design and for sources-appropriate community partnerships and encourages opportunities for faculty and student scholarship based on the service learning experience. Programs of study across the university have been encouraged to provide service learning course options that allow students to meet this requirement in relevant and engaging ways. In the spring of 2010, discussions commenced to incorporate service learning into the political science curriculum. While the choice of program seemed to conform to national norms, university values, and departmental learning objectives, some unique challenges had to be overcome.

Political Science is a small department whose major fields of study are being reengineered following a thirty-year absence of leadership. It was necessary to consider whether a department, which in 2010 was staffed by just one full-time faculty member and three adjunct faculty members, could sustain an additional curricular challenge. The decision to proceed was made after considering the research on high-impact practices for the student populations of first-generation, female, minority, and at-risk learners that Carlow University serves (National Survey of Student Engagement, 2010). It was determined that a university committed to empowering women and to teaching in the Catholic social tradition had to rise to this challenge. We defined the following factors as necessary prerequisites to provide an effective and efficient service learning experience:

- Skills must be embedded in the classroom.
- Service learning courses must be incorporated into the major.
- Service learning must contribute to teaching advocacy skills.
- Service learning must be sustainable—that is, offered no more than once during an academic year and be capable of replication.
- Service learning must be in a course rotation that complements departmental needs working with limited or contingent faculty.

POL 101: Introduction to American Government is offered every academic year. A service learning section of this course was created in the fall of 2010 and designated in the course catalogue as POL 101-SL. POL 101-SL is to be offered in the fall of even-numbered years to capitalize on election seasons. POL 350 was created as a special-topics course shell for courses that would both address the needs of community partners and provide a pathway for upper-level political science students to participate in service learning. While there has been much focus on the impact of service learning on student civic engagement, less attention has been paid to the impact of service learning on teaching about conflict and the ways in which conflict can be remediated. This study was prompted by a curiosity to determine if service learning could have an impact beyond its traditional use as a tool to promote citizen engagement.

CASE 1, POL 101-SL: INTRODUCTION TO AMERICAN GOVERNMENT

The pilot for POL 101-SL, the service learning section of POL 101, commenced in the fall of 2010, which was a gubernatorial election year in

Pennsylvania. One section of POL 101-SL and two sections of POL 101 were offered on Carlow's main campus. Four additional sections of POL 101 were offered at the university's regional campuses across southwestern Pennsylvania. The pilot included POL 101-SL and the one section of POL 101 that served traditional, full-time day students (a total of forty-four students). Sections of POL 101 that served students in the accelerated degree program, a group traditionally exempt from the service learning requirement, were not part of the study.

Before classes commenced, approval by the institutional review board (IRB) was received to administer pre- and post-testing of both the service learning (POL 101-SL) and nonservice learning (POL 101) sections of this course. The purpose of these tests was to examine students' civic attitudes at the beginning and at the conclusion of the semester.

Both the service learning and nonservice learning sections of the course had parallel learning objectives, a common textbook, and met the university's requirements for designation as a writing-skills integration course, as well as the political science and economics content area of the core curriculum. POL 101 and POL 101-SL provide an introduction to American government. Introduction to American Government is the gateway course to the major in political science and to the minors in political science, public policy, and prelaw. Students in other disciplines, who are fulfilling core curriculum requirements, often constitute the majority of enrollees. Fall semesters are particularly exciting, as students can watch, analyze, and even participate in electoral politics and community events.

POL 101-SL was designed to meet the outcomes that Janet Eyler and Dwight E. Giles Jr. identify as having the most profound impact on the development of citizen engagement—that is, programs that "have well articulated goals related to course content, [and are of] duration long enough to build relations and extensive reflection" (Eyler and Giles 1999, as cited in Hepburn, Niemi, and Chapman 2000, 618). To summarize, the goal of service learning in political science should be to change students' attitudes toward civic and political engagement. Research shows that students often view *political engagement* as more "corrupt, dirty, and dishonest" than *community service*, such as providing meals or shelter (Walker 2000, 647). Therefore, pre- and post-testing across POL 101 and POL 101-SL was designed to measure potential change in attitudes toward civic engagement.

After consultation with the coordinator for service learning, a template for a service learning class was created. POL 101-SL would be based on a service theme that would allow the department chair to maintain connections to a community partner and would be accessible to any other department member who in the future may teach POL 101-SL. This was an intentional design to ensure the sustainability of the class across rotations and instructors. The initial template of service learning was designed around the theme of elections and election issues. POL 101-SL would be offered in rotation in the fall of even-numbered semesters to coincide with major electoral events and to increase the availability of community programming such as working on election campaigns, which department members could access for students' site placements.

Department faculty maintain relationships with several community nonprofits, such as the League of Women Voters, A+ Schools (school governance monitoring), and the Program for Deliberative Democracy ("the Program"), which became the community partner for POL 101-SL in the fall of 2010. At that time, the department chair also served as the chair of the Program's advisory board. Students in POL 101-SL were engaged in a formal role in the Program's deliberative poll, titled "The Future of Government in Allegheny County."[2]

POL 101-SL students were trained by the Program's staff to serve as rapporteurs during the deliberative poll. Each student was assigned to work with a group of citizens engaged in dialogue involving financial and structural issues facing the municipal governments in Allegheny County. The role of the rapporteur in a small-group dialogue is to assist the facilitator by taking notes and by assertive listening—that is, engaging in techniques such as playback to clarify a deliberant's point. Students were taught to remain neutral even when faced with conflict among the members of their group. This was a skill-building activity that complemented the writing-skills integration requirement of the course and reinforced content learning. Students prepared for their participation in the event by reading the deliberative poll's background document, "Local Government at the Crossroads: Critical Choices for Our Communities" (Program for Deliberative Democracy 2010), and were fortunate to have the author as a guest lecturer in class.

On the day of the deliberative poll, students joined with over three hundred residents of communities in Allegheny County to discuss and reflect on the financial challenges facing the municipalities within the county. Students witnessed the conflict between residents from more affluent communities and those from smaller, less financially secure ones over issues such as consolidation or elimination of municipal services, elimination of county jobs, and in some cases mergers between contiguous townships. While discussions were impassioned, students witnessed residents sharing their views (some factually supported, others not) and working through conflicts, even if resolution on issues was not completely reached.

Students began to recognize that, armed with the tools of dialogue, strong views can be voiced without becoming disruptive. Conflict, in this instance, empowered the residents—all of whom had read the background document before participating in the deliberation—to make strategic suggestions to meet the financial challenges in their communities. At the conclusion of this event, students engaged in a written reflection exercise and class discussions on the impact of deliberative conversations on democratic decision-making.

By the end of the term, students in POL 101 and POL 101-SL had completed the traditional scope of material expected in an introductory course, with special emphasis on writing. Students in POL 101-SL had an additional "text" in the fifteen hours of community service.

Methodology

Pre- and post-testing was conducted in POL 101 and POL 101-SL to elicit the following information:

- Was a change in students' attitudes toward civic and political issues more pronounced among students in POL 101-SL than among students in POL 101?

- Were students in POL 101-SL more likely to see conflict as a necessary and constructive part of democracy than students in POL 101?

- Can service learning be sustained at both departmental and institutional levels?

The pre- and post-tests used an IRB-approved, modified version of the Public Service Motivation Scale (Perry 1996). Students in POL 101-SL were pre- and post-surveyed by the university's service learning office to determine both their general impression of service learning and their particular experience in POL 101-SL. These surveys employed a metric common to traditional course evaluations and also elicited general demographic information from each student. At the end of the final examination in POL 101-SL, students were asked to indicate their willingness to be contacted for additional follow-up in future semesters. (Note that their answers had no bearing on their grade. Students were asked to circle either "yes" or "no.") Seventeen of the twenty-two students enrolled in POL 101-SL indicated their willingness to be contacted. These students constituted a focus group that participated in additional discussions regarding service learning and its relevance to their majors. This focus group provided additional insights into directions for departmental and university service learning programming.

Focus groups were conducted under a February 2011 extension of the August 2010 IRB covering the original pre- and post-testing for the service learning course. The following questions were put to the focus group:

- If you took the course to fulfill your SL [service learning] requirement at Carlow, how did that impact your initial attitude towards the course? Toward the service project?

- Did you have any sense of what the service might entail? Did the related course content influence which SL section you took?

- For political science majors: What made you choose the SL version of POL 101?

- If you are a nonmajor, what ideas did you have about political science before enrolling in the course? How did the SL impact your understanding of political science (if at all)?

- What were your expectations for the SL part of this course? How did this course meet or challenge your expectations?

- How did the SL project in this class compare to what you thought you would be doing? How did it compare to what other students have told you about their SL courses?

- What was the most valuable aspect of this course for you?
- What was the least valuable aspect?
- What would you tell other students about this course? About SL?
- Do you think there is a difference between SL and civic engagement? If so, what is that difference?
- Would you continue to be involved with any of the projects? Why or why not?

Survey Results

There was a statistically significant level of difference between students in POL 101 and POL 101-SL for four of the twenty-two questions on the modified Public Service Motivation Scale (Perry 1996). These questions, which reflected Tobi Walker's (2000) concerns about civic attitudes, were:

- Q. 8: Politics is a dirty word.
- Q. 13: I am one of those rare persons who would risk personal loss to help another.
- Q. 17: The give and take of policymaking doesn't appeal to me.
- Q. 19: I don't care much for politicians.

This change in attitudes reflected those expected to result from sustained meaningful community engagements as described in the literature on service learning. (We acknowledge that a confounding variable is the instructor, and we can debate whether this change is a function of service learning or instructor.) Additional *t*-tests examined the change in means on the pre- and post-surveys across these sections. While all changes in means moved in the expected directions—that is, for example, students agreed *less* strongly that politics was a dirty word—none proved to reach the level of statistical significance on these paired sample tests.

As POL 101-SL was a writing skills course, it facilitated assessment of student learning through an examination of individual students' service learning reflection assignments and in cumulative moments across the course beyond the post-testing. For example, the course's final examination included an extra-credit question that asked students to reflect on the following:

> Please... connect your service experiences to the full semester's learning. What have been the clearest points of connection for you between the service and the curriculum? Which concepts, if any, came to life through the service? Or, was it the other way around: service experiences made more sense when you studied the theories that they informed. Cite examples.

Sixteen of the twenty-two students chose to answer this question. Eleven answers supported the premise that service learning experiences help illuminate material in the class or texts. Representative answers included the following comments:

> The class curriculum made more sense to me after doing the service activities. I like to experience what I learn and this hands-on approach helped me grasp concepts better. I understand voting and the importance of being active in democracy from my service. (Sophomore, psychology major)

> I think the class concepts became clearer through service. When we read about voters, deliberative democracy and thick government it was all pretty confusing but by seeing the deliberative democracy event, the concept of the thick government became clear and a lot more realistic. (First-year, major not yet declared)

Five answers suggested that the reverse was more often true—that is, the class and texts explained the service experiences. A representative answer in this group included the following reflection:

> This class and the service learning helped me understand different issues and policies. It also helped me to become more motivated and interested in politics. Class concepts helped me understand the service-learning activities and it gave me more value because I was able to understand them. The Debating 4 Democracy [D4D] helped me learn how to get my voice heard and help others get their voices heard. And in class, learning the different offices from local to national, I can now say "okay, I or a group has a concern, who should I approach?" I know now [sic] who to approach and how to do so because of what I learned in class and at the D4D workshop. (Junior, minor in political science, declared during the semester)

Focus-Group Results

Seventeen students participated in the focus group and 25 percent of that group had participated previously in a focus-group experience. The minority representation in the focus group paralleled the demographic of POL 101-SL. All students in the focus-group sessions indicated that they had enrolled in the "SL" section of the course to meet the university's service learning course requirement. They all had reservations about the service component of the course, in particular their ability to find the time to complete the required fifteen hours of service. While some students commented that they would not have taken the service learning section if it had not been required by the university, all but one participant expressed that they found the service learning to be valuable. In terms of expectations, one student commented:

> I thought I would be taking a class and then volunteering on site. I liked how it was connected with the course content—that's not what I had expected.

Others commented that participation in the deliberative poll allowed them to learn about the political process in a more concrete way. One student said:

> In class we talked about voter apathy versus engaged individuals—I felt like the Deliberative Democracy project helped me see that people are not apathetic, which we always assume. Even just average citizens have issues they care about and want to talk about but they need a process like this to bring them into the dialogue.

In addition, several students remained in contact with the Program for Deliberative Democracy and participated in other events, often with members of the group for whom they had served as a rapporteur.

Students noted they were concerned about the number of required hours but commented that the course was well designed for them to reach this goal. Students were asked if they preferred to have had a variety of civic-engagement projects or if they would have preferred to focus in more depth on one project. One student commented:

> Just the Deliberative Democracy project would've been enough value for this course. Quality trumps quantity and one good, thoughtful experience is super-important. It's important that service learning is not busy work.

Student responses were mixed regarding whether they planned to be committed in the future to the type of civic-engagement efforts to which they were exposed in POL 101-SL. Two students said they would be enthusiastic to participate in another deliberative democracy event; however, while one of the students commented that the deliberative poll event was "really cool," neither felt inclined to follow up on his or her own (see chapter 4). Another student commented that she would not stay involved in these specific projects but said:

> I will say I pay more attention [to politics] now when I watch TV and I have some apps on my iPhone for news.

The statistical findings of this survey are neither profound in their challenge to established literature nor often reach statistical significance. However, when considered in combination with the qualitative findings, as well as national trends in service learning, they suggest that service learning has a positive impact on curricular delivery from the classroom to the departmental level.

Beyond the curricular insights that the students' responses provide, they also highlight issues regarding the sustainability of student service efforts and questions for practitioners in the discipline. For example, should service learning focus on building sustained partnerships between the university and community organizations, or should service learning focus on ways to empower students to value civic engagement over the course of their lives? Research and practical experience suggest that there are various design and execution strategies that will allow colleges and universities to make strategic and sustainable commitments to service learning. Therefore, it is argued that the greater impact of service learning is in its ability to foster life-long values of civic or community engagement and an appreciation of and tolerance for conflict as a necessary part of the democratic process. This can be accomplished even when students have their first exposure to service learning in an upper-level course, as the second case study illustrates.

CASE 2, POL 350 SPECIAL TOPICS: THE STRUCTURE OF CONFLICT—LOCAL TO GLOBAL

Implementation of service learning in courses specifically focused on conflict enriches coursework by encouraging students to apply the knowledge and analytical tools gained in the classroom to remediate the issues that are drivers for discordance in communities. Students, in collaboration with faculty and community partners, can be engaged to develop research projects, collect and analyze data, and share their results and conclusions with the organizations and agencies that require the information, as well as with their professors. This type of work benefits community organizations, enhances the student's theoretical understanding of conflict, and, in certain instances, provides the students with exposure to working within a diverse, international environment, even within the boundaries of the student's own community (Tilghman 2007).

POL 350: The Structure of Conflict—Local to Global was developed to provide upper-level political science students with tools to understand and analyze the difficult choices that policymakers face when they design and undertake measures to intervene in conflict. The course instructs students to better evaluate the outcomes of actions taken and alternatives eschewed and to identify the underlying ethical issues that are embedded in the decisions and actions of practitioners in the field of conflict resolution. A service learning component was added to provide students with the opportunity to experience how decisions relating to conflict resolution are executed in the field and the impact individuals and institutions can have in transforming conflict (see chapter 4).

The service learning experience connected students with community mediators in an undertaking known as the Lawrenceville Dialogue Project (LDP). Initiated in August 2008 and still ongoing, the LDP was created by the nongovernmental organization (NGO) Mediators Beyond Borders in cooperation with Pittsburgh's Center for Victims of Violence and Crime. This project involved a series of facilitated dialogues among the Somali and non-Somali populations in the Lawrenceville neighborhood of Pittsburgh. At the conclusion of this course, students drew on both theoretical and field experience, as they participated in critical and evaluative discussions on issues relating to the role of individuals and institutions in peacemaking and peacebuilding at the grassroots level.

Background of the Lawrenceville Dialogue Project

In 2004, Pittsburgh was selected as a relocation site for approximately two hundred Somali refugees. This group consisted primarily of female heads of households, with from seven to ten children per family. Prior to their resettlement in the United States, many members of this group, in particular the children and young adults, had lived most of their lives in Kenya's Kakuma refugee camp, where there was little access to schooling, job training, and health care and insufficient preparation for the challenges that would come with life in America. The Somalis who resettled in Pittsburgh were semiliterate in their first language and had no knowledge of the English language. Their cultural, linguistic, and social differences impeded their adaptation to city life and made them vulnerable to both abuse by, and conflict with, their adoptive community in Lawrenceville (DiMola and Lunsford 2007).

At the time of the Somalis' resettlement, Lawrenceville was primarily an ethnically and racially homogeneous neighborhood of approximately eleven thousand residents. The neighborhood is an amalgam of families, whose ancestors worked in the factories and steel mills at the turn of the twentieth century, and young professionals and artists, who were attracted by the neighborhood's affordable housing and commercial space. Lawrenceville was chosen as a resettlement site because of the availability of low-income housing, its proximity to several major bus lines, and the presence two of the city's largest public schools, Arsenal Elementary and Arsenal Middle Schools.

Arsenal Middle School serves children ages ten through thirteen in grades six through eight. Children of the Somali families were enrolled in Arsenal Elementary or Arsenal Middle School. As Arsenal Middle School's student demographic became more diverse, primarily through the introduction of the Somali children, there was a corresponding rise in ethnically based violence within the student population (DiMola and Lunsford 2007). This violence was not contained to incidents within the school. Children and their parents were in conflict at public places within the community, such as shops, fast-food establishments, and the health clinic. These incidents deepened the rift between the Somali and non-Somali populations and had deleterious impacts on the Lawrenceville community. Adult and juvenile arrests among both Somalis and non-Somalis increased, property values declined, and businesses relocated out of the area (DiMola and Lunsford 2007). Community leaders joined with the principal of Arsenal Middle School and enlisted the assistance of Mediators Beyond Borders, a community organization, to create an initiative that would both remediate violence in the school and create understanding between the Somali and non-Somali populations in the neighborhood.

The LDP was developed as a series of community dialogues and mediations designed to end the violence and bridge the divide between Lawrenceville's Somali and non-Somali populations. The instructor of POL 350 was a founding member of Mediators Beyond Borders and a designer of the LDP, which provided the capacity to include this project as the service learning component of POL 350.

Students in POL 350 began their work by framing the following questions:

- What strategies need to be implemented that will allow the Somali and non-Somali communities to peacefully coexist and to ensure the rights of both groups are respected?

- What techniques of group dialogue can community mediators employ to create a more inclusive community?

The LDP became the vehicle that catapulted students from consideration of theoretical concepts of conflict and culture to working on conflict and community mediation within a group from which they were culturally, linguistically, and socially dissimilar (see chapter 4). The project utilized community partnerships that were developed with the Pittsburgh Refugee Center and the Center for Victims of Violence and Crime, in addition to Mediators Beyond Borders.

Creation of the Service Learning Component

Creation of the service learning experience involved three steps: education in the classroom, action in the community, and student reflection. A curricular unit was developed that provided students with information on the history and culture of the Somali people and on the refugee resettlement process. The goal was to ensure that students understood refugee resettlement and the particular challenges involved in resettling the Somalis in Pittsburgh. Students began by viewing the film *Rain in a Dry Land*, a documentary that follows the relocation of four Somali families in cities across the United States. Following the screening, students participated in a facilitated discussion with the director of the Pittsburgh Refugee Center, an organization that works on issues related to refugee resettlement and whose director is a Somali national. This interaction allowed the students to explore more fully the problems facing refugee families, as well as the financial and logistical challenges faced by the various agencies and NGOs that assist in relocation efforts; these were issues that the students would experience directly when working with the Somali population.

The second step involved moving the students from the classroom into the community. The faculty member drew on community partnerships developed with Mediators Beyond Borders and the Center for Victims of Violence and Crime to facilitate the students' introduction into the community. Since Lawrenceville was a community actively in conflict, it was necessary for the faculty member and the community partner to ensure that there would be opportunities for students to become introduced to and to work with the community to the various degrees with which the students would feel comfortable. Initially, the students accompanied members of the Center for Victims of Violence and Crime and Mediators Beyond Borders to community board meetings that were attended by local government officials, services providers, and families from the Somali and non-Somali communities in Lawrenceville. At those meetings students heard the concerns of representatives of the Somali and non-Somali communities, as well as the challenges identified and solutions proposed by the businesses, agencies, and institutions located in the Lawrenceville neighborhood.

As the project progressed, students worked with leaders from the Somali community to conduct interviews of Somali families regarding their perceptions of life in Lawrenceville. Students who were trained in the techniques of leading a dialogue participated as assistants to seasoned community mediators to facilitate conversations among community groups in settings that increased positive interaction and cultural learning, while other students worked in Arsenal Middle School on the creation of a peer mediation program. All of the students' efforts were focused toward building relationships among the various groups within Lawrenceville to foster the sense of a shared community. At the conclusion of the field experience, students produced a case study with outcomes and evaluations. The purpose of the case study was to create a blueprint for replication of facilitated dialogues by other communities.

The third step of the service learning experience required students to reflect on their field experience by considering how it contributed to their understanding of conflict and the strategies used to manage conflictual relationships. Students had the following comments:

Working with the families increased my interest in learning more about conflict by studying it in the field.

I became more involved and interested in why the conflict occurs by participating with a community in crisis.

Students' appreciation for conflict management was reflected in the following responses:

When people were able to exchange information both groups stated they appreciated the opportunity to get to know each other. The non-Somali families wanted to know how they should address the Somalis when they see them on the street. The Somali families wanted everyone to know that they are hard working.

Solutions were generated to address concerns regarding viable employment for Somalis and opportunities to work together. Two suggestions were a community garden as a way for the Somalis to use their indigenous skills as farmers to contribute to the community by both teaching gardening and growing produce that can be revenue generating or shared. The second suggestion was the development of a Somali restaurant that would again capitalize on the talents of the Somalis while establishing a place where a common gathering place could be established.

The Somalis expressed a desire to participate on an on-going basis in community and civic activities. The community development organization agreed to play a role in making that possible.

Outcomes

The students helped to facilitate the integration of an African refugee group into a Pittsburgh neighborhood. This experience had a pronounced impact on the students. For example, prior to participating in this project, none of the students had any previous interactions with persons from Somalia, with refugees, or with the organizations that aid in the refugee-resettlement process. In addition, since the project was locally based, several of the students were able to continue to work with these organizations and within the Lawrenceville community.

The project's success as a vehicle for a service learning experience can be attributed to the use of the service learning model in the development and execution of the curricular content. In POL 350, the instructor advanced a collaborative work environment between the students and the community mediators. This partnership promoted interdisciplinary research, teaching, and fieldwork on issues surrounding the resettlement of a refugee population. Students experienced, firsthand, practical solutions to the complex issues of refugee resettlement from the perspectives of both the Somali and non-Somali communities in Lawrenceville.

Our rationale for incorporating service learning into the teaching of conflict studies is that disciplinary, interdisciplinary, and multidisciplinary inquiry is essential to enhance the quality and to deepen the commitment of students' understanding of what drives conflict and the challenges to its remediation. The opportunity for students to work in and with a community in conflict furthers their understanding of the course material and the intellectual methods of the field while meeting community-defined needs.

In 2011, the American Political Science Association's Task Force for Political Science in the 21st Century recommended that

> political science should continue to internationalize its curriculum by, for example, encouraging open discussion and communication about sensitive issues in the world, particularly as they relate to people of different political environments, backgrounds, beliefs, and cultures. This can also be done by emphasizing global citizenship that connects what is local and what is global and stresses the importance of breaking away from a purely Westernized view of the world. (APSA 2011, 36)

Incorporation of service learning into the teaching of conflict responds to this recommendation. Students learn strategies for remediating or resolving conflict that allows communities in crisis to safely and effectively address sensitive and provocative issues and empowers students to view themselves as agents of change. The service learning experience also facilitates student engagement with economically, ethnically, and socially diverse communities.

Service learning can be an effective tool in teaching about conflict both for courses where the subject of conflict is as explicit as in a course on the structure of conflict or as subtle as in an introductory course on American government that introduces conflict as part of the democratic process. In both instances, a service learning component can provide students with a framework for understanding conflict that can be meaningfully structured by disciplinary knowledge, informed by practice, and crafted by practical skills engaged in the civic and community sectors.

Notes

1. Carlow University mission statement can be found at http://www.carlow.edu/Vision_Mission_Values_Philosophy.aspx.

2. A deliberative poll gathers a representative sample of the community to discuss and respond to questions on pressing local, regional, or national issues. One of the functions of deliberative conversations is to engage the public in informed, moderated discussions on potentially controversial or politically charged issues to reduce the possibility of community conflict. The program Local Government at the Crossroads was created to address issues facing the future of municipal government in Allegheny County. The county has experienced diminished revenues, which has impacted its ability to continue to deliver quality services to county residents. There were conflicts among communities regarding disparities in payment for and receipt of county services. The deliberative poll was an effort to provide citizens with some background material on the issues, such as funding for county services, fiscal challenges facing local governments, delivery of services, and how services might be affected by a choice to pursue options such as raising taxes, reducing services, and changing the way services are delivered (Program for Deliberative Desmocracy 2010).

SEVEN

Field-Based Service Learning Pedagogy and Its Effects

PATRICIA A. MAULDEN AND LISA ELAINE SHAW

> Through this experience I not only learned about Liberia and working in a postconflict environment but I learned about myself and how I work and function within that context. This is something I don't think you can learn sitting in a classroom.
>
> —2011 Liberia field experience student

This chapter explores the long-term effects of the reciprocal-engagement model developed by the authors over six years of teaching field-based service learning courses.[1] The field-based pedagogy research project explored shifts in understanding, abilities, perceptions of the self, and conceptualization of possibilities attributed, at least in part, to experiential engagement in field-based service learning courses. In the sections below, the role and understanding of reciprocity and service will be explored in relation to field-based experiences. The conclusion discusses pedagogical and experiential effects of field-based service learning courses for both faculty and students. The courses upon which this chapter draws occurred in Liberia from 2010 to 2012.

The field-based experiential learning model developed for the courses in Liberia, which was subsequently used in Colombia, West Virginia, and Brazil, provides students with a "real-world" setting in which to link conflict theory to conflict resolution practice. The learning model developed as instructors pondered how to structure a field experience where students observe contextual realities, reflect, make assessments, discuss resolution approaches, and closely engage with context culture, local societies, and postconflict dilemmas. Many discussions were held during the planning for the initial field experience, as taking students to Liberia, a country still emerging from twenty years of war, presented many challenges. These discussions, as well as the designers' previous field experiences in conflict zones, framed a course model that focused the curriculum experientially, ethically, and theoretically. To accomplish a theoretically informed, ethical experience that would give students the chance to work with individuals and communities in the field, instructors determined that engaging country partners as contextual experts would be a first step. Building on faculty's already existing relationship with a local organization in Liberia, the student and faculty team were able to connect with other partner organizations in different areas of the country. As our contact network spread, potential opportunities for students to work with organizations in various communities across Liberia increased.

Aligning with local experts and working on locally developed projects allowed students to learn from our partners and for our partners to learn from the students. This reciprocal process presented students with dilemmas that challenged the certainty of theory and previous course-based analyses of context and of processes of conflict and resolution. These dilemmas required individual and group critical thinking and reflection, leading to at least the potential for deeper levels of learning and more nuanced understanding. This dynamic forms not only the basis of, but also the reason for, the development of the reciprocal-engagement model. The initial field course in 2010 allowed the instructors to test the nascent framework, allowing reflection in action as part of the field experience but also reflection on action upon our return. Postexperience student evaluations and discussions brought revisions that were formalized in the model presented in this chapter. The trips in 2011 and 2012 brought additional field-based and postexperience reflections from students, local partners, and instructors. These comments and suggestions helped instructors to organize activities before, during, and after the field course in more effective ways.

Since 2010, eighty students and eight faculty members participated in service learning field experiences, which have a similar structure:

- Each group works directly with local organizations.
- All activities and projects come from community-member requests, local partner organizations' needs assessments, and ongoing in-country project work.
- Two faculty facilitators accompany students for a period of two weeks to one month.
- Students are divided into teams to conduct in-field workshops and activities.
- In-field workshops and activities include conflict assessment and mapping, resolution process designs, trainings, mediations, group workshops, and project implementation.

In Liberia, students conducted workshops on conflict mapping, facilitation, mediation, and communication skills. They also assisted local organizations with family reunification and worked with local practitioners to strengthen their assessment and facilitation approaches. Additionally, the teams ran a workshop to help high school students set up peer mediation programs and helped a community organize its celebrations of the Day of the African Child.

Service learning field experiences as developed through the reciprocal-engagement model give students (and instructors) an opportunity to experience or resituate themselves in an ongoing or postconflict context. This potentially includes living without many of the amenities generally taken for granted, having theories and conclusions called into question, developing empathy for and a more comprehensive level of understanding of parties in local conflicts, learning more deeply about themselves, adapting individual ideas and wishes with those of the community (both students and partners), and finding a broader awareness of conflict dynamics and resolution possibilities. Students enter the service experience with certain types of knowledge (primarily academic) while lacking other types of knowledge (contextual and experiential). As the process unfolds, students and instructors find a nuanced view of power, expertise, humility, and strength. The service encompasses working with local actors on locally determined projects, sharing with them, when appropriate, knowledge or skills that might be useful for future projects. The values and practices of this model allow a level of learning and experience far beyond a tour or series of lectures. Students intensively and experientially struggle directly with themselves, with local partners and communities, with difficult circumstances, with their coursework, and with their assumptions (Lambright and Lu 2009, 425, 428; Bringle and Hatcher 1999, 113). The struggle and its effects make the reciprocal-engagement model of service learning a powerful and rewarding educational opportunity.

The following sections review academic and experiential pedagogy, explore in detail the reciprocal-engagement model, and conclude with a discussion of lessons learned and potential opportunities to enlarge and expand the field-based experiential model. As experiences vary significantly across contexts, however, only the Liberia case will be explored.

Academic and Experiential Learning Pedagogy

A service learning intensive field course can be very demanding, requiring that instructors maintain a high level of awareness of student activities, stresses, group dynamics, and learning. In addition, instructors must keep ongoing organization and community relations strong, reach out to potential partners, and manage logistical realities that can seem ever changing. This high level of active engagement warrants that two instructors work together.

During the academic year, instructors begin to prepare students to understand the conflict and community context and to have a grounding in conflict theory as well as assessment and resolution skills. The academic component of the model includes a mandatory reading list, suggested readings, and a two-part pre-trip paper that analyzes and explores theories underpinning contextual dynamics and conflict resolution or peacebuilding approaches. The second component calls for students to reflect on their own expectations, strengths, weaknesses, and uncertainties. This first written assignment establishes a baseline for the exploration that will occur throughout the field experience around the linkages and the tensions between theory, practice, and context as well as the learning, reflections, and experiences of the student. While in the field, student teams complete project analyses for each site visit, workshop, training, or planning session. These assignments allow for reflection, synthesis, and review to become an inherent part of the ongoing individual and group process of learning. In addition, students and faculty engage in debriefing sessions at the end of each working day to examine the links between experience, context, and conflict resolution theory. Debriefing also surfaces assumptions, expectations, biases, fears, and other concerns about the work as well as about individual responses to the physically difficult and emotionally challenging environment. Finally, the integration essay submitted a month after the end of the course readdresses issues from the first assignment and expands students' written reflections about their own learning and change processes.

Experiential learning within this pedagogical frame is conveyed to students in pre-trip meetings and orientation seminars once the team arrives in the field. Once it is situated, hands-on activities, lecture presentations (often by community members or organizational personnel), site visits to communities, organizations, and markets, and locally organized activities such as cultural festivals give students contextual insight. Being present in a war-torn, conflict-ridden, semisecure, or environmentally devastated place can bring a new sense of the world and can call into question individual ideas about ongoing policies of war-to-peace transition, attention to human rights, or access to basic resources. In the case of Liberia, policy documents, government representatives, and international organizational reports painted a very rosy picture that was quickly obscured by what students and faculty experienced in the capital and in rural areas. The picture altered further as local community members talked about their lives, their struggles, and their fading hopes for change. Each student engaged with this quandary in various ways, but, as emerged during debriefing sessions and personal meetings, all were significantly impacted. The final assignment, submitted one month after returning home, allowed the students time to further reflect on the effects of the work. The articulation of these effects formed a significant portion of their final assignment.

Reciprocal-Engagement Model

The previous sections established the service learning field course as an experientially based learning opportunity. The reciprocal-engagement model itself merely frames that learning from a pedagogical and theoretical standpoint. This section explores the model's components (critical thinking, multilevel learning, shifting power relations, resituated experience, and reflection) and their practical implementation in Liberia.

The diagram below depicts the model's components as a framework or pattern that facilitates student engagement. The items in the right-hand column—theoretical understandings, personal assumptions and biases, practice experience, and limited contextual knowledge—name some of what students and faculty bring with them to the field course academically, experientially, theoretically, personally, and ethically. The model and the pedagogical framing of the course posit that prior experience and knowledge will be challenged when in the field. The model also proposes that it is in the experience of working with those challenges that learning happens.

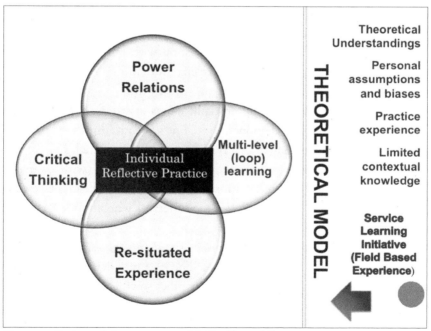

Figure 7.1. Reciprocal-engagement model. *Maulden and Shaw 2010.*

CRITICAL THINKING

Critical thinking can be considered a reasoning process that involves identifying assumptions, raising questions, clarifying issues, and developing affective attitudes such as humility, courage, and confidence (Sedlak et al. 2003, 100). The role of humility in the field cannot be overemphasized, particularly as students and faculty may easily default to the view that the individuals with whom they are working are somehow "less" or "lacking," based on their own notions of knowledge, capacity, or intelligence. This will be explored further in the power and resituated-learning discussions, but it also has a role in the critical-thinking aspects of individual reflective practice at the heart of the model.

The reasoning process can also bring in elements of metaphor, moving somewhat beyond the observable and perhaps a bit beyond the affective as individuals and groups come to understand and experience one thing in terms of another. Metaphors involve language, thought, and action and are very important in field courses, impacting how students and faculty structure perceptions, get around in the Liberian world, and relate to the residents (Lakoff and Johnson 1980, 3–6). The meanings ascribed to a metaphor can vary significantly between cultures, societies, or even individuals. For example, an initial workshop with our Liberian partner organization (a nongovernmental organization doing community and family-reconciliation work) focused on ways to think about conflict and conflict assessment, or mapping. Initially, we, as instructors, did not consider using a PowerPoint demonstration, but in communications prior to our arrival we learned that such a presentation was expected. One of the first slides in the presentation likened conflict to an iceberg (with a refreshingly cool photo) and to a tree, as most dynamics are underneath or beyond the observable or the articulated. For the Liberians who attended, the iceberg meant very little. The tree, however, had significant conceptual value as everyone either knows how to "brush farm" (plant, tend, and harvest produce) or knows someone who does. The idea of a living thing, in this case a tree, growing up from the seed of conflict sown in the parched earth of context resonated strongly and elicited very astute analysis and dynamic concept maps. When the iceberg model was explained (frozen water gathering mass as a glacier and breaking off into the icy sea, its bulk below the surface but a small part above the waves), the connection to experiences around conflict continued to be outside of Liberian experience and, while interesting, difficult to relate to everyday life. Increased critical thinking and personal growth for students and faculty came, as they began to see the world through local eyes.

MULTILEVEL LEARNING

Building upon and linking with critical thinking as discussed above, multilevel learning can be framed as an individual's process of engagement with a particular context and the subsequent adaptation and construction of meaning, understanding, and knowledge that results. In essence, as cognitive, affective, and experiential parts of the self, engage with the environment, knowledge and understanding can develop (Peschl 2007, 137). The reciprocal-engagement model gives form to course designers' views that students engaging in conflict analysis and resolution fieldwork in a context not their own have the opportunity to experience a profound change in themselves and potentially to share ideas or experiences that can offer some type of change for individuals with whom they work.

As an example, the student and faculty team worked with our field partner organization around family unification. Specifically, they assisted in finding ways to facilitate the return of street children to their homes and communities. In that activity the team found that a very brief assessment had been completed regarding what had happened in the home or the community prior to the child either leaving on his or her own or being forced out. Often the existing report was no more than three or four sentences on a half sheet of paper and, other than the child, did not name the parties involved or give a description of the situational dynamics. The evidence of this limited data appeared in the low rates of children (aged five to fourteen) being welcomed back and the high rates of children that repeatedly left their homes. We discussed this trend with the organization's practitioners, asked them about their reunification work, and heard about time constraints and limited staffing. The organization's directors noted that, with the help of the student teams, they could accomplish three months' work in one month. We asked them questions about their processes, and together we worked to devise a more comprehensive assessment strategy. When we returned the following year, one of the practitioners involved taught us how he had significantly improved his practice far beyond what we had discussed and the practitioner had enrolled in university to study social work. Six years later, he is the director of a human services agency and has graduated with his degree.

Over the course of three years, these consultations resulted in the organization developing standard protocols that included conducting interviews with additional family and community members and finding out more information about what caused the child to leave home. While more time-consuming, the additional information proved useful in providing long-term reunifications. This example highlights knowledge gained by students and organizational staff. Students experienced directly how difficult it could be to negotiate with family and community members to facilitate the return of a child. Organizational staff already knew of these difficulties but learned that additional information gained through assessment often led to more positive results.

The example underscores the processes linking learning and change, moving from "reacting and downloading" to "redesigning and adapting" and finally to "reframing" (Peschl 2007, 138–39). This pattern can be considered in terms of levels or loops, ranging from zero to three (Romme and Van Witteloostuijn 1999, 439–40):

- The zero loop implies ignoring changes, bad outcomes, or anomalies in the environment.

- Single-loop approaches involve consolidating ideas or behaviors, carrying on in the same way only more so.

- Double loop requires the modification of underlying norms, policies, or objectives, a reframing or transformation.

- Triple loop increases the deepness of learning about the diversity of issues and dynamics, linking learnings past and present together in a way that produces new strategies for understanding.

As a case in point, at the request of our organizational partners one of the student and faculty teams traveled to a remote city in Liberia to observe a hearing on a long-standing land dispute. At the community leader's invitation, the team members introduced themselves, were recognized as guest meeting facilitators, and took their seats among those present. During a particularly difficult community discussion, one member of the team raised a hand to speak and was recognized. At that point the team member proceeded to tell the community leader and those concerned how they needed to solve the problem. This person had a particular approach that had been used in a different part of the world but assumed would fit almost any context. The audience listened politely as the team member shared this conflict resolution approach without critically considering the role of observer or the potential that in this context the approach would neither be welcome nor effective. The approach came not from a position of humility, as discussed in the critical thinking section, but from a position of certainty. At that meeting, which did reach settlement, perhaps assisted by the presence of outside observers as well as by disputants finally willing to offer apology and acknowledgment, another student commented, "After all that, they settled the thing themselves." Our Liberian partners fully understood the contextual usefulness of outside observers as an intervention strategy, something that the team did not fully consider. The experience proved a strong learning experience and a reminder that in the end local problems need local solutions worked through by community members.

Power Relations

The previous discussion focused on the links between critical thinking and learning through experience and reflection. The exploration now considers power in relation to social organization and control of resources (Contu and Willmott 2003, 285–87), as well as knowledge and cultural determinations. In the Liberia field project, it was the community members and grassroots organizations that possessed expert knowledge and understanding of contextual dynamics. They also held power in their ability to navigate complex social relationships. Students came with varying sets of skills and knowledge that needed to be adapted or replaced to effectively "fit" within the Liberian context. This "fitting" process required critical thinking and learning levels, as discussed above, but also incorporated existing power dynamics. The field experience format allowed students the opportunity to work their way through "fitting" appropriately within the context, acknowledging power dynamics in new ways, incorporating learning levels in this process, and reflecting not only on their environment and on those in it but also on themselves.

A fundamental point of departure for the field experience design is the idea that students and faculty work together as a community of practice. As much as possible, challenges are explored by the community, and subsequent learning is shared. From an internal perspective, the evaluative power of the faculty "over" students remained, but faculty teams worked to ensure that it was the students who took the lead in planning and conducting workshops, trainings, and activities. Through this process, the student and faculty teams had multiple opportunities to have their assumptions, their values, and their attitudes challenged. Daily debriefings, private discussions (student to student, student to faculty, faculty to faculty), and project-reflection analyses provided ways through which these challenges could be examined. Individual and group reflection served as the intersection for critical thinking and purposeful learning, as students and faculty systematically brought a sense of inquiry to experiences, preparing the ground, so to speak, for deeper learning throughout their field experiences (Amulya 2004).

Exploring power dynamics and tensions between the external (global or state) and local (community or individual) also formed an important aspect of each field course. Participants entered into the postconflict or conflict-prone context with certain assumptions, whether implicit or explicit, about local individuals and communities. Often these were based on internationally focused articles, United Nations documents, and so forth. With those ideas, theories, and understandings in mind, students often had a difficult time seeing community residents as people with skills, capacities, knowledge, and understandings. In other words, the power that community residents held was either not discerned or remained unacknowledged by team members, perhaps as it did not match with what was "brought in," as depicted on the right-hand side of the reciprocal-engagement model.

Stefan Andreassen (2005, 971) notes the reductive repetition motif that frames such contexts and communities as possessing, in terms of development, a "core set of deficiencies for which externally generated 'solutions' must be devised." Oliver P. Richmond (2011, 53) explores the "relative value ascribed," in terms of liberal peacebuilding, to the local (lower) in relation to the international (higher). From those points of view, agencies and individuals that come from the outside to help put the country back together again claim the power, the resources, and the expertise that allows them to do so in good conscience. Peacebuilding literature (Mac Ginty 2011; Philpott and Powers 2010; Richmond 2010; Murithi 2009) reflects the ongoing debates about the efficacy or indeed the ethics of this paradigm. Instructors of the Liberian course tried not to make the same errors. Removing assumptions, however, is a difficult proposition and one that requires much reflection as much of the literature builds on these subliminal messages. Overall, the students did come to recognize and respect the incredible strength, intelligence, awareness, and stamina of our local partners and community members. Cultural and social activities brought together the student team and local residents. These events played an important role in breaking down restraint, allowing friendships to grow, and fostering changes in perception between students and Liberian residents.

Resituated Experience

As explored up to this point, the intersection of critical thinking, learning processes, and power, while embedded quite literally within the field-site context, centers the academic and experiential aspects of the field study. This section views the relationship between thinking/learning, power, and that resituated or unfamiliar state. For instance, living conditions in Liberia were somewhat spartan. Students and faculty stayed in guesthouses, took bucket (cold water) showers, had interrupted access to electricity and the Internet, and traveled in uncomfortable, crowded vehicles. Transport often arrived late, usually due to fuel-access issues or needed repairs, which forced the teams to wait. These experiences were the norm contextually, but for some team members they were far outside of the norm experientially.

Another example involves the use of hand sanitizer. In Liberia at this time (before the outbreak of Ebola), all greetings involved shaking hands.

As students encountered varying levels of hygiene, plumbing, and running water, several would break out their travel-size hand sanitizer bottles (clipped to their backpacks) immediately after greetings. Often the greeted individual had full view of what was happening. Discussions ensued about the role and responsibility of being "a guest in someone's house" and the message that such an action transmitted. The individual concerns for hygiene were greater, at least in the beginning, than concerns for positive engagement with our Liberian colleagues. Another difficulty students encountered were the Liberian approaches to gender. Despite postconflict programs for women's empowerment and gender equality, students experienced social and cultural tensions about gender and the subsequent strong pushback to maintain traditional gender roles. Expressions, actions, and expectations for female behavior angered several young women and caused tension with our partners and within student groups. The team debriefings and group analysis reports often included gender concerns, as well as other unfamiliar or disturbing situational dynamics.

Despite debriefings, students occasionally complained to the faculty and on one occasion to our local partners. Each Friday, the students and faculty met with local partners to discuss the week's activities and to plan for the following week. Each of the student teams presented their project work to the plenary session that included all of the practitioners, directors, and employees of the partner organization. During one of these sessions, a group commented on the uncomfortable experience during a long drive. The team advised the partner organization that purchasing and installing upholstered seats with seat belts should be a high priority as the transport was clearly dangerous and felt unsafe. The reciprocal-engagement model posits that experience and learning can be understood "as a generated social practice in the lived-in world" (Contu and Willmott 2003, 284). The student group's public statement reflects the *core set of deficiencies* frame presented earlier. The lived-in world of Liberia differed substantially from the lived-in world of a suburban American campus, and a higher value was clearly ascribed to the latter, which in consequence set the standard for what ought to be.

Our partners listened politely, but in the organizational meeting with directors and faculty, it was made clear that the student comments offended them. The faculty team, in consequence, worked to repair the relationship with its partners throughout the remainder of the field experience. Subsequent debriefing sessions with students began to focus more explicitly on how limited resources are allocated locally, on how the "relative value ascribed" impacted what outsiders might think important in relation to what residents determine as important, and on reminding the teams that we were in essence guests in their house (see also chapter 2). The faculty team approached the event as a learning opportunity, a way to rethink or reframe frustrations inherent in the work and to analyze assumptions and values. Discussions focused more specifically on the emotional effects of witnessing deprivation on every side, about getting to know residents not as abstractions but as colleagues, while at the same time acknowledging that we would be able to leave and they would not. Some students engaged strongly in these discussions, talking about their own assumptions and how they were changing, what they learned from our partners, and so on. Other students did not. Each of the students, however, reflected upon these discussions and experiences in debriefing sessions, team meetings, written field reports, and in faculty-to-student discussions. Issues such as discomfort, waiting, heat, humidity, torrential rain, mud, and so on had been discussed in pre-trip meetings, but at that point they were hypothetical. Faculty and students from previous field experiences explained contextual constraints (contrasting with life back home) and presented materials to give an idea about working and living conditions in Liberia. That said, experiential learning occurs in part through the struggle with the unfamiliar or the contextually encountered.

Resituated embeddedness (the contextual encounter) gives students and faculty an opportunity to reconsider their own values and their own roles and to very briefly "live" the context as much as possible. The resituated experience could be considered as merely spending time in a different place. The reciprocal-engagement model, however, attempts to facilitate a process of reflection, learning, and increased awareness of not only context but also individuals and groups within the context. In other words, the model encourages students and faculty to purposely re-embed their own situatedness, think critically, and learn about types of resources and power that individuals, communities, and grassroots organizations share with them. The students, community members, and grassroots organization personnel work together in all types of peacebuilding work, becoming temporary communities of practice. This often meant that the students and faculty received power and resources *from* the local partners, bestowing a degree of legitimacy (in the eyes of the larger local population) upon novices in the context. In effect, local partners and community members extended an invitation to appreciate how peacebuilding practices work in Liberia and offered students opportunities to work with those practices and perhaps add to them. As students participate in this type of *praxis* or reciprocal, dynamic, reflexive engagement (Hansen 2008, 40), they can benefit in ways that would be impossible with only classroom experiences, readings, and objective discussions and theorizing.

As has been discussed in some detail, the theory (in terms of the model) and the practice (in terms of student and faculty engagement) can be fraught with tension and ambiguity. Regardless or perhaps because of tensions and ambiguity, processes of critical thinking, multilevel learning, shifting power relationships, and resituated experiences can allow students a cognitive, emotional, theoretical, and experiential space in which to reconsider, deepen, and restructure their own assumptions, goals, and understandings. Shifts do occur, as evidenced by discussions during daily debriefing sessions, project-reflection analysis reports, private conversations, final essay reflections, post-trip surveys, and post-trip group meeting dialogue. They do not, however, always occur (Lambright and Lu 2009, 428). A few additional factors that could enter into the equation include individual ideas of the person, how the "other" is valued, comfort with uncertainty, and ability or willingness to set aside previous assumptions.

The long-term effects of this model of service learning cannot necessarily be predicted, but indications can be determined. Of the eighty students participating in the service learning field courses through 2014, an estimated 75 percent reported very significant shifts, 20 percent reported significant shifts, and 5 percent reported minimal shifts. Students self-determined how they understood shifts in their own understandings and ideas. Distinctions were also made, in relation to existing interests or worldviews or the level of change in personal or professional focus that occurred in response to their field-study experience.

The ultimate object of the field study is to move students and faculty beyond abstract conceptualizations of theory *about* a postconflict or conflict-shaped social environment to a new understanding *of* the complex social, economic, political, and human dynamics embedded within the context (Hettler and Johnston 2009, 102–3; Batchelder and Root 1994, 346). The explicit incorporation of reciprocity as a foundation for social interactions and engagement and as the rationale for how those interactions should occur (Ish-Shalom 2011, 974, 987) was a consistent building block of the project. The pedagogical intersection of reflection, power, resituated experience, critical thinking, and learning encourages analyzing individual and group political, social, economic, or cultural particularity within the field experience (Ish-Shalom 2011, 991). That said, the ways in which reciprocity and engagement played out experientially with students and faculty often proved surprising, as indicated in the anecdotes throughout the chapter and the additional comments below.

The process began immediately upon arrival in country. During initial encounters with the context, students and faculty hovered between thriving (the rush of the new environment and the excitement of "being there") and coping (managing with the superficial inequities and lack of resources). The stresses of the work, context, community living, homesickness, and so on strained nerves and patience from time to time. Students (and faculty) assisted one another through discussion, time alone, and social activities. Confrontational behaviors occasionally happened within the small working groups, and these were debriefed in various ways. Feelings of helplessness in the face of such rampant deprivation overwhelmed some; others coped by making promises to local residents that were impossible to fulfill. Some students temporarily removed themselves emotionally and occasionally physically from project work. The faculty team viewed each emerging dilemma as a teachable moment for the individuals involved, as well as for the group, and worked to provide appropriate support for each student.

At the same time, however, friendships between students and partner staff developed, free-time activities were coordinated and enjoyed, and upon return to the United States many students kept in contact with their new friends and colleagues. During the post-trip group meeting, approximately one month after our return, students were beginning to wax nostalgic about their experiences, remembering the difficulties certainly but focusing more on the quality of the experiences. This transition took time, and students described the more difficult than expected return to warm showers and the shock of walking into a grocery store, seeing the abundance, remembering the want, and bursting into tears. One way to examine this dynamic in more depth is through the ecological model of justice and well-being as outlined by Isaac Prilleltensky (2012, 10–11). The model links levels of fairness (and attendant individual well-being) with conditions of justice, the scale moving from optimal justice to persisting conditions of injustice using the emotive and participatory descriptors of thriving, coping, confronting, and suffering. As the field-study model focuses on resituated experience and intentional embeddedness, students inevitably encountered and experienced all of these descriptors.

As explored throughout this chapter, on the one hand, a service learning field course puts both faculty and students into a context of uncertainty, emotional strain, and physical challenge. On the other hand, it allows faculty and students to engage in peacebuilding and conflict resolution work with local organizations and residents who passionately believe that they can help their communities become more peaceful and more just. The student and faculty experience of moving from theory to practice in a conflict-prone country such as Liberia can be extremely fraught. It can also, however, provide insight, understanding, and a powerful determination to work for peace and justice. The strength of the field-based experiential learning approach lies at the heart of these dilemmas, with the potential for personal transformation and renewed purpose.

Note

1. The authors would like to thank Martha Mutisi, who helped get the program started; our Don Bosco colleagues Hashmi Pusah, Sharon Nelson, John

Monibah, and Joe Wiah; the Reverend Tolbert Thomas Jallah Jr.; our friends at the Lutheran Guesthouse in Monrovia; Linda Keuntje; Susan Hirsch; Agnieszka Paczyńska; Andrea Wisler; the faculty and student cohorts of 2010, 2011, and 2012; and finally the inimitable Glea Don Bosco.

THREE

Effecting Change

EIGHT

Making Change Makers

Integrating Service Learning into NGO Management Courses

MARYAM Z. DELOFFRE

Universities and colleges are under increasing pressure to demonstrate the policy and practical relevance of their pedagogy and programs (Balboa and Deloffre 2015).[1] To take one example, a 2010 United States Institute of Peace report finds a striking discrepancy between the knowledge, skills, and abilities (KSAs) provided by conflict analysis and resolution (CAR) graduate programs and those desired by employers (Carstarphen et al. 2010). Although graduate programs emphasize KSAs such as theories of CAR, courses on political issues such as governance and human rights, and country- or region-specific knowledge, employers seek job candidates with field experiences, applied CAR skills, and training in technical skills such as program planning (Carstarphen et al. 2010, 4). All employers rated applied experiences that bridge theory and practice as the most valuable qualification for positions related to CAR (Carstarphen et al. 2010, 7).

Likewise, a 2014 survey of 400 employers and 613 college students conducted for the Association of American Colleges and Universities, finds that 60 percent of employers (business and nonprofit) indicated that they were much more likely to consider hiring a recent college graduate who has completed an applied-learning or project-based learning experience. Additionally, 80 percent of employers stated that during the hiring process it is very important to them that recent graduates demonstrate the ability to apply learning to real-world settings (Hart Research Associates 2015, 6–7). How might CAR graduate programs supply these highly desired project-based and applied-learning experiences in the classroom? Service learning—an experiential approach where students collaborate with community organizations to plan and implement a project—is one pedagogical method designed to increase opportunities for students to engage in project-based and applied learning.

The international peace and conflict resolution (IPCR) master's program at Arcadia University has the specific objective of integrating experiential learning throughout the curriculum to foster understanding of conflict zones, peacebuilding, and development.[2] My course, Non-Governmental Organization (NGO) Management, trains students for work in the nonprofit sector. The course provides an introduction to traditional topics in NGO management, such as program planning, implementation, and evaluation and includes a semester-long service learning project. This chapter draws on my experience developing, coordinating, and managing a service learning partnership with the American Friends Service Committee (AFSC) headquarters in Philadelphia, Pennsylvania.[3] AFSC is a Quaker organization committed to pursuing lasting peace and justice through nonviolence and civic engagement in multiple sites in the United States as well as in Africa, Central America, the Middle East, and Asia. As of this writing, fifty-one graduate students have completed twenty-five projects for nine different programs and departments—including Grants and Development, Security Management, the Office of Public Policy and Advocacy, Planning and Evaluation, and International Programs—in AFSC offices in Philadelphia, Washington, DC, West Virginia, and Minnesota.

My experience designing and managing the service learning program has been extremely positive. The projects add an invaluable practical element to the course, and I often see students' faces light up as they make connections between lectures and their work for AFSC. Interactions with AFSC have also enriched my understanding of NGO operations and help me ensure that the course is policy relevant, includes cutting-edge methodologies, and reflects best practices in the field.

I begin by defining service learning and discussing its benefits for student learning and professional growth in four areas: academic development, civic responsibility, practical skills, and interpersonal skills. Next, I explain how to design a course with a service learning component, specifically showcasing my experience with AFSC, and consider how two critical elements—multiple sites of interaction and reflection—optimize student learning. I then draw on data collected from surveys of students and project supervisors, as well as de-identified and anonymous excerpts of students' reflective journals, to assess the impacts of the service learning project on both students and AFSC. I find that overall the program positively impacts student learning and creates value for AFSC. Finally, I discuss the challenges and constraints of service learning projects and proffer four essential ingredients—project relevance to the course, student empowerment, expanded time, and reflective practice—for effective project-based courses.

Considering the Academic and Professional Benefits of Service Learning

When I started designing the course, I knew that it would be challenging, and perhaps overwhelming, for students to grapple with the complexity of nonprofit management in one semester. I did not want students to complete the course feeling as if they had only scratched the surface of NGO management and thus started researching innovative pedagogies that could bring the classroom material to life. Service learning seemed to fit my course objectives and the experiential focus of the MA program. Robert G. Bringle and Julie A. Hatcher define service learning as a "course-based, credit-bearing educational experience in which students (a) participate in an organized service activity that meets identified community needs and (b) reflect on the service activity in such a way as to gain further understanding of the course content, a broader appreciation of the discipline, and an enhanced sense of civic responsibility" (1999, 179). Students attain academic goals and experience personal growth while simultaneously serving partner organizations' needs through completion of an applied-learning project (Snell et al. 2015, 373; Hébert and Hauf 2015, 37).

As also discussed in chapter 7 in this volume, all activities and projects were suggested by community organizations who benefited from students' time and resources to fill organizational needs and accomplish unmet goals (Lester 2015, 281).

Service learning projects provide students with benefits and value in four primary areas: academic achievement, professional skill development, civic responsibility, and personal growth. First, service learning fosters higher-order learning; students demonstrate a deeper understanding of concepts and are able to apply theory to real-world situations. In political science degree programs, service learning has been shown to positively impact students' political knowledge, attitudes, and behaviors (Battistoni 2000, 615). As chapters 6 and 7 in this volume also show, service learning projects contribute to meaningful curricular enhancements, improved content learning, and attainment of learning objectives.

Students who participate in service learning activities also perform better on tasks that require creativity and innovation, and they develop strong writing, problem-solving, and critical-thinking skills (Hébert and Hauf 2015, 38). Ali Hébert and Petra Hauf (2015) use a pre-test/post-test experimental design to compare the academic performance of students who participated in a service learning project against a control group. They find that students who participated in service learning did not show improved academic performance as measured by quantitative indicators (e.g., final examination grades); however, those students demonstrated an increased understanding of course concepts and were more capable of providing correct answers (Hébert and Hauf 2015, 44).

Second, service learning enables professional development in two areas: skills acquisition and employability. Through service learning, students practice highly sought-after skills, such as leadership, teamwork, communication, and problem-solving (Lester 2015, 281). Students report higher levels of improvement in interpersonal skills, such as verbal communication, leadership, and teamwork, than students who did not undertake service learning (Hébert and Hauf 2015, 46).

Project-based experiences help students differentiate themselves on the job market, which enhances their employment prospects. Mary Sprague and R. Cameron Percy's study of the impacts of project-based practicums finds that students list projects on their résumés; discuss the practicum during job interviews, particularly as a concrete example of a teamwork experience; submit their final, polished projects as a work sample; and seek career advice from contacts made during their practicum (2014, 100).

Third, depending on the design and objectives of the service learning projects, students might develop civic responsibility. Research in political science and business shows that service learning has positive impacts on the development of democratic civic values and attitudes as well as deepening understandings of social responsibility (Battistoni 2000, 615; Lester 2015, 281). By partnering with communities and community organizations, service learning projects increase students' awareness of societal problems and might ignite a desire to make a difference (Hébert and Hauf 2015, 39). Hébert and Hauf (2015) find that, compared to the control group, students who participated in service learning more strongly believed that they could make a difference in their community and that contributing to their community was important. Moreover, students in the experimental group were more strongly inclined to participate in community service the following year than students in the control group, suggesting that the effects of service learning are sustained over time. Chapter 6 in this volume also finds some positive, albeit weak, effect of service learning on enhancing attitudes of civic responsibility and engagement.

Finally, service learning has a positive impact on personal, attitudinal, moral, and social outcomes (Bringle and Hatcher 1996, 223). Service learning is linked to increases in self-esteem, empathy, self-efficacy, and improvement in relationship building skills (Snell et al. 2015; Hébert and Hauf 2015).

Designing a Course with a Service Learning Component

Embedding a service learning project within an academic course requires advanced planning and organization. About six months before my NGO management course was offered for the first time, I identified several peace and justice NGOs located in the Philadelphia metropolitan area. I did not have established relationships within these organizations, so my initial contacts were cold calls. I was fortunate that AFSC was immediately responsive and eager to collaborate on this new initiative. My AFSC liaison convened a meeting of program directors who expressed interest in the initiative, and we met to discuss the objectives, structure, and timeline for the service learning projects. We agreed on a project-proposal template and issued a call for project proposals to AFSC program directors. The template requires AFSC program directors to define project goals and objectives, list the responsibilities of the AFSC staff and the students, and specify project outputs.

The project proposal is my first check on ensuring that the project scope is sufficiently limited and feasible, that students have or will acquire adequate skills to complete the project, and that the project objectives are clear. Once I receive the proposals, I provide feedback to project supervisors and request revisions to pare scope and improve clarity. Sufficiently narrowing the scope and improving clarity of projects are two common challenges more fully discussed in a later section. To preview the survey data, students commonly express frustration with project clarity, writing, for example, "I think the main thing most of my peers and I struggled with was the initial clarity of each assigned project. We had to follow up several times in order to truly understand what it was we were supposed to do."

On the first day of class, students read the project proposals, and each student identifies his or her top three choices. Scott W. Lester suggests that students are more engaged and productive and also exhibit a greater sense of commitment when they are interested and enthusiastic about the project (Lester 2015, 286). Students perform better and produce more polished outcomes when they perceive the project is of value, which produces a positive result for the community organization and builds the reputation of the degree program (Lester 2015, 286). When composing the groups, I take into consideration student interest in the projects and student skill sets, as well as student personalities and leadership styles, to ensure that teams are well rounded.

During the second class meeting, the students and I travel to AFSC headquarters for an introductory meeting with project supervisors, AFSC executives, and support staff. To prepare for the meeting, students read several background documents on AFSC's mission, values, and programs and explore the organization's website. The introductory meeting includes a general orientation and breakout sessions where the student groups meet with project supervisors to exchange contact information, further discuss the goals and objectives of the project, and decide on a communication strategy. Students take notes during this meeting and prepare a project plan, using standard templates (e.g., a Gantt chart), for the third class session. I review the project plan, provide feedback on projected timelines and deliverables, and require that students make revisions prior to submitting the plan to their project supervisors.

In designing a project plan, students practice developing and implementing a planning tool learned in class. The project plan also serves as a second check to ensure that the project scope and objectives are reasonable and clear. I instituted this practice in response to student and AFSC feedback. For example, one student commented that "a more clear and concise research or project plan should be in place so as to reduce the amount of questions each group has in the beginning phase of the relationship." Prior to assigning project plans, student teams would lose precious time at the beginning of the semester trying to understand project goals. For example, the International Programs Department submitted a proposal with several objectives, including "to create and share stories of AFSC's international work," without specifying scope (AFSC runs multiple programs in fifteen countries) or clarifying procedures (How would students create stories? Would they need to collect data?). Upon further discussion, the team identified a more feasible objective: design an impact assessment of AFSC's flagship dialogue and exchange program, specifically the World Social Forums in Tunisia and Brazil. However, this back-and-forth meant that students had less time for data collection and project implementation.

The project plan fosters these conversations earlier in the semester and also serves as a tool to track progress and team member responsibilities. Another important advantage of the project plan is that it creates a deadline for scheduling group meetings, check-ins, and deadlines. As indicated by the survey data, student satisfaction with project clarity increased after I began assigning project plans.

Designing Course Elements to Optimize Learning

Experiences alone do not automatically generate learning; experience may stimulate critical thinking and generate understanding but may also reinforce stereotypes and exacerbate social inequalities when unguided (Bringle and Hatcher 1996; Bahng 2015). Two ways in which I deliberately and carefully guide learning are through the use of multiple sites of interaction and of reflective journals.

MULTIPLE SITES OF INTERACTION

Robin Stanley Snell et al. (2015, 376) find that strong relationships between students and project supervisors positively impact project effectiveness, and repeated interactions help group members articulate and refine project goals. Depending on the nature of the AFSC projects, some students might work remotely, communicating primarily via Skype, phone, or email, while others visit headquarters frequently and interact with their project supervisors in person. Given this variation, my AFSC liaison and I incorporate two group site-visits during the semester. The first is the orientation discussed previously that introduces students to AFSC's mission, values, executive officers, and project supervisors. During the last week of the semester, the class travels to AFSC a second time for an organization-wide meeting where students formally present their final projects. The final presentations allow students to practice public speaking in professional settings as well as learn how to disseminate project outputs. This forum also provides an opportunity for the broader AFSC community to provide feedback on student work and to see how the students have added value and contributed to the organization. The two meetings also serve as professional networking events for the students.

In addition to the formal meetings, I arrange for AFSC staff members—not necessarily project supervisors—to be guest lecturers in class. Guest speakers supply diverse perspectives and demonstrate how the theoretical concepts and constructs learned in class are used in practice (Lester 2015, 290). For example, the director of communications and the director of marketing presented on the development and implementation of a recent advocacy campaign during which AFSC trained over twelve hundred people ("birddogs") to question the US presidential candidates about corporate influence in politics and the for-profit prison industry during the Iowa and New Hampshire caucuses. This guest lecture detailed the development of the campaign from the inception of the theory of change to the monitoring and evaluation of advocacy outcomes and complemented my lectures on program planning with real-world examples.

Finally, opportunities periodically arise for students to make presentations to and interact with various stakeholders and programs in AFSC. For instance, students presented their research on AFSC's support of Occupy Wall Street movements nationwide to members of the board of trustees. Most recently, students presented their evaluation of AFSC's security-management initiatives to members of the security committee. These frequent, meaningful interactions with AFSC staff facilitate communication, improve project outcomes, and introduce students to AFSC's organizational culture and values.

REFLECTION

Reflection is the process through which students link classroom content to the service project, thereby transforming experiences into genuine learning (Eyler, Giles, and Schmiede 1996; Bringle and Hatcher 1999). Students reflect by noting observations, asking questions, and examining actions taken in the service learning context, including interactions with project group members and successful or failed attempts at designing and implementing project components. Through reflection, students enhance their critical understanding of the course topics, engage in higher-level thinking and problem-solving, and improve their ability to assess their own progress. Moreover, techniques such as reflective journals, collaborative projects, and group decision-making are more effective at assessing higher-level learning than traditional tools such as lectures and exams (Hébert and Hauf 2015, 44).

Reflection also promotes personal development by enhancing students' self-awareness, sense of community, and appreciation of their own capacities. Through reflection, students analyze concepts, evaluate experiences, form opinions, and examine and question their beliefs and values. Lester suggests that "this ability to reflect on how they were able to grow is critical to maximizing the value of any service learning / leadership development experience. When reflection activities are a regular part of the course and serve to clarify personal values it enhances the quality of the course" (2015, 285).

Effective reflection is guided and purposeful, occurs continuously, intentionally links service objectives to the course objectives, and requires frequent feedback from the instructor (Eyler, Giles, and Schmiede 1996). I require students to write weekly in a reflective journal that is stored online and shared with me. Online journals provide a space for students to reflect continuously, while also granting the professor access for the purposes of providing feedback, monitoring the project, and observing student progress and growth. I use the comments feature on the online document to provide feedback on student reflections.

Guiding reflective practice means providing students with structured prompts to scaffold their reflections. Unstructured prompts, such as "Reflect on your service learning project this week," foster uncritical, disorganized observations that do not elicit insights or proactive solutions to attenuate future problems. Structured prompts are designed to guide the formation of personal goals and objectives, encourage strategic thinking and problem-solving, facilitate formulation of proactive solutions to problems, and foster the ability to view a situation from multiple perspectives. I use three types of structured prompts to guide student reflections, as displayed in table 8.1.

The two examples below contain excerpts from unstructured and structured journal entries to facilitate comparison of the types of reflection elicited by each prompt. In the example of an unstructured entry, the student discusses feelings of "frustration," "nervousness," and "confusion" but does not try to problem-solve, reflect on how to address these emotions, or how to plan, work, or interact differently to mitigate the problem. This type of reflection might be beneficial to the student in that it permits him or her to acknowledge emotions but does not guide and empower the student to develop proactive tools to resolve similar situations in the future.

Example of Student Reflection (Unstructured Entry)

Today I actually participated in one of the AFSC #OccupyWallStreet Conference Calls. I was nervous because there were staff members on the call from all over the country and [my supervisor] not only wanted me to introduce myself to them, but he wanted me to explain to everyone what my project was for my internship with AFSC!

Table 8.1. Structured prompts for use in reflective journals

Structured Prompts	Description
Specific questions	1) Write a letter to yourself that outlines your goals for this semester and for the service-learning project. 2) Find three dream job advertisements for employment in the non-profit sector. What skills are required? What skills can you hone and develop during this class? How might you develop networks to help you acquire your dream job? 3) Re-read your letter to yourself and reflect upon your progress towards your goals for the semester.
Three-part entry (Bringle and Hatcher, 1999)	Divide your entry into thirds. Section 1: describe an aspect of the service experience. Section 2: analyze how course content relates to the service experience. Section 3: comment on how the experience and course content can be applied to your personal or professional life.
Critical incident entry (Bringle and Hatcher, 1999)	Analyze a significant event or incident that occurred during the week. Think through either set of prompts below, note your thoughts and reactions and articulate the action you plan to take in the future. 1) Describe a significant event that occurred as a part of the service-learning experience. Why was this significant to you? What underlying issues (societal, interpersonal, personal) surfaced as a result of this experience? How will this incident influence your future behavior? 2) Describe an incident or situation that created a dilemma for you in terms of what to say or do. What is the first thing you thought of to say or do? List three other actions you might have taken. Which option seems to be the best response to you now and why?

And [my team members] were not there with me.... Not only was I nervous because I would be explaining the project to the very people [my team members] and I were collecting data on, but because [my supervisor] was on the call and because [my team members] and I are still a bit confused as to what exactly it is we are supposed to be recording. I was nervous that I would mess up the explanation and get something wrong and then not only would [my supervisor] be upset but so would all of the other AFSC staff members!

By contrast, in structured entry 1 below, the student notes similar emotions but then troubleshoots how to solve the problem in the future. Structured entry 1 notes frustration with the scope and ambiguity of project goals but brainstorms solutions that might help alleviate frustration and create better outcomes.

Examples of Student Reflection (Structured Entry)

1. A recent dilemma that we experienced as a group was when we came up with a work plan and thought we understood the purpose of the project and then received an e-mail from our supervisor that did not align with our work plan or purpose. It has been a mildly frustrating road from the start because of how vast and vague the project is . . . and our difficulty understanding the ultimate goal. . . . We decided to create a new work plan based on what we understood from the e-mail. . . . . Three other things that I would do now, looking back on the situation is to e-mail our supervisor with our current work plan, explain our confusion, and to set up a meeting through Skype or in person. Looking at these three options I feel that setting up the meeting is the best idea to address the communication issues we are having to create a work plan that satisfies both parties.

2. My experience working with [my team member] has made me realize that I can be a little bit more relaxed and easy-going than other people sometimes, but I also understand that from [my team member's] perspective my laidback attitude could either make him more anxious or help to relieve his anxiety. Perhaps that is something I should keep in mind when setting deadlines, in order to be more conscientious [sic] of the fact that [my team member] and I are slightly different in that way.

Structured prompts also permit students to express self-awareness and recognize how their personal attributes and characteristics affect their interpersonal interactions. In structured entry 2, the student recognizes that she is "laidback," that this orientation is different from that of her team members, and that these differences in work styles negatively impact group dynamics and notes a solution that might accommodate all team members. The student is also able to see the situation from multiple perspectives and place them in context, which is illustrative of the deepest kind of reflection (Bringle and Hatcher 1999).

Impacts on Students and AFSC

The NGO management course with the service learning component has run in the spring semester in 2012, 2013, 2014, and 2016. This section discusses survey data collected in the spring of 2012, 2013, and 2016.[4] Following the final presentations and papers, I send out electronic surveys to AFSC project supervisors and the students. The average response rate was 82 percent for the AFSC project supervisor survey and 76 percent for the student survey. The strong response rates suggest that the data are meaningful and representative of those who participated in the project. Given the small sample sizes, it is important to note that these data are instructive rather than generalizable. In addition, the survey questionnaire changed slightly from the first version (2012), which included more open-ended questions, to the current version, which includes more-structured questions. This change reduced the sample size (n) for some questions.

To start, students were asked to indicate overall satisfaction with the service learning project. On average, 83 percent of students stated they were highly satisfied or satisfied. In the qualitative open-ended responses to this question, students said the service learning projects were valuable because they supplied an opportunity to apply theory and coursework in real-world settings. To illustrate, a student wrote, "It was a great opportunity for us to apply some of the coursework into a 'real world' situation. It also allowed me to experience the challenges that come with working for an NGO." Another explained, "It bridged the gap between theory and practice; students were able to get real exposure to working for an NGO and what sort of things they would be doing; it provides a realistic perspective of how an organization functions; I could see some of the things we learned in class unfold in front of me as I was working with AFSC." One student noted, "Working on our project, which was to improve program planning at AFSC, my partner and I were able to use examples that we had learned about in class, and directly apply them to our work."

Students overwhelmingly agreed ("strongly agree" and "agree") that the AFSC project provided specific academic and professional benefits associated with service learning, as shown in figure 8.2. Eighty-nine percent of students strongly agreed or agreed that the AFSC project increased their

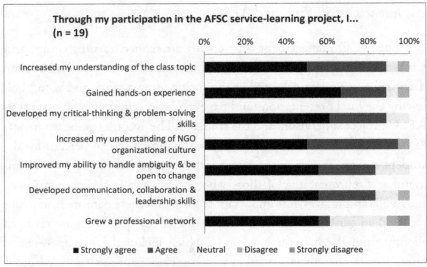

Figure 8.2. Student perceptions of AFSC project benefits.

understanding of the class topic and helped them develop critical-thinking and problem-solving skills, and 84 percent said it fostered development of communication, collaboration, and leadership skills. Ninety-four percent of the students reported an increase in their understanding of NGO organizational culture. Sixty-two percent of students strongly agreed that the project enabled them to grow a professional network they could use for future employment or internships.

Another benefit of service learning is an increase in civic engagement and sustained involvement in social justice activities and volunteer work. In order to measure their level of civic engagement after the service learning experience, students were asked, *How likely are you to volunteer for AFSC or another peace and justice organization in the future?* Since I did not conduct a pre-test survey, these data are not an indicator of an *increase* in civic engagement or responsibility, as it is possible that students already rated highly on these measures prior to participating in the projects. In the 2013 survey, 88 percent of students indicated that they were highly likely or likely to volunteer again; 13 percent said they were unlikely to do so.[5] In the 2016 survey, 30 percent of students indicated that they were more likely to volunteer than at the beginning of the semester, 50 percent stated they were slightly more likely to volunteer, and 20 percent said it was about the same.

Making Change Makers

Students also place an imprint on community organizations by providing human resources, conducting analyses, introducing new ideas and outside perspectives, injecting energy and enthusiasm into the organization, and supplying volunteer hours (Sprague and Hu 2015, 264–265). Community organizations report that they use students' work to address organizational, departmental, and community needs and the students' contributions have long-lasting impacts on the organization (Sprague and Hu 2015; Sprague and Percy 2014).

Both students and AFSC project supervisors were asked to identify the ways in which the students contributed to the organization, and each survey respondent was able to make multiple selections. Figure 8.3 shows how often each selection was chosen by category of respondent. AFSC project supervisors and students agreed with equal frequency that the service learning projects contributed human resources to the organization.

In general, students overestimated the value they contributed to the organization. For example, while 50 percent believe they contributed new ideas and perspectives to the organization, only 33 percent of project supervisors selected this option. This finding is not necessarily problematic; Snell et al. show that if students believe they provided useful resources to the community organization, then this perception serves as a source of satisfaction, self-efficacy, and self-worth (Snell et al. 2015, 386).

Qualitative comments from AFSC supervisors provide a more nuanced view and suggest that students contributed to the organization in

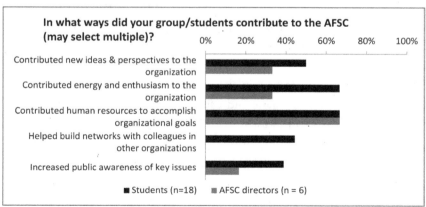

Figure 8.3. Contributions of service learning project to AFSC (project supervisors and students).

both tangible and intangible ways. To illustrate, 67 percent of students believed they contributed energy and enthusiasm to the organization, while only 33 percent of project supervisors selected this option. However, in qualitative comments, supervisors indicated appreciation for the curiosity and enthusiasm that students showed for the projects: "The students were engaging and high energy. Their presence challenged us to look at ourselves differently." One supervisor noted the students "helped us to see our work from a different perspective; provided practical suggestions for improvement; contributed to an expanded understanding of our work in relation to the larger NGO world."

The majority of project supervisors stated that the students produced both useful and meaningful work. To illustrate: "The Maryland prison report was excellent—with some tweaking we will be using it in the coming year as a support paper for funding. In addition the civic engagement paper is going to provide background for an upcoming staff retreat." The AFSC submitted several grants written by the students to funders, and one grant to support community building in Haiti was successfully funded. AFSC supervisors also highlighted the longer-term impacts of the students' contributions: "My group was a pleasure to work with and they produced some fantastic deliverables that my colleagues were impressed with and will be used well beyond the students' time at AFSC."

Partner organization satisfaction provides academic programs with a valuable indicator of the quality and utility of the academic and professional training they offer (Sprague and Hu 2015). Partner organization satisfaction is also imperative for sustaining the service learning relationship and expanding the pool of future projects. To measure AFSC project supervisor satisfaction, I asked whether supervisors would participate in the service learning project again and whether they would hire an Arcadia student in the future (Sprague and Hu 2015, 269). Figure 8.4 displays the results of these survey questions.

Ninety percent of AFSC project supervisors surveyed indicated that they were highly likely or likely to participate in the service learning program again. Results from the second survey question were mixed. Fifty-five percent of AFSC project supervisors indicated that they were highly likely or likely to hire an Arcadia student in the future, 33 percent were unsure,

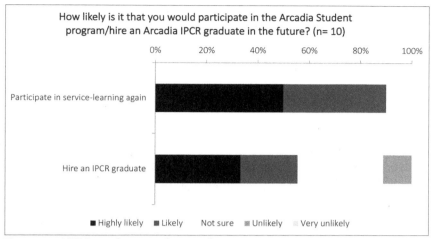

Figure 8.4. AFSC satisfaction with service learning projects.

and 11 percent were unlikely to do so. One explanation for the discrepancy between high satisfaction with the projects and the service learning program and the lower likelihood to hire an Arcadia IPCR graduate might be that students complete this course in the second semester of their first year before they have completed their coursework and training. Thus far, we have successfully placed two Arcadia IPCR graduates in a full-time position and four students in internships at AFSC.

Challenges and Constraints

Embedded service learning projects are prone to common challenges and constraints, including the time and resource commitment required from the professor and the students, paring down project scope, communication problems between the student groups and the community organization, and conflicts among the student team members (Hébert and Hauf 2015, 38; Sprague and Percy 2014, 102; Lester 2015, 288). The short duration of the projects, in particular when embedded in a semester-long course, makes it challenging to design projects that address authentic problems or needs while also aligning with course curricula and student capabilities (Snell et al. 2015, 393). Likewise, community organizations report several disadvantages of service learning projects: students are sometimes unprepared, unreliable, unprofessional, and uninterested in the project or the organization; the academic calendar and students' competing obligations complicate efforts to communicate and build relationships with students; and some organizations report that the time and resources they commit outweigh the benefits (Sprague and Hu 2015, 265; Snell et al. 2015).

Qualitative comments from project supervisor surveys echoed some of these concerns: "It was quite time-consuming working with students who struggled with some group dynamics and procrastination issues," and "Work quality was excellent, but time commitment was very little. 2–5 hours a week are not enough." Another project supervisor stated, "It's difficult to sometimes schedule time with the students. I know they have other classes and need to attend the NGO class. But fitting in more in-person time with students would be great (somehow!)."

Students were asked to rate on a five-point scale (highly satisfied to unsatisfied) their satisfaction with various components of the project. Figure 8.5 below displays the results of this survey question. On average, 66 percent of students were highly satisfied or satisfied with the clarity of the project assignment. Moreover, there is a noticeable upward trend over time: in 2013 no students were highly satisfied with the clarity of the project compared to five in 2016. This upward trend in student satisfaction with project clarity occurred after I instituted the project-plan assignment, which suggests that designing a project plan empowers students to clarify

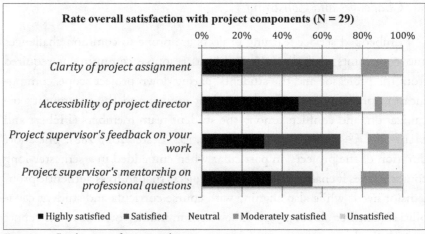

Figure 8.5. Student satisfaction with project components.

project goals and objectives early on and improves satisfaction with the service learning experience.

Snell et al. argue that constructive learning relationships between students and project supervisors serve as a powerful source of encouragement and motivation for both parties (2015, 386). AFSC project supervisors have been extremely generous with their time and take seriously their role in training and coaching students to become productive future colleagues in the CAR field. Students hold generally favorable views of their project supervisors' accessibility and guidance. Seventy-nine percent were highly satisfied or satisfied with the accessibility of their project supervisor, 69 percent were highly satisfied or satisfied with supervisor's feedback, and 55 percent were highly satisfied or satisfied with the supervisor's mentorship on questions related to professional development.

Best Practices and Conclusion

To conclude, I identify best practices intended to assist professors in developing successful, productive, and meaningful service learning courses in CAR programs. Service learning produces the best outcomes when projects include the following four ingredients.

First, it is essential that the service learning project be complementary to the course so that students view the academic content as a resource for gaining insight into their projects and their projects serve as practical applications of course concepts and techniques (Snell et al. 2015). The first iteration of the service learning program included multiple projects focused on research, event planning, or information gathering that did not directly relate to the course content. As my relationship with AFSC has strengthened and deepened, I have provided more specific guidance as to what types of projects would create natural synergies with the course, requesting projects related to program planning, grant-writing, strategic planning, and evaluation. These targeted projects have helped increase student satisfaction and performance. In addition, activities such as directed writings (reflection), small group discussions, and class presentations also further integrate the service learning project into the course (Bringle and Hatcher 1996, 222). Finally, including multiple modes and sites of interaction—guest speakers, student presentations to the organization, networking events—between students and the community organizations improves embeddedness, enhances communication between project supervisors and students, and improves project outcomes.

Second, increasing project relevance to the course improves student commitment to the project, which Snell et al. (2015) argue is essential to producing successful outcomes. Professors can encourage and generate student commitment by empowering students with shared ownership for project outcomes, roles, and responsibilities. Requiring students to complete a project plan not only introduces them to a tool in program management and planning but also permits students to actively clarify, select, and delimit project goals, objectives, and outputs. Project plans also enable students to track progress toward project goals, which engenders a sense of accomplishment and a genuine perception that their efforts are making a difference in the organization.

Third, traditional semester-long courses with an embedded service learning component are prone to time and resource constraints. Sprague and Percy suggest designing a course that convenes multiple times a week where the instructor meets at least once a week with the full class or each team and other class time is reserved for meetings with project supervisors, for work on project tasks, or for conducting interviews and site visits (2014, 93). Professors undertaking a service learning course for the first time should consider requesting additional credit units for the course to afford students and the professor adequate time to meet both the objectives of the academic course and the service learning project.

Finally, effective service learning must include regular reflective activities that encourage students to link the service experience to the course content and to learning objectives. Instructors should provide regular feedback to students on reflection activities to guide students on how to improve and develop reflective practice.

Notes

1. I thank my partners at AFSC, particularly Lisa Oliveri, for wholeheartedly engaging in the service learning program, mentoring students, and providing an enriching educational experience. Without the support of AFSC, this project

would not have been possible. I am especially grateful for skillful research assistance by Cameron Allen.

2. For additional information about the program: https://www.arcadia.edu/academics/programs/international-peace-and-conflict-resolution.

3. American Friends Service Committee: http://www.afsc.org/.

4. Surveys were not administered in 2014 due to extenuating circumstances.

5. This question was not asked in the 2012 survey.

NINE

When Context and Pretext Collide

Reflective Practice as an Ethical Framework for Field-Based Learning

GINA M. CERASANI AND RJ NICKELS

Practice is key to the study of conflict resolution. Both undergraduate and graduate students seek opportunities to apply the theories they have learned in their courses to real-world conflicts and to practice skills, such as conflict analysis and dialogue facilitation. In this chapter, we tell the story of our unique experience with field-based experiential learning as graduate students, which includes the lessons distilled from that experience and the application of those lessons to a field-based course we instructed. A key lesson drawn from these experiences is that fieldwork requires us to make in the moment decisions that have ethical implications and that student practitioners need an ethically oriented process to guide them through such decisions.

The field of conflict analysis and resolution (CAR) has long been concerned with questions of ethics and purpose. Many scholars have focused on the necessity of those engaged in the practice of CAR to attend reflexively to questions of power, motives, context, and the potential risks to parties involved (Avruch 2003; Laue and Cormick 1978; Nader 1980; Warfield 2002). Our chapter's title references anthropologist and scholar Kevin Avruch (2003), who describes the practitioner's ethical obligation to consider the culture and conflict history of the context where she works and also her own position and purpose in reference to that context. Though Avruch's emphasis is on practice in international contexts, we believe that the same principles apply in other circumstances, including those where students are learning and practicing in unfamiliar settings and locales. In CAR education and pedagogy, ethical considerations inform both the content of what is taught and the methods employed. This is particularly relevant for experiential learning programs, which often require instructors and learners to engage in CAR activities that may have material consequences for community members. We will describe our efforts to balance our roles as instructors and students, and the pretexts for our activities, with our changing and incomplete understandings of the contexts involved. Our choice to use reflective practice (RP) as a framework for these programs was driven largely by our belief that CAR practice, and the teaching thereof, is well suited to the reflexive activities that routinize ethical consideration and multiple-loop learning (for a discussion of multilevel learning, see chapter 7).

In the two field-based experiences that serve as case studies in this chapter, we relied on RP to guide our decision-making, to help us learn from our mistakes, and to provide a process for working through ethical challenges. Our success with RP in our field-based experience as graduate students led us to build the field-based course we later instructed with RP as the foundation. Following Avruch's dictum to give attention to the rich exploration of context and pretext "to orient us beyond instrumentalities of efficacy, and toward self-critique and reflexivity" (Avruch 2003, 363), we integrated RP activities into our projects and programs from the outset. By developing an adaptive and flexible framework for our explorations in unfamiliar territories, we prepared ourselves and our students to address practical and ethical challenges not foreseen prior to engaging in field-based activities.

In the sections that follow, we examine the role of field-based learning in the CAR field, and we identify crucial elements of an instructor's role in field-based programs. Later in the chapter, we offer our model of RP and describe how it served to organize and guide both field-based programs presented here. Finally, we consider the two programs as exemplars of the RP model for guiding ethical decision-making when working in the field with student practitioners.

Field-Based Education in Conflict Analysis and Resolution

Conflict analysis and resolution is a practice-oriented field, and both undergraduate and graduate CAR students are eager to practice their budding skills in the classroom and the field. CAR instructors employ various types of experiential activities in classrooms, including role plays, dialogues, mediation, and focus groups to provide students with opportunities to develop new skills and engage in conflict-resolution practices in a constructed, controlled environment free from concerns of potential harm to parties in conflict. In this environment, the focus is on learning, and students are expected to make mistakes (Cantor 1997; Jenkins 2010).

An alternative to classroom-based learning, or perhaps the next step toward becoming a CAR practitioner, is field-based learning. Opportunities for students in the field may take the form of internships, projects, or service learning programs. In CAR field-based learning, a key feature that makes it distinct from experiential learning in a classroom is that students are immersed in a conflict, often situated in a community, even if they do not directly intervene in a conflict. When students enter the field they are still learning, but the stakes are higher, and both instructors and students must attend to potential ethical pitfalls (Bringle and Hatcher 2000; Cohen and Kinsey 1994).

In this chapter, we examine two forms of field-based education: service learning and an academic project. Service learning programs combine facets of traditional community service programs with an explicit educational component. In the CAR field, the "service" element of service learning typically involves intervention in a conflict, employing conflict-resolution techniques, such as facilitated dialogue and training workshops. Because the interveners are nascent practitioners who are still students, such programs avoid complex interventions that require expertise beyond what most students possess. Academic projects share many qualities with service learning programs, but one way in which they tend to differ is duration. Although the length of both varies, service learning programs usually take place during spring or summer breaks for one to four weeks, while academic projects may last for a year or more. An academic project involving graduate students has the potential to provide opportunities for immersion in a community, extensive and prolonged conflict analysis, and the design and implementation of relatively complex interventions.

We will draw from two specific field-based programs to provide examples in this chapter. The first was a student-led project developed under the aegis of the Applied Practice and Theory (APT) program for CAR graduate students at George Mason University. The APT program provides students with opportunities to apply the practical and theoretical knowledge they have acquired during their studies in a real-world setting under the supervision and guidance of an experienced faculty member. As a form of field-based experiential learning, the APT program gives students the chance to test their education in real-world settings, reflect on the gaps in their knowledge and training, and adjust to changing conditions and emerging understandings in real-time. While this model does not necessarily have a traditional instructor, the involvement of a faculty adviser serves as both a pedagogical resource and a safeguard against ethical risk.

Similarly, the Service Learning Intensive (SLI) program offers undergraduate CAR students opportunities to apply acquired knowledge and skills to address conflict in the field. The SLI program was created by the Undergraduate Experiential Learning Project (UELP), a three-year project at George Mason University's School for Conflict Analysis and Resolution funded by a grant from the US Department of Education and described in the introduction to this volume. This program placed undergraduate CAR students, guided by faculty and doctoral students, in settings with parties experiencing conflict to apply theory to practice by designing theory-informed approaches to resolution. The UELP initiative developed international SLIs in Liberia and Colombia and a domestic course in Charleston, West Virginia (considered here). In a later section of this chapter, we describe both the APT and SLI approaches in detail, and we consider the role of RP as a crucial tool for navigating conflict and ethical dilemmas in a field-based setting and instructing students in the principles and techniques of intervention.

Role of Instructors in Field-Based Learning

The primary benefit of CAR field-based learning is that it offers students a unique opportunity to engage in conflict resolution practice by intervening in a current conflict with guidance from instructors. Instructors play a crucial role in such programs, as they are ultimately responsible for the outcomes of any intervention and also for ensuring the robustness of the learning experience for students. These dual responsibilities require instructors to find an uncomfortable balance in which they must guide and support students while also giving them space to attempt new practices and potentially to fail. In so doing, instructors must continually monitor interventions and make quick decisions about whether to interfere with a student-led process. A primary ethical consideration when making such a decision is potential harm to the parties in conflict (see also chapter 1).

It is important for instructors not to insulate students from the ethical challenges that may arise during an activity or program. In fact, teaching students to notice and articulate possible ethical dilemmas is a key opportunity in field-based learning. In addition to teaching students particular skills and concepts, instructors in field-based activities model and teach frameworks and systems for intervention. Developing activities and assignments that embody the principles and practices being taught allows students to participate without possessing mastery of the subject and helps instructors identify where guidance and further instruction may be needed.

Reflective Practice

The idea of developing an ethical orientation through action, observation, reflection, and adaptation extends back to Aristotle's notion of practical wisdom; our approach likewise encourages learning through the application of principles and acquiring new knowledge through doing and reflecting. In *The Reflective Practitioner*, Donald Schön (1984) marries a critique of technical rationality to a reconception of professional practice in which attending to one's own expectations, surprising or unexpected outcomes, and gaps in knowledge is central to the cultivation of expertise. This process, termed "reflective practice," has been adopted in various professional and educational settings, including medicine (Taylor 2010), education (Hartman 2010; Sellars 2014), and conflict resolution (Cheldelin, Warfield, and Makamba 2004).

At the center of Schön's model of RP is the idea that as practitioners are educated, they come to espouse particular theories of how systems work and that as they are practically trained, they constantly test these "theories-in-action." With experience comes greater tacit knowledge, which gives practitioners the ability to act quickly and spontaneously without considering every choice explicitly. However, when confronted with changing or unfamiliar conditions, unexpected developments, or other confounding circumstances, practitioners can "reflect-in-action," or consider how their tacit knowledge shapes their expectations and performance. By considering where there may be gaps in the practitioner's knowledge or a misapprehension of the situation caused by a flawed theory-in-action, practitioners can modify their reactions in ways that produce useful insights. For example, an expert conducting a well-worn training with a new audience may discover midcourse that the material carries cultural meaning previously overlooked or unnoticed.

At this point, she may interrupt the program to caucus with a colleague or change the language being used on a hunch that draws on other tacit knowledge. In addition to reflecting during action, practitioners can come to "reflect-in-practice," which broadens the scope of examining the intersection of real-world experience and theoretical understanding to the level of career, profession, or field. In addition to its practical value, RP is inherently oriented toward (if not a guarantor of) ethical work. This stance exhorts practitioners to make their assumptions explicit, allowing them to consider the values and priorities grounding their theories and attend to the consequences of their work. Its effectiveness is grounded in the willingness of experts to identify their ignorance by noticing mistakes and improve their techniques through responsible experimentation. In contrast to systems that rely on authorities for answers and guidance, RP insists that practitioners reconcile (or modify) their assumptions through the work they do.

As a pedagogical tool, RP offers teachers a method for encouraging students to interrogate theory, engage with fellow learners, and design projects and research that are both experimental and ethical. While Schön's work focuses chiefly on solitary practitioners, others have applied the approach in environments where students or practitioners reflect collaboratively. In addition to finding adherents in the fields of mediation (Lang and Taylor 2000), nursing (Bulman and Schutz 2013), and CAR (Warfield and Pfund 2013), it has also been used to frame curriculum development (Stowe 2006). Noel J. Stowe, working in the field of public history, discusses the utility and appropriateness of using RP to help "students learn high-order skills of question asking and question framing as they refine their abilities to set and re-set a problem so that it can be shaped toward ethical ends" (2006, 50). It is important to note that public history as a field shares with CAR an explicit ethical imperative to do work that serves a greater common good. While CAR may lack uniformity in its various disciplinary codes of ethics, the field was indubitably formed to address intractable and harmful conflicts. In conflict conditions, where events can dramatically change an intervener's calculus of what is needed or appropriate, RP can serve to help practitioners evaluate the ethical weight and implications of their actions. By explicitly and reflexively considering unfolding contexts in relation to their purpose as interveners, RP enables practitioners to answer Avruch's challenge to appreciate the complexity and interrelation of conflict context and practitioner pretext. (For a discussion of the role of identity in understanding context and pretext, see chapter 3.) The reflexive stance developed in RP helps practitioners act ethically and learn to identify dilemmas as they arise.

In addition to serving an ethical purpose, RP is a practical tool for practitioners encountering new or unexpected information about conflicts and/or parties as an activity unfolds. RP intentionally attends to gaps in knowledge as potential sites for the generation of insight, a concept well suited to CAR work, where understanding of the conflict is always partial and information is often acquired from parties with strongly biased perspectives. In addition to identifying gaps in understanding, reflective techniques can be used to reconcile apparently contradictory narrative accounts of a conflict (see Daniel R. Brunstetter and Daniel Wehrenfennig's description of The Olive Tree Initiative in chapter 3). In CAR practice, a key technique is knowing what questions to ask, what information to listen for, and how this information changes the practitioner's theory-in-action of the conflict. This can be accomplished by individual practitioners but is particularly effective when teams reflect during or following particular activities. Much CAR work is carried out collaboratively, and it is crucial that teams share a common understanding of the conflict. A benefit of working in teams is that some members may notice developments or new information not picked up by other members. By reflecting regularly during an intervention (a training, workshop, longer project, etc.), practitioners can improve their work and effectiveness. When students are being taught CAR concepts and methods, RP can serve as a powerful pedagogical tool. It links the students' knowledge and expertise regarding theories of CAR with their research of a conflict, thereby connecting their ongoing observations and evolving understanding. It can also serve as a "scaffold" to bring students toward a shared understanding of a conflict. Engaged and reflective discussions about their individual preferences, biases, and beliefs can result. For students (particularly undergraduates) with little practical experience, conducting CAR activities can be unsettling and overwhelming. RP normalizes the concept of being surprised or decentered during professional practice; it reminds learners that when a process does not proceed as precisely as planned, it is not necessarily the product of poor preparation. Rather, unexpected outcomes can be sources of valuable information and critical to improving one's work.

When designing a CAR intervention, thoughtfully and carefully matching the planned activities to a theoretical understanding of the conflict is crucial. All CAR processes extend from particular understandings of the nature of conflict, and which understandings are most appropriate in a given circumstance can vary depending on the information available, the access the practitioner has, and the potential implications of practices for the parties and communities involved. RP assumes that the theoretical understanding of a particular situation is functionally accurate and based on the expertise of the practitioner. However, good practice is contingent on observing what happens during episodes of practice, particularly as new and unexpected information emerges, and then revising one's theoretical understanding to make sense of this information. The cyclical process of experiencing, observing/reflecting, reconceptualizing, and experimenting based on a new theoretical understanding is at the center of RP; it draws on the work of learning theorist David Kolb (2015), which expands on social psychologist Kurt Lewin's theory of group dynamics and learning.[1]

(For another application of Kolb to teaching ethics in fieldwork, see chapter 3.)

In CAR interventions and projects that involve multiple activities over time, RP can help practitioners select or revise activities using information generated earlier in the process. For students, using RP to help devise effective practices and techniques emphasizes that good CAR work cannot always be fully designed prior to engagement in the conflict setting. Being able to adjust and adapt during the course of a project is an important skill, as is the ability to communicate the evolving understanding between team members and to participants. In the two projects described here, the activities central to RP were key, both to the instructors' approach to the projects and also the activities taught and deployed.

Field-Based Learning in Prince William County, Virginia

In 2008, we developed an APT project to address a community conflict surrounding immigration in Prince William County, Virginia. Our APT team consisted of three MS and two PhD students, all of whom shared a concern over the developing conflict but who differed broadly in their academic and personal perspectives on the issues. Under the guidance of faculty adviser Dr. Wallace Warfield, this fifteen-month-long project explicitly embraced RP as a key method for organizing the investigation and interventions conducted by the team; we explicitly referenced Schön, Kolb, and Lewin in our efforts to build the project. Practically, this took the form of regular and candid discussions of our operating assumptions about the conflict and the parties, our personal and professional biases on key issues, and how developments during the project had informed our judgments and understanding.

Professor Warfield, a veteran CAR professional, helped the team develop a set of practices to ensure that the project maintained a reflective stance. He emphasized the utility of RP as a learning frame for novice practitioners and budding scholars because of its focus on integrating observation and experience into dynamic theoretical assessments of conflicts. Another key benefit of this approach was that consistent reflection revealed the ways in which changing conditions affected our personal judgments and feelings about the conflict. The team attended closely to developments that surprised us or confounded our expectations; we routinely considered the fit between our actions and our ethical framework as initially construed and whether new information demanded reconsideration of that framework. This approach also highlighted the importance of multiple perspectives, muting distinctions that might otherwise have introduced hierarchies (e.g., knowledgeable PhD students versus novice master's students) into the project. This helped our team operate without status-based barriers despite differences among project participants.

Before engaging individuals and groups within the community, our team conducted extensive research into the conflict and its history. The Prince William County Board of Supervisors had recently passed a resolution that directed police to check the immigration status of anyone they suspected to be undocumented and to partner with US Immigration and Customs Enforcement to hand over those people found to lack documentation. This resolution and related issues polarized residents of the county and resulted in intense and sometimes violent conflict. Stakeholders included community groups, activist groups (both pro- and anti-immigrant), religious leaders, business leaders, and government officials, among others. We developed a theory of the conflict as we understood it, using analytical lenses acquired during our studies, and posited outstanding questions requiring more investigation. Developing multiple theoretical perspectives illuminated gaps in our knowledge and potential blind spots in our theorizing; for example, we wondered why certain parties (pastors, civil rights activists, and others) would remain silent when it appeared to contradict their "typical" roles. A closer examination of the discursive dynamics of the conflict revealed how online activity was regularly used to intimidate and silence figures who spoke openly about their convictions or concerns. We learned that a key nativist organization that supported the resolution, called Help Save Manassas, managed a blog that "named and shamed" those who disagreed with its position and that this had the effect of silencing some in the community who feared repercussions. This process helped us more explicitly develop our theory and assumptions about the conflict, which we used when considering our intervention strategy.

Our group decided early on to include regular conversations about ethics and ethical dilemmas in our group process. These conversations created space within this academic and practice project for critical consideration of the ethical implications of our choices and actions. In the early part of the project, there was open disagreement and dissent in the group. Some members favored impartiality over explicit political commitments, and others disagreed about the risks of offering assistance to a community in crisis despite our inexperience; however, the intentionality of the practice prepared us for difficult conversations, and intragroup friction was rarely disruptive. As a group, we heard each other's concerns and discussed the implications of our decisions on the group as a whole and its members as individuals; all choices were reached by consensus. We resolved to develop an explicit set of ethical commitments to be referenced during our work as conditions changed and our understanding of the conflict evolved. For example, the team resolved that we would commit to the inclusion of all voices in our project's interventions. We would shape our work to be welcoming of all parties regardless of their positions and would work to construct spaces in which those voices could be heard and elaborated.

Over the course of our interview research, however, we discovered that our project was unlikely to produce constructive interactions with all parties. We quickly learned, upon interacting with particularly strident anti-immigrant individuals and groups, that further conversation was neither welcome nor useful. Having done a good deal of background research and plenty of theoretical preparation, the team found the rejection in situ especially challenging. Our research had indicated that although the discourse around immigration and immigrants had become polarized, there remained space for discussion with parties not perceived as aligned with one side or another. We expected to be able to approach and interview both pro- and anti-immigration actors, but it quickly became clear that there was no space for "neutral" or "nonpartisan" actors in this context. The process of engagement itself was sufficient to position us as "taking sides," which significantly threatened our ability to abide by our ethical commitment to include all voices. In addition, it became immediately clear to us that some people at the center of the conflict itself—specifically, unauthorized immigrants—would be unlikely or unable to participate directly in programs open to a broad range of participants. For them, speaking out publicly constituted a grave risk. The team discussed this dilemma at length, debating whether excluding these people de facto made our project too ethically problematic to continue. Ultimately, we decided that we could proceed, with the caveat that even though they would not be direct participants, we would consider the potential indirect and secondary impacts our actions could have on this group. We also endeavored to identify proxies for "voiceless" parties for inclusion in project activities and extensively researched the statements and publications of parties unwilling to meet with us. In this way, parties we could not bring directly to the table were nonetheless closely considered in the project's development.

Once the group began conducting activities within Prince William County, each intervention was followed by an extensive debriefing session with the entire team. Members would recapitulate the theory and assumptions that led to the development of the activity, outline the expected constructive outcomes, and then describe how our experiences either met or confounded our expectations. We were encouraged to identify moments in the intervention when we noticed unexpected responses from participants and how these affected the activity as it played out. In addition, we theorized about what may have led to these unexpected turns, drawing both on our theoretical knowledge and our unfolding understanding of how these moments changed the intervention. As the project continued, the group became more and more adept at observing and noticing these moments during activities and more skilled at interpreting them and recasting our understanding of the conflict.

In one particularly notable incident, the team found itself reevaluating its position as an "outside intervener" and the depth of our understanding of those experiencing the conflict directly. We had been invited by a local official to conduct a conflict resolution training program as part of a neighborhood conference aimed at helping residents respond constructively to challenges among neighbors. Although none of us had extensive training experience, we had considered pedagogical interventions as a potential component of the project. We designed a two-part training program. The first half involved presenting concepts and ideas from the field (e.g., basic human needs, escalation, reflection and mindfulness, and constructive communication), and the second half involved a role-play activity based on a fictional neighborhood dispute. We initially delivered this training at a City of Manassas–sponsored conference on neighborhood issues open to a broad spectrum of residents and officials. While the turnout was modest (about a dozen people attended the workshop), the process worked largely as planned, and the participants were broadly receptive to the material. The team debriefed extensively on the experience, and though we did note some minor problems, they were more technical than substantive (e.g., time management for the didactic section, room logistics for the participatory section).

When our team was asked to present the workshop at a second conference designed for property managers and homeowner association officials, we readily agreed. We elected to keep the format broadly the same but were given more time to present. This workshop had more attendees (roughly thirty), and we looked forward to sharing our expertise with the group. After presenting the "concepts and ideas" section to the group and soliciting feedback, however, the team members were surprised to hear sharp and unvarnished criticism from participants. One concept presented was nonviolent communication, Marshall Rosenberg's system of discussing volatile and emotional topics in de-escalatory and reflective language (2003). Multiple participants made clear that, in their experience, such "soft" techniques would invariably be ineffective (and possibly deleterious) and that direct confrontation and decisive actions were called for in the fictional dispute. A few people invoked personal stories about neighborhood problems that were better addressed with "tough tactics." As students and novice practitioners, we were quickly positioned as naive and out of touch, and this prompted both in situ and postmortem reflection by the team. We reconsidered our expectations of success based on prior experience and noted our failure (a) to notice that the audience, though similar, was meaningfully different from our first group of participants and (b) to appreciate that training folks already embroiled in active conflicts requires more groundwork to establish a legitimate platform from which to teach. As our group proceeded to other interventions, such as workshops and facilitated dialogues, we used these insights to inform our preparations, and this experience both revealed valuable information about the conflict and useful knowledge about how to practice in the field.

For our APT team, RP provided an excellent framework around which to design, deploy, and continually develop our field-based project.

Through conversations in which assumptions and biases were surfaced, we were able to build stronger bonds within the team and identify potential problems in advance. Under the guidance of our faculty adviser, the team used reflective techniques during and following our interventions to test our theories-in-action and used our observations to adapt our practices to be more effective. We identified potential ethical challenges and used our experiences in the community to inform and expand our understanding of the risks and possible liabilities of our work in addition to expected benefits. Lastly, we were able to include routine practices of reflection in our project that cemented the techniques of observation, questioning, reconsideration, and engagement that characterized our work in the community.

Field-Based Learning in Charleston, West Virginia

In the summer of 2012, we instructed a three-week, six-credit course in Charleston, West Virginia, for undergraduate students. The course was designed to incorporate both service in the form of conflict resolution and learning through reflection. It was also guided by a philosophy that values students as the primary architects and practitioners of interventions in real-world conflicts, with instructors serving an important role by providing frameworks for analysis and intervention and by guiding students through a process of RP. In this SLI, students intervened in a conflict between residents and staff at the Charleston Job Corps Center. Job Corps is a US Department of Labor program that offers residential-based education and vocational training to low-income men and women sixteen to twenty-four years old.

We decided early in the process of designing the Charleston SLI that it would be grounded in the RP model that had served our APT team so well. Before our group traveled to Charleston, we met with the students every day for a week to prepare for our time in the field. During this week, in addition to covering topics from logistical issues to Appalachian culture, we introduced and established RP as central to the SLI. To initiate engagement in RP, we provided students with readings describing the practice, we encouraged them each day to consider the theories, both implicit and explicit, that inform their actions and approaches to conflict, and we set aside time each day to reflect on the day's experiences.

As with the APT project, we decided to engage the students in a discussion about the purpose(s) of the project, the ethical principles and commitments that would inform our work, and potential ethical problems or challenges we might face once in West Virginia. With guidance from the instructors, the students considered their own position as outsiders, undergraduates, and learners, reflectively asking and answering questions about the limits of their expertise, the value their work might offer to Job Corps, and their own biases and preconceptions about Charleston and the people there. They came to consensus on principles, such as a commitment to candor and transparency about their status as student-learners, the inclusion and prioritization of youth residents' voices and perspectives during intervention practices, and the explicit consideration of the potential effects any "reporting out" to Job Corps management might have on participants.

During the course of the program in Charleston, students engaged in multiple forms of reflection. They maintained daily journals in which they had the opportunity to reflect on their individual experiences in written form. Group meetings with all students, held each evening, allowed students to share reflections on their own experiences and to hear those of their colleagues. Furthermore, each small group completed a project-reflection form once their work on a project was finished. This process encouraged collaborative reflection on intragroup dynamics, interactions with partners, and the experience of working on the project. Finally, when appropriate, students engaged in reflection with community partners or others with whom they were working.

We spent much of our first week in Charleston at the city's Job Corps Center. The center's director had requested conflict resolution training for Job Corps residents; he and other staff wanted to provide residents with skills for resolving conflicts constructively. We decided that our students should conduct focus groups with the Job Corps residents to identify the typical conflicts in the lives of the residents and to learn how they manage those conflicts. Our students would analyze what they had learned through the focus-group sessions, and they would develop short, simple conflict resolution training for residents that would address the conflicts that had surfaced in the focus-group discussions.

Upon our arrival in Charleston, we created a daily schedule that included evening sessions for time to reflect with the students and sessions that immediately followed in which we would reflect as instructors and plan for the next day. Through our own RP, we quickly discovered that the process of reflecting was not intuitive for students, and we decided to address it by meeting briefly with the students each morning to inquire about their expectations for the day. We wanted them to explicitly identify their expectations and the assumptions, or theories, on which those expectations rested. Once instituted, this practice helped some students develop a deeper RP, as they became more aware of the theories and assumptions upon which their expectations were based, and they could reflect on how those assumptions affected their expectations and actions.

As one example, several students shared an assumption, or a theory-in-action, that the Job Corps residents would likely be troubled youth who would resist conflict resolution practices or training. They developed this theory from their own experiences with the types of people they expected the Job Corps youth to be, as well as through minimal research on the Job Corps program and the Charleston center in particular. In reflections the evening after the students conducted focus groups with Job Corps residents, many reported that they were surprised by the nature of the engagement with the residents. In particular, they noted that the residents expressed appreciation for the conversation design (i.e., they were seated in a circle, and our students asked the residents questions) and were more forthcoming in their responses than the students had expected.

Through RP, and in particular through discussions during our evening reflections, students expressed awareness of and concerns related to power imbalances and structural conflict at the Job Corps Center. They recognized that conflicts between center residents and staff, which residents identified during focus-group sessions, were shaped by systems of discipline in place at the center and larger systems outside the center. Some students wondered if, by teaching residents to resolve conflicts more effectively, they were teaching them to be compliant in the service of a potentially unjust system. In describing what they perceived as an ethical dilemma, they drew from Johan Galtung's theory of structural violence, which describes violence that is "built into the structure and shows up as unequal power and consequently as unequal life chances" (Galtung 1969, 171), and considered how it might apply to this case and inform their actions.

Similarly, students were concerned when the Job Corps Center's administrator requested a briefing from the students to learn the results of their analysis of the focus-group sessions and their recommendations for reducing conflict in the center. In particular, students worried that by providing such a briefing they might inadvertently breach the confidentiality they had promised the center's residents when they conducted the focus groups. In this case, the students' ethical concerns stemmed from established norms and practices in the conflict resolution field. Through a discussion grounded in RP, the students developed a briefing that they thought would provide useful information while respecting the confidential nature of the discussions with the center's residents. They had the opportunity to learn through this process how to work through the challenge of balancing competing interests.

Constructing these field-based learning programs on a foundation of RP did not prevent all missteps. Nor did it ensure that we or our students always made the right decisions. However, when confronted with ethical concerns, the RP model provided a framework for thoughtful consideration that explicitly identified and tested our theories and assumptions.

Students benefit from participating in field-based CAR courses because in such courses they have experiences that are unexpected and often unsettling. To make sense of those experiences they must draw from their knowledge of the dynamics of conflict. Field-based learning requires the application of theory to practice in the moment, so that through such courses students not only learn conflict resolution skills, but they also deepen their understanding of the theories of the field.

RP helps students and instructors adapt to changing conditions in the field, new information, unexpected turns, and incomplete understandings of conflict. Its ethical orientation makes it ideal for participants in field-based programs, where students and instructors engage with ethical challenges and make ethical decisions in controlled but spontaneous environments. The techniques of RP can be used to develop processes of continuous reconsideration of new information, surfacing of biases and assumptions, and evaluation of risk.

We have experienced field-based learning both in the roles of students, participating in a year-long APT project for graduate CAR students, and of instructors, coleading an SLI for undergraduate CAR students. Our experiences as students, particularly with regard to the inclusion of RP as a fundamental component, informed the design of the program we instructed. In both programs, as is typical in field-based courses, we encountered multiple surprises and situations in which we were unsure how to act, but we had to make decisions, sometimes quickly. Both presented ethical challenges and difficult decisions. As graduate students, we intervened in a conflict that included undocumented immigrants and parties who sometimes used threatening or violent language. In the service learning program that we instructed, we provided support and instruction to students who intervened in a conflict that involved young, mostly minority residents who lived in a secure facility and staff who were often frustrated with the way the residents handled conflicts.

RP provides a useful ethical framework for decision-making in field-based courses. By making the implicit explicit, RP challenges us to surface the theories that inform our actions, confront our biases, and critically examine the connections we make between theory and practice. By guiding students through RP techniques informed by rigorous research and real-life interactions, instructors can cultivate both intervention skills and professional habits that may enable them to become ethical and competent practitioners. The RP model applied to experiential learning is an optimal method for helping students learn practical ethics as they take their initial steps into the world of CAR.

Note

1. Lewin, an early associate of the Frankfurt School of critical theorists, was particularly concerned with the way that reflexivity allows individuals to adapt to exigent and unfolding conditions while avoiding the risks of "groupthink." We believe that this impulse comports well with Avruch's belief that CAR practitioners

must consider how culture, context, and pretext are entwined in ways that are not immediately apparent and that both "problems" and "parties" can be problematic when viewed acontextually. We also believe that both teachers and learners in CAR should develop skills to examine their intentions, values, and actions as products of a cultural context in relation to distinct contexts that have produced conflict. This multifaceted mode of observation and analysis allows practitioners to make better ethical judgments when questions or concerns arise.

TEN

Cultivating Transformation in Field-Based Courses

ALEXANDER CROMWELL

For students in the international peace and conflict field, traveling to a conflict zone to hear from those who have lived through the violence can be extremely meaningful.[1] The experience exposes students to a wide array of opinions not available to them in their home country and to the complexities of the conflict experienced by people who lived through it. In this chapter, I explore the transformations that students experience in these programs and how they come about. Specifically, I argue that students attending field-based courses in areas of conflict experience two important transformations that make them better prepared to work in the conflict resolution field. The first is that they learn to reflect critically on their role as interveners in conflict. The second is a new or renewed motivation to work to resolve the conflict. I also explore in detail some processes for supporting these transformations. Three essential components for facilitating these transformations are meaningful contact with local people, allowing enough space and flexibility for these interactions to happen, and an intentional focus on reflective practice to maximize this learning.

This chapter brings together theories from study abroad and peace and conflict studies to explain the transformative phenomena experienced by students who attend field-based courses in conflict areas. My argument is that these transformative experiences make them better conflict resolution practitioners. The discussion in subsequent sections furthers theory on transformation in field-based courses in the international peace and conflict field by providing concrete examples of transformations experienced by students in these courses, analyzing them systematically, and connecting them back to the literature explored in this chapter.

The Benefits of Studying Abroad in Conflict Zones

In many disciplines, there is a wide gap between scholarly theories and the day-to-day work in which practitioners engage (Cheldelin, Warfield, and Makamba 2004). The international peace and conflict field is no exception. Students express that coursework in peace and conflict is too theoretical and challenging to apply to jobs related to mitigating international conflict (Aall, Helsing, and Tidwell 2007). Pamela Aall and her colleagues argue that these programs should make learning in their courses more experiential so that students can see how these theories apply in the "real world." In a special report produced by the United States Institute of Peace on the relationship between graduate programs in peace and conflict studies and professional practice in the field, Nike Carstarphen, Craig Zelizer, Robert Harris, and David J. Smith (2010) find that roughly 50 percent of employers believed that students' academic programs had not adequately prepared them for their jobs, whereas 90 percent of faculty and 80 percent of students thought that graduating students were sufficiently equipped for these positions. These findings highlight different views held by educators in international peace and conflict, the students attending these programs, and specialists working in the field regarding the type of experience that students are gaining from these graduate programs.

What kind of experience do students need to work in jobs related to international conflict? Carstarphen et al. (2010) find that peace and conflict employers said that experience abroad was the most important training for students who want to work in the field. Additionally, Kimberly Franklin (2010) argues that employers working in fields with a global reach consider skills associated with studying abroad, such as cross-cultural understanding, to be important indicators of qualified job candidates. Therefore, one of the most important ways for students interested in working in international conflict to prepare themselves for this work is to get international experience.

Employers are not the only ones who value study-abroad experience. Students who attend these programs typically describe the experience as "life-changing" or "life-transforming," a response so common that it has become cliché (Selby 2008). Educators also see these effects in their participants (see chapter 3, this volume). Vasiliki Anastasakos (2013) recounts her experience teaching multiple study-abroad courses in Turkey and Costa Rica, where she saw her students develop increased openness and respect for people from different religious and cultural backgrounds. She also describes transformations in the global understanding and relationships they built with the people they met. I experienced similar transformations traveling as a student and staff member to Syria, Israel/Palestine, Serbia and Croatia, and Indonesia on four separate study-abroad programs focused on conflict resolution. I have also seen profound transformations in Indonesian and Pakistani youth who studied abroad in the United States. In interviews that I did with these students, many of them described these programs as "life-changing." They expressed the belief that they had become more open-minded and had more positive views toward other religious and ethnic groups from their experience in the program (Cromwell n.d.).

Transformative Learning and Shifts in Consciousness

Clearly, something valuable is happening in these experiences. But what does "life-changing" actually mean? Transformative learning theory explains the process and outcome of these "life-changing" experiences. The originator of the theory, Jack Mezirow (1978 and 1997), describes this transformation as a shift in a person's "frame of reference." A frame of reference is how one sees the world and makes sense of their experiences. Mezirow argues that shifts happen when a person is confronted with an experience that contradicts their previous beliefs, where they must reconstruct their understanding through critical reflection. Many times this shift occurs as a result of discourse because meaning is constructed with others through dialogue (Mezirow 2003). When people are confronted with something at odds with their frame of reference, they experience a "disorienting dilemma" (Mezirow 1978; Taylor 1994), also known as "disequilibrium" or "dissonance" (Che, Spearman, and Manizade 2009; Kiely 2005). People can easily integrate low-intensity dissonance into their mental framework, but when they experience high-intensity dissonance, it requires a change in their frame of reference, leading to transformative learning (Kiely 2005). High-intensity dissonance usually involves a strong emotional reaction caused by this new interaction (Brewer and Cunningham 2009), such as hearing from a victim of mass violence. When a student encounters something so completely at odds with their previous experiences, it is almost impossible to maintain the same assumptions they held previously. Kiely (2005) argues that this type of dissonance results in transformative learning. Study-abroad courses are full of opportunities where students experience high-intensity dissonance (Brewer and Cunningham 2009) because these courses are often designed to push students out of their comfort zones and put them face-to-face with unanticipated challenges (see introduction, this volume). Moreover, study-abroad scholars emphasize the value of disorienting dilemmas and dissonance resulting from study-abroad experiences for their possibility in stimulating transformational moments (Brewer and Cunningham 2009; Che, Spearman, and Manizade 2009; Trilokekar and Kukar 2011).

But how does a shift in frame of reference explain what students experience when they attend field-based courses in conflict areas? The literature reviewed thus far in this chapter describes transformations that students generally experience in study abroad, but to fully understand the potential of studying abroad in conflict zones for peace and conflict students, it is important to contextualize these transformations within the literature on peace and conflict. One goal for educating students in peace and conflict is to transform attitudes in support of a culture of peace (Iram 2006), and one way to do this is through facilitating "shifts in consciousness." Shifts in consciousness are personal transformations in perception that occur through reflection, dissonance, and other experiences that can lead to individuals developing new ways of thinking about how to cultivate peace (Nan 2010). The shift in frame of reference explained by transformative learning is the same as a shift in consciousness because both involve a change in thinking stimulated by some sort of dissonance. Though these disciplines use slightly different terms, they both describe this same phenomenon of a "shift" as a central outcome of either the transformative learning or peace education processes. For the purposes of this chapter, I will use the term "shift in frame of reference" to describe this change. This emphasis on the same construct illuminates a direct compatibility between transformative learning and conflict resolution education and highlights the necessary emphasis on transformative education when teaching conflict resolution. This parallel between the two fields also shows the particular value of study abroad when working with students in the peace and conflict field because of the transformative possibility of these courses. By providing students with the opportunity to move outside of the narrow viewpoint of their frame of reference, they can become more effective peacemakers because they will learn to value the perspectives of people living in the conflict zone. Many scholars in the peace and conflict field argue for the importance of learning from local populations and working with them when trying to resolve a conflict (e.g., Avruch and Black 1993; Gopin 2009; Lederach 1995 and 1997). Field-based courses can facilitate this learning because they provide direct contact with these populations.

In the pages that remain, I focus on transformations experienced by participants in two programs for conflict studies students run by the Center for World Religions, Diplomacy, and Conflict Resolution (CRDC) at George Mason University. The first program brought students to Israel/Palestine for ten days in 2012. The second took students to Serbia and Croatia for roughly ten days in 2013. I served as a graduate student and staff member for both courses. Additionally, because simply attending a study-abroad trip does not guarantee that a student will gain the benefits that have been discussed so far in this chapter (Bennett 2008; Brewer and Cunningham 2009; Deardorff 2008; Ogden 2006; Savicki 2008), I will explain some of the components in these courses that were essential for these transformations to come about. The questions guiding this inquiry are: What transformations do participants experience in study-abroad courses in conflict areas? How do these transformations happen, and what factors explain them? The answers to these questions highlight why study abroad is particularly important for students interested in peace and conflict and show transformations specific to the peace and conflict field, while contextualizing them within the conflict literature.

Descriptions of the Two Programs

The course in Israel/Palestine was a program for graduate and undergraduate students focused on developing reflective practice skills for peace practitioners. Reflective practice is a person's ability to examine their current and previous behavior working in their profession and to use this knowledge to enhance theoretical understanding of best practices in their field (Schön 1984). For peace and conflict practitioners, it refers to engaging in this process before, during, and after conducting any form of conflict resolution or peacebuilding work (Cheldelin, Warfield, and Makamba 2004). Reflective practice also involves reflection on the ethical challenges involved in intervening in conflicts and being mindful of how one's biases influence their peace work, all the while learning from the process to be better practitioners (Gopin 2009). Therefore, the goal of the course was for students to develop intentional processes of personal reflection that would connect conflict resolution practice to theories they had learned. They were instructed to think about their role as interveners before entering the region, while they were in the conflict zone, and once they returned home. To this end, students were required to reflect on their presence in the conflict through daily journaling as well as regular debriefing sessions. When journaling, students examined their experiences in great detail and explored their insights on the conflict gained from interacting with local people on both sides, as well as what they learned about conflict resolution practice from evaluating their personal engagement and the intervention as a whole.

Students stayed at a hotel in East Jerusalem for the duration of the program. The program included daily sessions with the course professor and meetings with Palestinian and Israeli politicians, academics, peace activists, Israeli settlers, and former Israeli soldiers. The group toured sites in Jerusalem and other important places with an Israeli and Palestinian peacemaker both present at each location, explaining common Israeli and Palestinian narratives of these sites and their historical significance to each group. Additionally, we visited the Tent of Nations, Yad Vashem (the Holocaust memorial), a refugee camp in Bethlehem, nonviolent leaders in Ramallah, and a Jewish Israeli settlement in the West Bank.[2] These highly diverse experiences were aimed at giving participants a sense of the complexity involved in the conflict by hearing multiple perspectives from a range of stakeholders. Many of the sessions in the course also involved discussions on the dynamics of the conflict that we experienced and the challenges involved in reflective practice while intervening in the Israeli-Palestinian conflict. The course was also an intervention in the conflict, as it offered the opportunity to fund and empower local peacebuilders on both sides by providing them with work as guides and guest speakers. Thus, the students were part of the intervention because attending the course contributed to the livelihood of these peacemakers.

The Serbia and Croatia course took graduate students to Serbia and Croatia to study the role of history and memory after mass atrocities, focusing on the impact of the 1991–95 Yugoslav wars on the region. The program involved daily classes and debriefing sessions with the instructor, meetings with various nongovernmental organizations (NGOs), government officials, and conflict experts from the local area, field trips to memorials and various nonprofit organizations, and some sightseeing. Students spent the first five days in Belgrade, Serbia, and the remaining five days in Osijek, Croatia. In Belgrade, students met with people from organizations such as Women in Black, the Youth Initiative for Human Rights, the Organization for Security and Co-operation in Europe, and the Helsinki Committee for Human Rights. In Osijek, they visited organizations such as the Nansen Dialogue Centre, the PRONI Centre for Social Education, Youth Peace Group Danube, and the Center for Peace, Nonviolence and Human Rights. Through all of these experiences, students had the opportunity to meet with actors working for peace and human rights at various levels and in multiple sectors in society. In this course, students were also required to journal every day about how their worldview was impacted by their experiences and what they learned from their various interactions throughout the program.

Faculty interested in teaching such courses may worry about the logistical and ethical challenges involved in leading a group of students to a conflict zone or postconflict area where tensions between groups are still high. As Agnieszka Paczyńska and Susan F. Hirsch mention in the introduction to this volume, for practitioners, taking careful precautions to "do no harm" in their own peacebuilding work is a challenge in itself. Therefore, bringing a group of students into such unpredictable contexts raises the possibility of students inadvertently doing or experiencing harm and a whole slew of unforeseen challenges that educators must be prepared for. Although the unpredictability of conflict contexts makes these challenges a particular struggle for faculty, the key to running such a course is to develop long-term relationships with local people living in the context whom the faculty member can trust. By maintaining consistent communication with these contacts about the situation on the ground and the prospective safety of the group and local partner in the field, faculty members can have a good sense of the possible risks in undertaking the course for the stakeholders involved. The educator following the advice of local peacemakers also models for students how they can most effectively intervene in their future as peace and conflict practitioners as well. By seeing the close trusting relationships the faculty member has with his or her network, students learn the types of relationships they should work to build in their own practice. Faculty can also better prepare students for the course through experiential learning activities that mimic some of the ethical challenges students may face in the field (see chapter 1). Therefore, though this chapter primarily focuses on lessons students learn through challenges in the field that may help them for future ethical dilemmas as peace practitioners, the unique challenges that teachers face in leading study-abroad courses in conflict zones need to be kept in mind when considering such a course.

Students Reflecting on Their Role as Conflict Interveners

One powerful change for participants across both of these courses was developing a critical perspective on their roles as interveners in conflict.[3] Students became familiar with some of the concrete challenges for peacemakers in conflict zones and learned how to reflect on these experiences to intervene more effectively in future conflicts. In the Israel/Palestine course, this was clear from the moment we arrived at the airport and dealt with Israeli security. Group members traveled separately, so we each had different experiences entering the country. I was planning to go directly to Ramallah in the West Bank to meet a Palestinian friend and was also traveling with a Muslim friend, and we were pulled off to undergo extra screening. We spent a few hours in special security, with each of us being interrogated individually. The man who interviewed me repeatedly asked why I had come to the country, and I kept explaining that I was there for a study-abroad course on conflict resolution. He asked if I knew any Arabs and if I would visit the West Bank. I had been told by my friends working in the region to keep my relationships with Palestinians secret for their protection and to not create too many questions, so I said that I did not know Palestinians and that I might visit the West Bank during the course but was not sure. He seemed unconvinced by my answers to his questions and made me access my email in front of him to prove that I did not have any correspondence with Arabs about my trip. He did not find anything. Finally, he asked me directly if I was planning on attending any protests. I told him that I was not. My response seemed to satisfy him, so he let me go.

I was frazzled by this experience, which made me aware of the pressure faced by conflict interveners when entering an area of conflict. In this case, I presume that I faced suspicion and questioning because of my friendship with Palestinians in the country. Many other students in the course also experienced these additional security measures because of stamps on their passports from majority Muslim and/or Arab countries that Israel has bad relations with or because they had Palestinian friends in the country. In addition, some students in the group faced enhanced scrutiny because of passports that indicated they were born in one of these countries or because they looked like they could be Muslim and/or Arab. These experiences provided important lessons on how to build trust when dealing with security forces who are suspicious because of one's engagement with people on the other side of the conflict or when one is seen as a member of the other side.

My education on the challenges interveners face continued in Ramallah. Later, I would appreciate how important it was to have this opportunity to meet local people and gain a deeper understanding of the challenges they experience in the West Bank before the program officially began. My friend and I went all around the city and met lots of terrific people. As I expressed how much I liked the West Bank, many people told me that they were trapped and that it was a horrible situation for them. I learned how challenging it was to get a permit to leave the West Bank and enter Israel. But I did not fully comprehend the challenges faced by Palestinians until I went through Kalandia checkpoint on our way from Ramallah to Jerusalem. The checkpoint looks like a huge prison, with gigantic, looming walls topped with barbed wire. People are required to line up, wait for a buzzer to sound, go through metal detectors, and hold up their permits to Israeli soldiers who sit behind bulletproof glass. This is a daily experience for Palestinians who work outside of the West Bank. They are at the mercy of Israeli soldiers who can shut down the checkpoint or strip-search them at a moment's notice. This is not to say that there are not legitimate security concerns for the Israeli people, but witnessing the checkpoint process raised serious questions for me as to the negative impacts of security measures that disenfranchise an entire group of people based on the actions of a select few. The experience gave me a taste of the humiliation that Palestinians experience on a regular basis and the emotional toll of working with populations that experience systematic injustice in conflict settings.

When our group traveled to a refugee camp in Bethlehem later in the trip, we witnessed the plight of many families that had been relocated as a result of the conflict in 1948, with the creation of the state of Israel, when many Jews and Palestinians were forced to leave their homes. Some of these Palestinian families have remained in Bethlehem since this time as perpetual refugees. We learned that the Israeli government controls their access to water and electricity; many times the only water they have comes from rainwater they collect in large jugs on their roofs. We also saw the clear wealth disparity between areas in Jewish West Jerusalem and Palestinian East Jerusalem in terms of the buildings, streets, and infrastructure. This disparity was amplified when traveling from Israel proper to the occupied West Bank. In addition, we heard stories from Palestinian activists of losing family members in the conflict.

These experiences had a powerful emotional impact on the students and me that affected us later in the program when we had a pair of young

Israeli politicians come to speak to the group. We were all very angry about the injustices we had seen and were not ready to engage in constructive dialogue. When both politicians shared their positions, our group reacted negatively toward them. One of the politicians denied the role of Israeli forces in the 1948 conflict between the two groups, stating that the Palestinians simply "left the land" or were not there to begin with. Once the floor was opened for questions, our students began attacking him, saying that he was ignoring the history of human rights abuses that Palestinians had experienced. They accused both politicians for being complicit in the exploitation of the Palestinian people. One of the politicians became defensive, stating that Israel had the "most moral army in the world." I became so angry that my body was literally shaking. I blurted out a question: "What is that based on?" A few other students chimed in, and both politicians became even more defensive, obstructing the conversation, which resulted in a negative experience for the presenters and those of us in the crowd.

The presentation had been designed as an opportunity to understand some of the complexity of different Israeli perspectives, but instead of listening to the presenters, the students and I reacted angrily, destroying any possibility for dialogue. And our actions left us with the dilemma of how to challenge unjust practices in conflict settings constructively and respectfully. Students became acquainted with the dilemma of the intervener, where they must learn how to manage strong reactions when trying to work with people on opposing sides of a conflict. That evening our class failed at doing this, and it resulted in the politicians becoming defensive and more rooted in their positions. This was an important lesson in conflict resolution on how to engage with people with whom one disagrees. Interveners need to work with all parties in the conflict whether they have the same perspective or not. Overall, this experience was valuable for reflecting on how to be respectful but strategic in such interactions and not let emotions take over.

The intensity of these experiences has stayed with me over the years and has been an important guide for my work in international conflict since. Being thrust into situations like facing Israeli security, going through checkpoints, and trying to dialogue with people one completely disagrees with pushes students outside of their comfort zones and forces them to adapt to the situation because of the dissonance they experience between their previous understanding of the world and these new experiences. This adaptation can create a shift in their frame of reference, as they struggle to manage their emotions and restructure their understanding of peacebuilding practice and the people in conflict contexts. The result can be important transformations as the students learn their limitations, the importance of flexibility, and how to be more effective in their future work in conflict areas.

Students also learned that interveners are never neutral and always have baggage associated with the area in the world they are from. In the Serbia and Croatia course, people reacted differently to our group depending on which side of the conflict they were on. Many Serbs had a negative perspective toward the United States because of its role in the Yugoslav Wars of 1991–95,[4] as well as the Kosovo crisis of 1999.[5] For example, on one free afternoon, I went with a few students to the ruins from the 1999 bombings by the North Atlantic Treaty Organization (NATO) of the Federal Ministry of Defense, located in the center of Belgrade. I had seen the towering wreckage a few days earlier on my initial taxi trip through the city and wondered why these central buildings still had not been repaired almost fifteen years later. While walking around the area, we met a security guard and spoke at length with him about the bombings and wreckage of the buildings. He shared with us the anger Serbs felt toward NATO and the United States for bombing central areas of their city when Serbia was invading Kosovo. He argued that Serbia had done nothing to provoke the wrath of the United States and its allies; he believed that the international community viewed Serbia as barbaric and aggressive and did not like that his country was seen in this light. We learned that the shells of buildings being left in the center of the city, unrepaired, allowed the Serbian people to show the American injustice against Serbs. The ruins support their position as victims and are used by politicians as a political tool to foster anti-American sentiment. Seeing the damage that had been done forced me and the rest of the students to reflect on the harm inflicted by our own country and to critically examine how our identity implicated us in various ways as outsiders studying the conflict. As a group mostly of Americans, we would need to be mindful of the anger toward us when trying to intervene in this conflict setting. We could not pretend that we were neutral, even if we wanted to be.

Another experience that made me, and many of the students, reflect on our role as Americans was when an activist from Women in Black took us out to meet people in the local community in Serbia. She cautioned us against telling people we were American and was adamant that we should describe ourselves as Canadian because of the negative sentiment toward Americans in Belgrade. So that night, everywhere the group went, we told people we were Canadian. Following this encounter, I became apprehensive about sharing my identity as an American and started to be a lot more careful about whom I told this to. This experience raised the issue of transparency and the ethical dilemma associated with being honest but strategic in sharing one's background in conflict interventions. In this particular experience, our activist colleague was worried about how people would view her for associating with Americans, and she requested that we cover this up. Telling people that we were Canadian limited our ability to build trust with people we met because the relationship was built on a lie. As a result, our group became aware of the challenges peace practitioners face in building trust with local people while also maintaining their personal safety, when disclosing parts of their identity may endanger them and their work during peacebuilding interventions.

However, there were also groups that reacted to us very positively simply because we were Americans. After visiting the Youth Initiative for Human Rights in Belgrade, we met with some Serbian students from the organization, who had four Kosovar Albanian friends visiting from Pristina in Kosovo. We learned from our new Kosovar friends about their experiences in 1999, when ethnic cleansing occurred in Kosovo and some of them were forced to flee the country and become refugees. They explained that the United States was viewed very positively and Bill Clinton was seen as a hero in the country because the United States had bombed Serbia (part of the Federal Republic of Yugoslavia at the time) and aided Kosovo during the conflict. Therefore, we were exposed to different accounts of the same events in 1999 and learned how different people would react to us depending on which group they were in.

The combination of these interactions taught us how a person's positionality deeply influences his or her ability to intervene in conflicts and win the trust of the people in a particular context. In such situations an important shift in understanding occurred for many of the participants, as we absorbed the perspectives of individuals who might not see our country as positively as we did. Seeing the wreckage of the ministry buildings and having conversations with local people likely caused high-intensity dissonance, resulting in a shift in perspective and transformative learning for each of us. At the same time, the many welcoming people in Serbia who were excited to meet us taught us about the complexity on the ground and encouraged us not to generalize too broadly about the overall population. These courses provided multiple opportunities for students to think critically about the challenges facing interveners in a conflict, the limitations of their own perspectives, and the perspectives that people in the conflict might have of them. This critical examination is essential for facilitating shifts in students' frames of reference and creating deep and meaningful transformations for students in these contexts. As Pushpa Iyer argues in chapter 3, in such contexts students are faced with dilemmas resulting from their identities, where the ethical challenges they experience push them to deepen their understanding of their positionality and their own ethical frameworks. She explains that this willingness to question one's identity and one's ethical reasoning is an important outcome for students that can help them be better prepared for ethical challenges they may face in future interventions.

Motivation and Commitment

The second key transformation for students in these courses is the strengthening of a motivation to help people living in the midst of the conflict, after students witness firsthand the injustices these people have experienced. This kind of witnessing can deeply impact students emotionally and make them care much more about people in the part of the world they travel to. I specified multiple instances earlier in this chapter where the other students and I were put in situations where we saw injustice that made us angry, such as the refugee camps in Bethlehem and the checkpoints surrounding the West Bank. These experiences created a desire in many of the participants to do something to address the conflict. Many of us were enraged by what we observed, and it instilled in us a passion to change the reality that Palestinians had to face. Before going to the region some of us knew about challenges such as checkpoints. But going there and meeting people who were struggling seriously shifted the way in which many of us thought about the conflict. It connected us to real people who simply wanted to have basic comforts we took for granted: freedom of movement, citizenship, safety for their families, and sometimes even basic necessities such as water and electricity. The high-intensity dissonance we experienced stimulated a transformation to the extent that we felt we could no longer simply sit by and let the injustice in Palestine continue.

However, many times it is unclear to students how they can channel this newfound inspiration into concrete action. They may want to help people in the conflict area, but they do not know where to begin, and they may question their ability to do so, especially as they are learning to critically examine their capability to intervene. For this reason, faculty and administrators facilitating these programs need to develop clear channels that students can tap into to do something with their motivation before it fades. As Yigal Rosen and David Perkins (2013) argue, the biggest challenge faced by programs involving international peace and conflict is maintaining over time the transformations that participants experience during the program. Additionally, Ned Lazarus (2011) finds that the most important component for sustaining change is the quality and consistency of follow-on programming. In my research on Pakistani youth who studied abroad in the United States, participation and connectivity with the Pakistan-U.S. Alumni Network or other community structures (such as a school where an alumnus taught and a university club that one was a part of) was essential for students to engage in continued positive action in their communities (Cromwell n.d.). These structures provided alumni with the logistical (and, in many cases, financial) support and legitimacy to initiate and sustain their projects. Out of the ninety alumni projects that I analyzed, 96 percent of them had some sort of structural or institutional support (Cromwell n.d.). Moreover, Daniel R. Brunstetter and Daniel Wehrenfennig (chapter 4, this volume) describe a step-by-step follow-on plan for after their students study abroad that illustrates how programs can develop a structure that supports students' concrete action and create clear opportunities for students to engage in this action. The steps move from creating a safe space for students to discuss their trip experiences and students giving presentations to the campus and the community, to alumni publishing their presentation content in an on-campus journal, to participants taking an additional course involving off-campus volunteering and a capstone project, to finally recruiting the next year's participants and joining the alumni network. The examples in these different programs highlight that when faculty design field-based courses in conflict zones, they should explicitly plan how they will harness students' motivation and provide support structures for them for once they return from the program.

After participating in the Israel/Palestine course, program alumni had the opportunity to channel their motivation into concrete action by supporting a CRDC event at George Mason University where the Palestinian ambassador to the United States spoke. The event was important because it opened up space for people to hear the Palestinian narrative. Students volunteered to find guests for the ambassador's speech and to help with the planning and implementation of the event. There were also many students who interned with CRDC and supported other projects because they were inspired by their experience abroad with the center and wanted to support its work in conflict areas.

One of the best examples of motivation leading to future action comes from the study-abroad course that I attended in Syria in January 2011. The course was focused on citizen diplomacy and building positive relations between Americans and Syrians. Little did we know that two months later protests would begin in the country, leading to a brutal civil war. My fellow students and I watched from afar as the conflict steadily got worse and worse, wondering what we could do to help. We finally had the opportunity to do something concrete when a young Syrian whom we had met during our time there could no longer remain in the country because of safety concerns. We created an online fund-raiser for him and were able to raise enough money to get him out of Syria and into Germany. Almost all of the students shared the campaign through social media or contributed money to help get him out of the country. Though students did not do much at first after the program ended, many of them helped our friend leave the country once there was a concrete way that they could contribute. Five years later, the program had still made an impact on them to the extent that they wanted to help this young man. Although the examples from both of these courses are anecdotal, they show behaviors that participants engaged in to support initiatives with people from the conflict region where they had traveled. These examples highlight the impact that motivation stimulated by these programs can have if intentional processes are developed for capitalizing on this passion to conduct further peacebuilding initiatives.

How These Transformations Happen

ALLOWING SPACE FOR EXPLORATION

The most valuable experiences in these programs are not necessarily part of the explicit course plan or schedule. In the courses described in this chapter, although the course content was important for understanding the conflict and really enriched the understanding of the students, some of the most transformative moments occurred in the evenings when the students stepped outside of the classroom and engaged with the local population. For example, dealing with airport security in Israel/Palestine was not a specifically planned part of course content. The faculty member had no control of the experience that individual students would have during this process, although he was able to prepare us to the best of his ability. However, the professor was aware that there was a likelihood that some students might have issues with security for various reasons, such as an Arab or Muslim background and ties with Palestinians. Knowing that students would face these kinds of challenges, the professor intentionally set up the course around reflecting on and discussing the experience of going through security and checkpoints, as well as what students were witnessing in terms of wealth disparity and injustices on both sides. This allowed these experiences to be a central part of the group's learning.

In the Serbia and Croatia course, many of our group's powerful experiences also occurred informally and during free time in the evenings. The examples given earlier—namely, seeing the wreckage of the Federal Ministry of Defense and meeting a security guard there, meeting young people from Kosovo, and engaging with local people in the community—were all experiences that were not structured as part of the course but were essential in facilitating the transformations explained earlier in this chapter. These were the spaces where discourse happened, allowing for exposure to new perspectives and stimulating participants to think in new ways. There is only so much interaction that can occur in class time and during official meetings with NGOs; thus, it is the one-on-one conversations outside of formal classes where relationships deepen and transformation can flourish. In his discussion of best practices of study-abroad courses, Selby (2008) describes the importance of providing enough flexibility in the course to let students explore and have valuable experiences on their own. An overly planned course does not allow time for these interactions and can potentially rob students of experiencing such transformations. However, for these experiences to have a transformative impact, they must also involve two key components: engaging with local populations and establishing processes of reflective practice to maximize learning from these experiences. In the Israel/Palestine course, the day that I spent in Ramallah before the program officially began was likely the most powerful for me. However, the relationships I developed with my Palestinian friends and the ability to reflect on my experiences with them and others throughout the course were essential for digesting the experience and making sense of it within the overall conflict context.

ENGAGING WITH LOCAL PEOPLE

Arguably, some of the biggest transformations that come about in these types of programs are a result of having contact with people living in the conflict setting. Meeting people in conflict settings allows students to understand people's attitudes in a deeper, more nuanced way because they can see and be part of their daily lives. When positive contact happens between groups across lines of difference, it can lead to the reduction of prejudice through decreased intergroup anxiety and increased empathy and knowledge developed between the groups (Al Ramiah and Hewstone 2013). This contact happens in intentional ways, such as in the meetings with refugees in Bethlehem and relationships that participants form with the guides on the Israel/Palestine course. However, it also happens in more flexible ways through relationships built with local people when participants have free time to explore and engage in meaningful interactions with them, as I did during my day in Ramallah and on other evenings with friends that I had made on my first day there. Brunstetter and Wehrenfennig (chapter 4, this volume) also emphasize the important role of students engaging with local people from various perspectives in their courses on the Israeli-Palestinian and Turkish-Armenian conflicts. They argue that such exposure deepens students' understanding of experiences of people on both sides of these conflicts and helps them "stretch" their own perspectives on the conflict and their roles as future peace and conflict practitioners. Jennifer M. Ramos (chapter 5) makes a similar argument about exposing students to various local stakeholders across the conflict in Northern Ireland.

In many ways, positive contact with local people is the most important part of these programs. Once students develop relationships with people in a place, they will be more likely to want to support people in the conflict. Without meaningful relationships forming, it is less likely that students will have a vested interest in working to resolve the conflict in the future. With the Syria course, it was our group's bond with our Syrian friend that made us want to support him in getting out of the country and compelled us to act on his behalf. However, the outcome of the contact really depends on the quality of the interaction between the groups. When the contact between groups is negative, sometimes students will have their stereotypes and prejudices reinforced and come away from the program with very little desire to engage with these groups in the future. For example, in the Israel/Palestine course, when the students met with the Israeli politicians and there were a lot of accusations hurled at the politicians, it is likely that neither group (our predominantly US group nor the Israelis) came away with a better view of the other group or more understanding of them. This negative experience could damage future interactions that these individuals have with the other group because they may now have an unfavorable view of the other group.

REFLECTION VERSUS REFLECTIVE PRACTICE

If there is no intentional reflection on the experiences that happen outside of the structured course plan involving local people in the conflict zone, students' transformations may not be as meaningful. Reflection is seen as a key component for experiential learning, as it helps to connect experience with theoretical knowledge that people possess (Brown, Roediger, and McDaniel 2014; Dewey 1933; Kolb 1984). Moreover, study-abroad scholars advocate for reflection as the most important part of maximizing what students learn in study-abroad experiences (Anastasakos 2013; Donnelly-Smith 2009; Selby 2008). However, for students of peace and conflict, simply reflecting on their experience in the program is not enough. There needs to be an intentional focus on reflective practice, where their experiences can inform their future practice and they can develop ways of reflecting consistently whenever they engage in peacebuilding work (Warfield 2002). Many of the authors in this volume argue for the importance of debriefing and reflective practice to improve their students' ability to approach future conflict situations. Attending these programs provides students with the opportunity to become reflective practitioners, by learning to critically reflect on their positionality and impact in all future peacebuilding that they do. This mind-set will also allow them to realize how they have an impact on situations by simply being present in the conflict zone. This was the explicit focus of the Israel/Palestine course, and I have detailed how the focus on reflective practice helped to cement this understanding and these transformations for participants in the program.

Even as I write this chapter and reflect on the lessons that I gained from these courses and explore more broadly the types of transformation they can facilitate, my ability to do so comes from what I learned about reflective practice in them. Therefore, a focus on reflective practice not only helps to maximize learning and transformation throughout students' experience in a field-based course but can also help them develop habits of reflection that can assist them throughout their future practice in the peace and conflict field.

There is still much work to be done to fully grasp the potential of field-based courses in conflict areas for creating transformation in their participants, what these transformations are, and how they happen. However, this chapter shows that these courses can provide space for serious reflection on the role a student can play in the conflict they are studying and in future conflicts, as well as how to effect change in the conflict zone and beyond. The most important transformations that participants experience in these programs are the cultivation of a critical understanding of their role as interveners in conflict contexts and the development of a conviction to work in the conflict setting that they visit. Three essential factors for facilitating these transformations are flexibility in course design, positive interactions with local people in the conflict context, and students learning the importance of reflective practice to augment what they gain from these experiences. The better the faculty member is able to allow space for exploration and meaningful contact with local people and to facilitate thorough reflective practice to help digest these experiences, the more powerful the transformations experienced by participants are likely to be. With continued analysis and assessment of field-based courses in conflict zones, faculty members can become more intentional about designing experiences that maximize the transformation of participants throughout their time in these programs and build sustainable programs to maintain these transformations once participants return to their communities.

Notes

1. I would like to thank the editors of this volume, Agnieszka Paczyńska and Susan F. Hirsch, for their detailed comments on multiple revisions of this chapter. I am also grateful to the faculty members who taught the courses examined in this chapter for their feedback: Marc Gopin for the Israel/Palestine course and Borislava Manojlovic for the course in the Balkans. Further, I am grateful to Leslie Dwyer and David Joseph Smith for their comments on the initial draft of this chapter. Last but not least, I would like to thank Tobias Greiff for his feedback on conflicts in the Balkans.

2. Settlements, in the context of Israel/Palestine, refer to housing developments for Jewish Israeli citizens to live on plots of land in the West Bank, East Jerusalem, and the Golan Heights, areas that have been occupied by Israel since the war of 1967. Settlements were and are highly contested spaces because they are considered illegal by the international community and Palestinians view them as the Israelis' method of slowly moving onto Palestinian land, undermining the possibility of a two-state solution that would adhere to the pre-1967 borders. The continued building of settlements has been a huge roadblock in the negotiations between the Israelis and Palestinians for this reason.

3. In this section, I will focus on my personal experiences in each course and extrapolate from them to make arguments about the transformations that occur for students, based on my experience as both a student and staff member during these courses. I have also been looking back systematically at similar programs as part of my dissertation, which gives me further insight on analyzing and interpreting these experiences.

4. The United States played a role as part of NATO enforcing no-fly zones in Croatia and Bosnia beginning in 1994. This led to many Bosnian Serb planes being shot down and the NATO bombing of Serb targets in both Croatia and Bosnia. The United States' major role during the Yugoslav Wars was in Bosnia, where there were three warring factions: Bosnian Serbs, Bosnian Croats, and ethnic Bosnians. The United States pressured the ethnic Bosnians and the Bosnian Croats to agree to peace in 1994. Most significantly, NATO initiated a bombing campaign in 1995 supporting ethnic Bosnian and Bosnian Croat forces against Bosnian Serb forces in the wake of massacres, such as the Srebrenica massacre perpetuated by Bosnian Serbs. This series of bombings turned the tide of the war against the Bosnian Serbs and led to the Dayton Accords that ended the war in late 1995.

5. The conflict began between the Yugoslav army (consisting of predominantly Serb forces) and the Kosovo Liberation Army in 1998. The United States was part of a NATO-led bombing campaign intended to address the humanitarian crisis in Kosovo resulting from the expulsion of Kosovar Albanians after the failure of observation missions and peace talks. NATO continued air strikes until a peace agreement was reached in June 1999. These bombings remain controversial because the UN Security Council did not authorize them. Russian and Serb elites describe them as a violation of the sovereignty of the Federal Republic of Yugoslavia, while some legal scholars describe them as a legitimate intervention because of the humanitarian concerns of protecting ethnic Albanians who were being targeted in Kosovo. For a summary of this debate, see Albert Legault (2000).

ELEVEN

To Hell and Back with Good Intentions

Global Service Learning in the Shadow of Ivan Illich

ANTHONY C. OGDEN AND ERIC HARTMAN

This chapter offers a review of and strategies to support ethical practices in global service learning (GSL) programming. These practices are considered in light of an historical reflection on Ivan Illich's speech "To Hell with Good Intentions," delivered in Cuernavaca, Mexico, on April 20, 1968. The first section considers the historical context and primary assertions in that forceful and memorable speech, along with a comparison of the state of international education in the 1960s and today, over fifty years later. The second section considers the development of GSL, a distinct pedagogical and partnership practice within field-based learning, with emphasis on community-driven principles and reciprocity. The third section advances a challenging case study of a university-sanctioned international service program. The fourth section then considers Fair-Trade Learning (FTL), a recent innovation within GSL that is intended to address several of the challenges surfaced within the case study (Hartman, Paris, and Blache-Cohen 2014). With awareness comes responsibility: challenges for administrators and universities are considered in the fifth and final section. Instructional activities that build on Illich's perspectives and FTL that have been designed for program leaders to encourage socially responsible and ethical community engagement are publicly available (see Hartman and Ogden 2014; Ogden, Hartman, and Lutterman-Aguillar 2014) at https://compact.org/resource-posts/ftl/.

Ivan Illich and "To Hell with Good Intentions"

How astonishing it must have been to the assembly of US volunteers gathered in Cuernavaca to hear Illich speak. No doubt they were excited to be in Mexico for the summer as volunteers, likely even beaming proudly at their own self-worth. Imagine Illich, in his biting and sarcastic style, beginning his speech by calling all those present hypocrites and proclaiming his opposition to their presence in Latin America as "North American do-gooders." Many must have wondered how this philosopher, educator, and Roman Catholic priest could be so offended by their benevolence and eagerness to "share God's blessings" with poor Mexicans. Some must have been disheartened or even angered to hear his critique of them as "vacationing salesmen for the middleclass, American way of life" and his claims that all they can do is create disorder. Illich exclaimed that their efforts might create just enough problems "to get someone shot after your vacation ends and you rush back to your middleclass neighborhoods." The damage, he insisted, would come at too high a price for any belated insight they might have that they should not have been volunteers in Latin America in the first place. Illich urged those volunteers to recognize their inabilities, powerlessness, and incapacity to do the good they intended.

A lot has changed since 1968. As Illich spoke in Cuernavaca, the war in Vietnam was still raging. Martin Luther King Jr. had been assassinated only weeks before. The Peace Corps had been established, and had recently hosted over fifteen thousand volunteers, the largest number in the organization's history. Radical student activism embroiled US campuses. Today, communication outlets have expanded to allow citizen journalism and dramatically improved access to global media coverage. Increased access to global communication, trade, and transportation has blurred the lines between the Global North and South, while advancing awareness of global interconnectedness, whether in respect to supply chains or pollution effects. The United States has been served by an African American president, openly gay and transgender individuals have held numerous public offices, and yet domestic and global patterns and policies point toward a resurgent nationalism despite decades of increasing support for global cooperation.

Much has also changed in the area of international education, particularly with outbound student mobility (see table 11.1). In 1968, fewer

Table 11.1. International education: the 1960s and now

	1960s	Presently
Education abroad	< 25,000, junior year abroad for elite students, Western Europe	304,467
Research	Research question: Study abroad leads to . . .?	Increasingly complex outcomes assessment
Experiences types	Study abroad, volunteerism, mission trips	Study, research, teaching, service learning, internships
Program types	Direct enrollment, consortia	Bilateral exchanges, faculty-directed, third-party providers, etc.
Facilitating institutions	Largely church or state mechanisms, universities	Church, state, nonprofit, for-profit, universities and colleges
Governance	Laissez-faire	Forum standards, code of ethics, Clery Act
Program length	Predominately semester or year	Largest growth is in short-term programming of less than one semester
Communication	Letters take eight days or more	Constant communication with and connection to home

than twenty-five thousand students were studying abroad, mostly in Western Europe (Ogden, Soneson, and Weting 2010). Whereas the majority of US students abroad once participated in junior year abroad (JYA), or full academic year programs, only 3 percent do so today (IIE 2015b). Of the nearly 305,000 US students who received academic credit for education abroad in 2013–14, over 62 percent chose programs of less than eight weeks in duration. The term "education abroad" is now preferred over the traditional term of "study abroad" to more accurately reflect the emerging range of outbound educational opportunities. These now include study abroad, research abroad, intern abroad, teach abroad, and service learning abroad. Volunteer programs and international mission trips continue to be offered but are often facilitated by religious and/or private organizations, often because such experiences are not credit-bearing. Because many US university and college students now seek international educational opportunities as part of their home degrees, a variety of modes of student mobility have also emerged. The most commonly utilized modes in 1968 were direct enrollment and bilateral exchanges (Hoffa 2007). Some regional and national interinstitutional consortia were also active at the time, such as the Institute for the International Education of Students (IES Abroad) and the Council on International Educational Exchange (CIEE). Today the most rapidly growing and popular mode of educational mobility in the United States is the faculty-directed program, or those programs in which a faculty member or members from the home campus facilitate student learning abroad (Spencer and Tuma 2002).

As education-abroad programming has expanded in size and scope, so too have the professional associations and governing structures that support it. Although already well established in 1968, the focus of NAFSA: Association of International Educators was initially to promote the professional development of college and university officials responsible for assisting and advising international students studying in the United States. It was not until 1990 that the focus of the association expanded to reflect other aspects of international education and exchange, including education abroad. With over ten thousand members located at more than thirty-five hundred institutions worldwide, NAFSA has become the world's largest, and arguably one of the most influential, individual membership associations dedicated to international education and exchange. Founded in 2001, the Forum on Education Abroad is the only US-based organization in existence today whose exclusive purpose is to serve the profession of education abroad. Recognized by the US Department of Justice and the Federal Trade Commission as a standards development organization for education abroad, the forum promotes best practices and excellence in curricular design, engages in data collection and research, conducts program assessment and quality improvement, and advocates on behalf of its members and the profession of education abroad. What might have once been described as laissez-faire in 1968, US education-abroad programming is now supported by a thriving professional infrastructure and a growing body of increasingly complex and sophisticated research and scholarship (Ogden 2015).

Although much has indeed changed since 1968, some attributes and components have remained constant. When analyzing Illich's core positions, the changes, or lack thereof, in GSL programming in particular, are apparent (see table 11.2). During the past decade, portions of the "Illich argument" against international service and the challenges of true partnership have periodically resurfaced. For example, Illich's rebuke that most students cannot

Table 11.2. Today's best practices in reflection of Ivan Illich's core positions

Ivan Illich's core positions	Best practices today
Volunteers tend to impose projects on local people rather than finding out what local people want and need.	More systematic approaches to ensuring various kinds of community voice. More local communities can say, "Go to hell."
Volunteers cannot help being vacationing salesmen for the middle-class American way of life since that is really the only life they know.	More students who do global service learning are from low-income and immigrant families or have lived in other countries. Best-practice programs include increasingly complex predeparture coursework and orientations.
Volunteers are naive and hypocritical because they are blind to poverty at home.	Programs are designed for students to make connections between home and abroad. Going abroad brings clarity to global processes and structures, including how they influence issues at home.
There is no way to meet with the underprivileged since there is no common ground to meet on.	More programs provide opportunities to hear the voices of local community partners and even to live with them.
Volunteers should not pretentiously impose themselves on others.	Many groups now invite students to come learn from and/or with them and to work together in solidarity regarding issues of poverty, human rights, peace, environment, etc.
Volunteers unwittingly make the US government more palatable to people who have been harmed by US economic and military policies.	Many groups incorporate sophisticated analysis of US policies into the educational design, working together with local community partners to educate students, from a critical perspective, about how US policies have impacted their communities.
Most volunteers cannot speak the local language where they plan to conduct volunteer work.	Pressure to allow students to conduct service learning or even internships with minimal or no language skills.
Students should come to study but not come to help.	Many groups deconstruct colonial mind-sets by focusing on collaborative learning and community-driven service.
There is no common ground on which volunteers can engage with the local host communities.	More programs are designing opportunities for volunteers to hear the stories and perspectives of local community partners and to live with them and engage in service together. Programs are moving from a "needs-based" model to a "strengths or assets" model.

speak the local language where they plan to conduct volunteer work appears to remain unchanged. There seem to be pressures to allow students with minimal or no appropriate language skills to participate in GSL programs.

Illich also stressed that there is no common ground from which student volunteers can engage with local host communities, other than perhaps those host members belonging to the middle class. Illich pointed toward an issue that remains a challenge: host community families, community organization directors, and local business owners who host students are frequently unrepresentative of the community as a whole. Many programs still do not design opportunities for students to have significant engagement with diverse local people, particularly with those community members who are marginalized. Often such groups provide service for "underprivileged" people without ever having meaningful interaction with them. Critiques of this phenomenon are many and varied (Crabtree 2008; Larsen 2015; Prins and Webster 2010). Despite the challenges, these critiques search for mechanisms of engaging on ethical terms. As Jennifer Kozak and Marianne A. Larsen summarize in a recent edited volume on host community impact:

> Rather than abandoning the idea of responsibility in the process of developing ethical ISL [international service learning] relationships, we need to accept that responsibility to the "Other" exists within a profoundly uneven, post-colonial world.... We need to be open to the possibility of our subjectivity emerging through situations in which we take responsibility for and with the "Other," who may be each and every one of us. We (in the global North) are complicit in the power-laden relationships of responsibility that are centered on the unfounded belief that we can "save the world" through service. (2015: 275–76)[1]

That is to say, most communities that receive international volunteers and service learning students would like to continue doing so but often under better terms, which frequently include deeper respect, reciprocity, and commitment to coplanning and coleadership (Reynolds, 2014; Larsen, 2015). The effort to engage ethically has positively impacted several of the issues identified by Illich. For instance, Illich resisted the practice of volunteers imposing a predetermined project idea on local people rather than asking what local people want or need. Best-practice programs today are employing systematic approaches to ensure community voice. Illich also argued that volunteers are generally naive and hypocritical because they are blind to poverty at home. Fortunately, there appears to be more awareness today of the need to design programs for students to draw connections between home and abroad (Slimbach 2016; Sobania 2015). In other words, the time abroad can bring clarity to and a deeper understanding of issues at home and the interconnections among oppression and marginalization everywhere. Illich welcomed those who came to travel or study but not those coming to "help." As guidelines and other standards for GSL are being developed, recognized, and adopted, more groups are trying to focus on balancing study and service. Many institutions and organizations are even moving away from the arguably colonial and hierarchical language of "service" and toward "partnership," "engagement," and "reciprocity."

Illich's "To Hell with Good Intentions" speech echoes forcefully and clearly today. It reminds education-abroad professionals and service learning educators that it is unfair to impose predetermined projects and service on local communities that are not empowered as equals and respected players or, as Illich frankly put it, able to "tell you to go to hell." Illich, the "maverick social critic," casts a long shadow on global community engagement and service learning, requiring those of us in higher education who support and advance GSL programming to reflect critically on our "good intentions" and the ethical implications of this work (Madar 2010).

What Is Global Service Learning?

Combining overseas travel and service has long been an interest of US students, reaching back to the latter half of the nineteenth century when they began to pursue overseas missionary and volunteer programs (Hoffa 2007). Although such programming still continues, there has been a dramatic increase in recent years in the number and breadth of credit-bearing education-abroad programs that feature some component of deliberate community partnership or engagement. As national participation rates in education-abroad programs continue to increase and diversify (IIE 2015b), coupled with strong student and institutional interest in service learning (Branan 2008; Hollander and Saltmarsh 2000; Staywyse 2012), more US students are seeking GSL opportunities and other forms of community-engaged learning.

According to the 2015 findings of the National Survey of Student Engagement (NSSE), 52 percent of all incoming US college and university freshmen indicate an interest in service learning programming (NSSE 2015). Of graduating seniors, 61 percent report having actually participated in some form of service learning while an undergraduate. Another 50 percent report having had an internship or some form of field experience. The NSSE data also suggest that the level of interest is even higher for students interested in education abroad. The 2015 edition of the Institute for International Education report *Open Doors* confirms increasing interest in international experiential programming. In 2013–14, just over twenty-two thousand students participated in noncredit work, internships, and volunteering abroad, which is nearly 75 percent higher than the number reported just two years earlier (IIE 2015b). Yet it remains difficult to capture the precise number of students who are engaging in this type of learning.[2] Both the NSSE and the *Open Doors* reports are further complicated by a lack of shared methods. The NSSE relies on student self-reporting based on their (the students') own interpretations of what service learning is, for example. Additionally, numerous organizations recruit students and organize service trips with them but do not go through university infrastructures and are thus not counted in *Open Doors* tabulations.

The education-abroad community has not been alone in its struggle to determine how best to characterize service learning. In 2008, the Forum on Education Abroad issued the first edition of the *Education Abroad Glossary*, with the goal that it be used as a conventional practice in both the profession and research (Peterson et al. 2007). The glossary denotes a "service-learning program" as "a subtype of field study program in which the pedagogical focus is a placement in an activity that serves the needs of a community" (https://forumea.org/resources/glossary/). The first edition offers this definition of "service-learning abroad" (or "community-engaged learning"):

> A specially designed experience combining reflection with structured participation in a community-based project to achieve specified learning outcomes as part of a study abroad program. The learning is given structure through the principles of experiential education to develop an integrated approach to understanding the relationship among theory, practice, ideals, values, and community.

Key to this definition is the emphasis on reflection and structured experiences. It falls somewhat short by not emphasizing community-identified needs or assets and by not stressing that the service and learning goals are to be of equal priority and that each enhances the other. Significant thinking in the field of service learning (Sigmon 1979; Dostilo et al. 2012) suggests service learning programs should be distinguishable by their intention to "equally benefit the provider and the recipient of the service as well as to ensure equal focus on both the service being provided and the learning that is occurring" (Furco 1996, 12).

The intention of GSL programming is quite clearly to equally benefit the student and the local host as well as to ensure focus is equally on both the service being provided and the learning that is occurring (Furco 1996; Jacoby 1996; Stoecker and Tryon 2009). For example, an engineering student participating in a service learning program in Tamil Nadu, India, that focuses on sustainability issues might apply the knowledge and skills learned in the program's associated course to collaborate with a local organization focusing on biodiesel, biosap, biochar, or pyolysis oil. While the program is intended to support capacity at the local organization, the program equally supports the students in better understanding issues in renewable energy, engineering in the Global South, and social justice and global service impacts. In this program, the focus is equally on student and community benefit.

It is the ability to recognize and distinguish quality among such programs that will allow the education-abroad community to develop better and more sustainable program offerings that set up students and host partners for success. According to Steven Jones (2011), well-designed and -facilitated service learning can greatly enhance student learning abroad by providing new opportunities for students to engage with the course material in real-world settings. Students can practice new skills and methods and gain international perspectives on their chosen disciplines and future professions. Students may become more willing and able to think critically about the utility of generalizing these experiences to their work at home. Service learning potentially allows students to develop close ties with the local community and begin building an international network of service and partnership. The role of the student shifts from visitor or observer to one in which he or she is seen as a participant or trustworthy colleague.

Whereas education abroad involves learning in new academic contexts, service learning in international settings provides a civic-engagement dimension, including concepts of global citizenship (Ogden 2010).

The service learning field itself has generated increasing scholarship on GSL (Bringle and Hatcher 2011; Kiely 2004, 2005; Hartman and Kiely 2014; Larsen 2015; Porfilio and Hickman 2011) and has recently improved its capacity to identify key components of reciprocity, such as beginning with community voice, direction, input, and deepening understanding of what constitutes knowledge as well as appreciating the diversity of locations from which it develops. Eric Hartman and Richard Kiely's definition of GSL, for instance, starts with intentionality in soliciting community input. They suggest GSL is "a community-driven service experience that employs structured, critically reflective practice to better understand common human dignity; self; culture; positionality; socio-economic, political, and environmental issues; power relations; and social responsibility, all in global contexts" (2014, 60). In a recent review of conceptual framing within the field, Larsen (2015) highlights many of the key commitments of this definition, while noting its increasing numbers of adherents. Larsen suggests:

> As an immersive pedagogy, GSL views the process of learning differently from ISL in focusing on concepts of power, privilege, and hegemony; the broader contexts within which GSL is played out, such as the global marketization of voluntourism; and the responsibilities of the GSL student by engaging the critical global civic and moral imagination.... GSL scholars and practitioners heavily emphasize the value of local knowledge in the community, and often refer to local and international NGOs they partner with in terms of co-educators.... GSL represents a more progressive understanding of what constitutes knowledge, the source(s) of knowledge, and how that knowledge is acquired through learning. (2015, 14)

As will be further explained below, GSL is also conceptually consistent with FTL, a strategy for reciprocity within global community engagement. While these concepts have been part of national and international presentations, conversations, and publications for at least five years, practices continue to reflect the full gamut of possibilities, including the kinds of patterns Illich so persuasively rejected. In the next section, an existing program is presented. That presentation is followed by a discussion of how stronger adherence to key concepts in the field would improve its educational and community impacts.

CASE STUDY: "SERVICE-LEARNING" IN ETHIOPIA

Given the increasing popularity of education-abroad programs that feature some component of community engagement, it stands to reason that program value and quality will vary both within and across institutions. As there are exemplary service learning programs and notable best practices in education abroad (Hartman and Kiely 2014; IIE 2015a; Nolting et al. 2012; Tryon, Hood, and Taalbi 2013), so too are there problematic programs that include elements that challenge conscientious education-abroad professionals and service learning educators. Consider the following case study, based on an actual program model:

> The Department of Athletics at a southeastern public university offers a goodwill "service-learning" tour each summer for twelve to fifteen student athletes to visit three rural cities in Ethiopia. The stated purpose of the tour is to improve the lives of the people living in this African country. Students travel with about ten other university athletes to spend one week there building or repairing homes, delivering food and sports equipment, and helping families in need. The year 2015 was the third for this tour, and in previous years student contingents have painted houses and delivered mattresses to people who were sleeping on makeshift beds of hay and cardboard. One year, they installed a sink at a water pump to give the village more accessible drinking water. Other student contingents have planted vegetable gardens and fruit trees at orphanages and done odd jobs in a leper colony. Most members of these previous groups had never been out of the United States. One of institution's athletic directors leads the tour each summer because he and his wife adopted a child from Ethiopia and have some familiarity with Ethiopian culture. The week-long trip costs about $4,000 per student, not including airfare. The group meets once or twice before departing so members can meet each other and familiarize themselves with travel logistics and health and safety protocols. No academic credit is awarded.

From the perspective of encouraging diverse education-abroad participation and locations, the program has several merits. It has been designed for student athletes, who have been traditionally underrepresented participants in education abroad. They visit Ethiopia, which has long been a nontraditional destination for study among US students. The program is ongoing, and students appear to be actively engaged in tangible service projects while in Ethiopia, some of which appear to be sustainable.

On the other hand, the program is problematic in many ways. It is only one week in duration, which prevents students from having sustained contact with the local communities in three different Ethiopian cities. There is no clear articulation of a community-identified need, and the selection criteria for the three locations are unclear. While painting residences, delivering mattresses, building a community sink, and planting gardens may be a valuable service, the extent to which the group consults with the local communities it is serving is unclear. Additionally, by engaging in charity (mattress delivery) and physical projects (community sink, vegetable gardens), the program runs the risk of reenforcing ahistorical and decontextualized global learning (Andreotti 2014). Critical inquiry would consider why some societies differ markedly in terms of resource access, whether and how "development" is necessary, what "development" is, and—if appropriate—what social, economic, political, cultural, and structural change may be important to support locally driven conceptions of moving closer to "the good life."

With respect to the Forum on Education Abroad's definition of service learning, the program is problematic in several additional ways. For example, it is promoted as a service learning tour but might be more aptly described as a volunteer or community-service initiative. According to Furco, service learning programs should be distinguishable by their intention to equally benefit the student and the local partner. In this particular case, the goal of the program—perhaps naively—positions the local community as the sole beneficiary. Student learning is not explicitly mentioned. Although GSL programs are generally embedded in some academic context, this program does not offer an academic course, any type of academic credit, or any explicit venue for structured or guided learning and reflection. Perhaps most pernicious is that without critical reflection within a context of GSL, the experiences in Ethiopia may allow students to reinforce preconceived notions about Ethiopia, Africa, or development that justify asymmetrical relationships between them and their community partners (Crabtree 2008; Sharpe and Dear 2013; Stoecker and Tryon 2009). Many of these problems could potentially be avoided when program leaders proactively intervene by facilitating meaningful, respectful, and balanced reflection (Hartman 2014; McMillan and Stanton 2014; Vande Berg, Paige, and Lou 2012).

In *Experience and Education*, John Dewey asserts that experiences such as these can be both educative and miseducative: "An educative experience is one that broadens the field of experience and knowledge, brings awareness to bear, and leads in a constructive direction, toward intelligent action. A mis-educative experience is one that arrests or distorts growth and can lead one into routine action, thus narrowing the field of further experience" (Dewey 1938, 25; Rodgers 2002). Consider the following quotes from students and program leaders taken from a series of local newspaper interviews in which they describe their time in Ethiopia:

— "It was successful and impactful ... because what you saw was not good."

— "You see homeless and poor people in America but it was amazing because it was like our bus had celebrities on it. The people would surround the players' bus like mobs of fans do for tour buses of rock-and-roll bands. Only these mobs were interested in the possibility of being provided food and money."

— "There's a limit to what we can do, but the important things is for the young people to understand the world is a pretty big place and we're in a pretty fortunate place."

— "To see these really good kids ... go and give back and actually understand and recognize that they received more than they gave is really one of the more rewarding things you can experience."

As Illich, in his acerbic critique, forewarned, these particular students arguably did not return from Ethiopia with a deeper understanding of their inabilities or a better sense of their capacity to make meaningful contributions. Rather, these quotes suggest that students and program leaders returned feeling successful in meeting the goals of the tour and better about themselves, their own communities, and their relative fortunes and advantages in life. They sure do have it better back here at home! Did these students have a miseducative experience? In fact, existing research suggest that unless students have structured experiences and guided reflection, they generally do not return with measurable gains in social responsibility or global civic engagement (Braskamp, Braskamp, and Merrill 2009; Hartman 2014; Hartman et al. 2015; Ogden 2010; Paige, Stallman, and Josić 2008). Students generally do not report a greater awareness of global interdependence or improved ability to evaluate social issues and identify instances and examples of global injustice and disparity. If the goals of GSL include supporting students' capacities to respect diverse perspectives and construct an ethic of social responsibility to address global and local issues, then their programming experiences must be designed with ethical and reciprocal global engagement at their core.

Ethical Service Learning, Reciprocity, and Fair-Trade Learning

FTL is a concept that slowly emerged through global community development and international education partnerships over the past thirty years (Hartman 2015a). We offer it here as a best-practice model that contains clear strategies for advancing mutuality and reciprocity in respect to community and student outcomes. Having grown from the voices and desires of a host community in rural Jamaica, along with deep reading of the community and international development literatures (Chambers 1997, 2012; Farmer et al., 2013), FTL presents an alternative to purely student-centered international education. Instead, FTL places equal emphasis on community-driven goals and student experience and learning. As an approach to individual and community development and transformation, FTL is attentive to the role that intercultural learning and service programming can play in community economic development, while simultaneously focusing on building global solidarity. Although FTL has been widely discussed (Hartman, Paris, and Blache-Cohen 2014; Prado, Quezada-Grant, and Warren 2014), clarity on its purposes through four "C" commitments has emerged more recently through practice and is published here for the first time. The four commitments, which are further explained immediately below, highlight that FTL is community-driven, requires caring credibly, is capital conscious, and continuously connecting.

The *community-driven* commitment in FTL applies to the entire program, including representation, planning, implementation, evaluation, and continuous improvement. This commitment is further enumerated in the full set of FTL standards (Hartman, Paris, and Blache-Cohen 2014), which provide a structured set of commitments centered on deep respect and reciprocity. Consequently, as much attention is paid to community-driven outcomes and to student learning about ethical global engagement.

The core commitment to deep mutual respect informs all FTL conversations. Profound commitment to community voice and direction throughout program design and delivery is representative not only of historical commitments within service learning (Dostilio et al. 2012; Furco 1996; Sigmon 1979) but also reflects best practices in global development partnerships (Chambers 1997). In the Ethiopia case above, steps taken to ensure community voice (and therefore buy-in and sustainability) are not evident.

Caring credibly refers to ensuring that any volunteering or service interventions are informed by the repeated, empirically grounded documentations of harms visited upon individuals in Global South communities because of good intentions naively mobilized (Better Care Network 2014; Hartman 2014; Evert 2014). Caring credibly requires systematic protection of vulnerable populations and avoidance of certain specific activities, such as short-term volunteering in orphanages and clinical medical volunteering among individuals who are not professionally certified. Numerous individuals and communities have been harmed, often unintentionally, as students "serve" patients and orphans. While orphanages are mentioned in the case study above, steps taken to ensure conscientious engagement, protection, and empowerment of this vulnerable population are not clear. Indeed, the global coalition of child rights advocates organized to discourage short-term service with orphans (because of attachment issues, risk of abuse, documented cases of trafficking, and other ills) would suggest that responsible engagement is not possible when the experiences are so brief (Better Care Network 2014).

Capital conscious indicates that FTL includes financial transparency coupled with deliberate efforts to enhance equity and ensure just remuneration. While the UN World Tourism Organization estimates that only 5 percent of tourism dollars spent in developing country communities typically stays in those communities (due to the location of ownership of many companies), the community association in Petersfield, Jamaica, that inspired the FTL model has carefully distributed hundreds of thousands of dollars of investment in a transparent budgeting system in which roughly 70 percent of programming dollars stay in the area. A large portion of the remaining balance goes to airlines (Hartman, Paris, and Blache-Cohen 2012). Aside from direct charitable philanthropy, intentionality of economic investment stemming from the Ethiopia program is not clear.

Finally, FTL prioritizes *continuous connecting*, in the sense that ethical and intentional travel includes efforts to build global solidarity. FTL therefore explicitly includes facilitated growth opportunities for community members, students, and other stakeholders to leverage the experiences toward lifelong global civil society and global citizenship commitments. There is no evidence that the Ethiopia program supported students' growth into responsible and continuous global civil society roles.

The concept of FTL and, specifically, FTL standards have immediate application for US education-abroad programs that emphasize community-engaged learning, particularly service learning programs. Compared with other frameworks for global engagement that involve undergraduate students, FTL offers an approach that is continuously and carefully attentive to holding community members and students in equal regard. FTL is mindful of the interaction and simultaneity of community and student participation, needs, vulnerabilities, and transformation. The extent to which FTL standards or any other framework will be adopted universally within education-abroad programming is precarious and will depend largely on the influential role and positioning of the campus-based education-abroad office.

Between a Rock and a Hard Place

As GSL becomes more popular among US students, the number of active stakeholders invested in this emerging mode of education-abroad programming is growing. Since the 1980s, higher-education institutions have begun to embrace community service and civic engagement. Supported by organizations such as Campus Compact, more institutions are utilizing service learning, both domestically and abroad, as a means to engage students in service and support their growth as critical and conscious citizens. Many institutions are now seeking the Carnegie Community Engagement classification as a way to have their commitment recognized (Driscoll 2006). Administrative staff members are similarly active players and are building international programs, including service learning and volunteer programs. This is most readily seen in the rise of alternative service breaks, or those service-oriented programs that engage student groups in some form of short-term community service, both domestically and internationally. Private-sector organizations are also present on US campuses and generally target student clubs and organizations with noncredit, international programming.

Charged with directing this motley chorus of well-intentioned players—at least as they relate to international experiences—is the campus education-abroad office. Seemingly caught between a rock and a hard place, it is the education-abroad office that is most often responsible for managing all aspects of international program development, management, and implementation. On one side are increasing student demands, new levels of faculty and staff engagement, greater attention and involvement from senior leadership, and private organizations vying for student attention. On the other side are mounting pressures for ensuring the health, safety, and security of students, managing institutional risk, upholding academic guidelines for quality and integrity, adhering to industry standards and best practices such as FTL, and maintaining collective aspirations for ethical and respectful service learning programs. Many offices are caught within the constraints of institutional policies that govern or restrict their responsibility and authority. For example, many education offices have responsibility for only credit-bearing, international programs, which in turn fortunately allows for the implementation of required faculty training, student orientation, outcomes assessment, and internal levels of oversight and approval. Noncredit programs are generally managed within the home sponsoring unit and thus operate independently of the education-abroad office and the support services such offices provide. The case study presents one very real example. Moreover, private-sector organizations offering non-credit-bearing international programs are seldom vetted or approved and most always operate outside of the education-abroad office. Education-abroad offices generally have little knowledge or provide any oversight of these programs but are often required to respond to program-related emergencies and student problems.

Though caught between the goals of international education and the vagaries of global student mobility, it is the responsibility of the education-abroad community to ensure the smooth development and implementation of quality GSL programs. Fortunately, there are a number of helpful resources currently available to education-abroad professionals that can be leveraged when working alongside senior leadership, faculty, staff or private-sector organizations. Of particular note is the GlobalSL.org website (https://compact.org/global-sl/), which amasses evidence-based tools and peer-reviewed research to support community-campus partnerships advancing global learning and cooperative development. It is edited and overseen by researchers and practitioners who represent diverse fields, all concerned with the question of how to responsibly and ethically grow partnerships between educational institutions and communities.[3]

The Education Abroad Faculty Toolkit (http://www.uky.edu/toolkit/), currently hosted and maintained at the University of Kentucky, also offers an array of pedagogically sound instructional activities that can be integrated into courses offered through education-abroad programs. It was designed with respect to two primary focus areas, global citizenship and academic development. Specific course objectives have been written for each focus area and are supported by an array of instructional tools that can either be integrated into course syllabi or facilitated as one-time activities. Each tool is explained in a one-page document that provides a brief description of the tool, noting its objectives, materials needs, and recommended method of evaluation. Each tool is supported with a student handout and/or related instructional documents. Additionally, scales to measure global citizenship and academic development are provided alongside abstracts from outcomes assessment studies that have used these scales. The toolkit is free and aims to provide a much-needed resource for those planning and directing education-abroad programs. Tools based on the Illich speech and FTL can be found on the Education Abroad Faculty Toolkit site at http://www.uky.edu/toolkit/to-hell-with-good-intentions and can be used to encourage students to assess GSL from a critical perspective, reflect on their motivations for engaging in such programs, and develop a better understanding of social responsibility and ethical community engagement.

~

Careful, conscientious, ethical, and responsible global engagement is rife with possibility. Considerable evidence demonstrates students who participate in quality global engagement experiences learn more deeply (Bringle and Hatcher 2011), have meaningful experiences (Kiely 2004, 2005; Porfilio and Hickman 2011), and contribute to communities in diverse and consequential ways (Larsen 2015; Lough and Matthew 2014; Reynolds 2014). Yet it is equally clear that this methodology of global learning and cooperative development is rife with risk. Students may solidify stereotypes, have miseducative experiences, and even harm communities (Crabtree 2008; Gorski 2008; Hartman and Kiely 2014; Larsen 2015; Lasker 2016). Contemporary GSL scholarship emphasizes not only an ethos of reciprocity and mutuality but also recognizes that all contact has consequences (Gorski 2008; Larsen 2015). A postcolonial perspective has been introduced into this effort, urging us not only to consider mutual consequences but also to ask "how and why it is that the impact of ISL on student learning outcomes has been framed as a problem to be studied and improved, while the impact of ISL on host communities has not. What are the socio-historical conditions that make it (im)possible for us to think about host communities in particular ways?" (Larsen 2015, 10).

This promising, historically grounded, critical vein of inquiry forces us to face the complicated history of service. Larsen references Edward Said (1979), explaining, "In service to the colonial, imperial project, the Orientalist paradigm allowed European scholars to represent the East/Orient as inferior and backward, and the West as superior" (Larsen 2015, 12). In such complicated space, FTL has emerged as a strategy for reciprocity. It is an approach that simultaneously engages the essential, complicated space of rigorous global education, with all of its attendant needs to unlearn, historicize, contextualize, and relearn, while also engaging the incredibly complex space of meaningful global development partnerships.

Attending to the four principles above, with close adherence to the entire standards set (Hartman, Paris, and Blache-Cohen 2014; Hartman 2015a), will significantly enhance the quality of student learning and community experience. Readily applicable, transferable, and downloadable teaching tools, partnership resources, videos, guidelines, and rubrics are available at https://compact.org/resource-posts/ftl/. Fifty years after Illich's compelling critique, some of the field's concepts and practices have begun to proffer a response—and a response that is grounded in desires and ideals that grew from the Global South. As international education and global development partnerships continue to move forward, a key task is to ensure that education-abroad administrators, faculty, staff, and students consider and address these important issues before engaging in GSL or similar activities. Too many institutions and young people continue to learn from the mistakes born of not first considering Illich (Bennett and Papi 2014; Biddle 2014) or neglecting to engage best-practice models born of decades of global development and education-abroad research and experience.

Notes

1. Kozak and Larsen further this argument supported by Eric Hartman (2015b), Benjamin J. Lough and Lenore E. Matthew (2014), Nora P. Reynolds (2014), and Cynthia Toms (2013).

2. The *Open Doors* annual report provides the most widely utilized and reliable dataset for US education-abroad enrollment. Unfortunately, the report does not yet differentiate between program types. *Open Doors* does not yet distinguish between volunteering, service learning, and other forms of community-engaged learning. In other words, credit-bearing service learning and internship participant numbers are not included in the above figures but are instead accounted for in overall credit-bearing enrollment figures.

3. The site contains (1) a GSL research wiki that pulls together research relevant to community-university partnerships, pedagogy, and student and community outcomes; (2) a tools and syllabi wiki that compiles resources relevant for

program development, reflective exercises, community partnership, and course development; (3) Web resources relevant to community-driven development, justice, human rights, and critically reflective experiential education; and (4) a blog for discussions relevant to partnerships for global learning and cooperative development.

Conclusion

Best Practices and Next Directions

SUSAN F. HIRSCH AND AGNIESZKA PACZYŃSKA

The chapters in this volume document the multiple levels of learning that students experience when they engage fully in a field-based course in a conflict zone. At the same time, the chapters also articulate the many concerns raised by such courses and emphasize repeatedly the necessity of careful planning before a course starts and vigilant monitoring throughout. With the intention of fostering instructors' ability to mount field-based courses, this conclusion begins with an overview of the best practices gleaned from the chapters. Subsequent sections focus on two areas of best practice that are key to ensuring the success of field-based courses: preparing students and preparing faculty. Our emphasis on careful planning notwithstanding, it is also the case that even the most prepared instructor of a field-based course in a conflict zone cannot fully anticipate all of the learning and personal transformation that students (and faculty) will experience while on a field-based course and afterward. The consequence is that those of us who take on these courses not only have to plan thoroughly, but also we must remain flexible, creative, and ready to leave our comfort zones to pursue the deep and myriad learning experiences promised by field-based courses. Field-based courses in conflict zones are proliferating, and new ideas are emerging all the time. Although limited, scholarship about these courses is growing. The final sections of this chapter outline new directions for research on field-based courses in conflict zones.

Overview of Best Practices

A number of best practices emerge from the chapters in this volume. They pertain to preparing students and faculty prior to the field-based course, developing ethical research and practice skills before and during the course, and ensuring that the course generates deep, transformative learning. Other best practices address how to forge the most effective links between field-based courses and the overall curriculum and how to engage most constructively and ethically with the communities and organizations with whom students and faculty partner during these experiences.

One of the most challenging aspects of field-based courses that take students into a conflict zone are the ethical dilemmas that they will face and the ethical choices they will need to make, often in contexts that are unfamiliar and stressful and frequently with little time in which to make choices. In particular, when working in conflict zones, ensuring that students do no harm is especially important. Training in ethical practice and ethical research skills is essential both prior to students going to the field and during the course itself. Not all situations can be anticipated, and therefore unexpected ethical dilemmas are bound to emerge during the course. Preparing students to consider ethics as they engage with communities and helping them to recognize common ethical challenges that may arise are essential. As the chapters in this volume make clear, these can include the tendency to commodify the learning experience, to objectify people (including local partners) whose lives appear so different, and to seek out "authentic" relationships and experiences without considering the economic and power dimensions that shape the entire experience. Studying ethical practice and research through prior coursework within the curriculum and in cocurricular activities helps prepare students for the ethical complexities of field-based practice and research. On-the-ground reinforcement of these lessons is an invaluable learning experience.

The authors in this volume also note the importance of critical reflection and reflective practice during the course as an essential component of field-based courses. Much of the learning happens through the reflection that students engage in, whether individually, in group discussions, or in conversations with faculty. It is therefore essential to incorporate ongoing reflection, dialoguing, and journaling into field-based courses. Such reflection activities facilitate the development of critical self-assessment skills and help students think about their positionality in the context in which they are situated. Depending on the nature of the field-based course, best practices for reflection can include one or more daily meetings, debriefings after any significant experience, and required daily journaling. Instructors should be aware that an action-packed course may not leave enough time for solitary journaling, and students can be encouraged to experiment with on-the-fly reflection strategies, such as audio-recording their thoughts and jotting notes to expand on later.

Reflective dialogues, often in the form of postactivity debriefings, allow faculty to guide students through the challenges of a field-based course where students are often pushed out of their comfort zones and confront difficult ethical dilemmas. Reflection also helps faculty in maintaining the often difficult balance between ensuring that students have the needed support and guidance while also allowing them to experience failure. A debriefing that dissects an activity that failed to go as planned is often the place where the most transformative learning takes place.

The quality of learning in field-based courses in conflict zones depends in part on how courses fit into overall curriculum as well as how a field-based portion fits into the broader learning objectives of a longer course. Students benefit when what happens in a field-based course or a service learning project is clearly linked to what they are doing in the traditional classroom as well as in their overall program of study. In other words, as shown in chapters 4, 5, 6, and 8, learning is deepened when there is a close connection between the theories students learn in the classroom and the service learning approaches or field-based practice and research in which they engage. Ideally, the overarching aims of a degree program, or even an entire institution, reinforce the orientation of the field-based course. For instance, a strong commitment to social justice or to building peace can be the frame for a course that reflects broader institutional values.

Finally, it is important to pay attention to how students and faculty engage with the communities and organizations with whom they work and partner. Ensuring that service learning and field-based courses are grounded in respect for local partners and that students and faculty are committed to the values of reciprocity, listening, and hearing what the communities have to say about what they need are basic principles that should underpin field-based courses. Coplanning and coleading with community partners should be emphasized and never sacrificed for the sake of convenience. Students and faculty need to be committed to learning from the communities and not seeing their own role as solving community problems. Rather, they need to be humble about what their role is. At the same time, the chapters emphasize the importance of developing clear and transparent expectations for what and how students and faculty will be engaging with the community or organization in order to minimize misunderstandings, unrealistic expectations, and ethical and moral lapses. Most chapter authors underscore the need to establish and maintain long-term relationships with the communities and organizations with whom the students work in order to foster trust and mutual respect.

For many of the volume's authors, finding constructive and creative ways to give back to the communities is essential. Examples include providing services that the community requests (a conflict assessment or a training, for instance), speaking publicly about what they have learned once they return from the field, and publishing their research results. Students and faculty should be aware of the subtle "convening" role that their presence as third parties might play in a community. In other words, they might be a catalyst for bringing together people who do not usually undertake activities together. Through this function, community members might be better positioned to address long-standing issues, or they might simply become more accustomed to being together, which might have benefits in the future. Long-term partnerships allow for the exploration of additional forms of mutual benefit, such as developing revenue streams for individuals and communities that provide services to the course participants in the form of lectures, food, materials, or housing. In terms of best practices, sustainability and "do no harm" should be the guiding principles for giving back to communities.

Preparing Students for Field-Based Courses

All authors in the volume underscore the point that preparing students for field-based courses in conflict zones requires significant attention prior to the beginning of the field component of a course. Preparation needs to go beyond the nuts of bolts of travel (e.g., what to pack, what shots are needed, what the dress code is) to involve providing students with knowledge of the context in which they will be working—the history, politics, and culture—as well as ensuring that students recognize their own positionality vis-à-vis the communities with whom they will be working. This preparation also involves equipping the students with the skills that they will need for the kind of practice or research to be undertaken during the course, be it facilitation, interviewing, or teaching conflict assessment skills, among others. In service learning courses, ensuring that students feel that they have ownership of their own learning is important. This sense of ownership is fostered by including students in the planning of the service learning experience, whether by involving them in the development of the course itinerary—where they will go, whom will they speak with—or through crafting of the project plans, which then allows them to monitor their progress in accomplishing the goals and objectives. Including students in the planning for a course will help them understand more fully why they are engaging in the work and thus guarantee strong commitment and concerted attention to the activities.

Preparing students adequately for these courses depends on getting them comfortable with a different kind of learning that contrasts with the typical classroom-based lecture and discussion. These courses work especially well within a curriculum where there are many other experiential learning opportunities and where innovation in teaching is valued by the institution. In our chapter, we discussed in-class experiential learning activities (ELAs) and argued that they are an especially effective way for introducing students to the complex social dynamics and the ethical dilemmas they will encounter during field-based courses. Through these activities, students also develop the skills that they will need to be successful in a field-based course (see chapter 1). Simulations and role plays can be crafted to develop particular skills that come into use during field-based courses, whether students are conducting a conflict assessment, facilitating a contentious conversation, or designing a training, among others. The activities can be adapted to short or long classroom sessions or can be run across multiple meetings, depending on the curricular and time constraints of a particular course. Likewise, they can be more structured, such as the ELA Community at Odds in Voinjama, Liberia: An Introduction to Conflict Intervention discussed in chapter 1, or allow more room for improvisation, depending on the learning objectives an instructor seeks to accomplish.

Because many of the field-based courses discussed in this volume expect students to engage with partners and others through intervention, the students require not only various forms of knowledge but also skill sets with which they have at least some experience. Through experience with facilitating a meeting, setting up a dialogue, or performing a conflict assessment, students can also hone the more intangible abilities that are useful in ethical practice, such as patience, confidence, efficiency, and good communication. Such abilities are difficult to teach, but personal levels of ability can be better understood and improved in a learning context. Courses focused on conflict resolution practice, especially those that take a reflective practice approach, can also be key sites for learning about and improving one's approach to practice in the field. These activities cultivate self-awareness and an ability to reflect on one's actions, including their consequences and significance. The connection between reflective practice and ethical practice can be seamless. In such courses students can learn a lot through reading and discussing case studies of ethical dilemmas and codes of conduct for ethical practice. Incorporating writing assignments that ask students to reflect on in-class or outside-class activities can also be a way to familiarize them with engaging in reflective practice. Many students are more familiar with and therefore more confident when writing analytical papers, in which their emotions, fears, doubts, and aspirations are not discussed or considered. Allowing students to acclimate themselves to putting their actions, perspectives, and emotions at the center of writing assignments gives them an opportunity to engage in reflective practice prior to participating in a field-based course. These assignments should also encourage students to reflect on the impact of their actions, perspectives, and emotions on others in order to foster critical thinking and perspective-taking. Moreover, through these exercises, students learn skills that ultimately might be useful to partners in the conflict resolution field.

Outside-class activities, such as dialogue processes, service learning activities, peer mediation programs, and some internships, can also accustom students to the kinds of engagement that they will experience in field-based courses. Various cocurricular activities can also be incorporated into the preparation of students for field-based courses. For instance, such activities as peer mediation programs, peace cafés, and dialogues provide the contexts where students can acquire specific skills that will prepare them for work they will be engaged in during a field-based course. They also offer students the opportunity to apply those skills in real-world settings yet in an environment that is familiar and therefore less stress-inducing. Students can practice mediating conflicts among fellow students or facilitating dialogues among members of the university community around deeply divisive and contentious issues, such as gun rights, abortion, and immigration policies, while being guided and supported by faculty mentors. Although these cocurricular activities unfold in a more familiar environment than the one students will encounter in a field-based course, nonetheless they allow students to experience the unpredictability of social interactions, whether it is a heated exchange between people whose views differ or the long silence at a dialogue table when no one seems ready to engage with others. By encountering these unpredictable interactions, they can become more familiar with their own responses and reactions in such contexts. Some of the ethical dilemmas that they are likely to encounter during field-based courses, such as how to respond to a complex social dynamic and how to not overpromise, can be experienced in these activities. Consequently, the students can reflect on their emotions and actions in such contexts as well as on how they recognized ethical dilemmas, how they resolved them (or not), and how they might respond when confronted with a similar dilemma in the future, perhaps on less familiar ground. Even when these activities are undertaken independently by students rather than as part of coursework, faculty can seek out opportunities to reinforce the connection between these activities and both classroom learning and field-based learning. Faculty support for practice activities held outside class could enhance the likelihood that these important connections are made.

A comprehensive approach to learning is the best way to prepare students, especially with respect to the conflict field. By this we mean coordination across courses and between courses and extracurricular activities. There are challenges to this kind of curricular planning as faculty are not always motivated to think in a concerted or coordinated way about what they teach and how they teach. Power dynamics in a department can make this a threatening conversation for those less empowered or lacking the skills to engage in experiential teaching. The increased reliance on adjunct teaching further compounds the difficulty of involving faculty in detailed discussions of curriculum that are ongoing year to year. There are few direct incentives for initiating these conversations or participating in them, and the risk involved can be daunting, especially for junior faculty and adjunct instructors. In short, finding the time and the political will for the kinds of discussions that will lead to curricular change toward more effective experiential learning can be difficult. In our experience the growth of experiential learning in our academic unit became the catalyst for broader curricular change across our degree programs. The lesson we learned is that, when space for discussion of curriculum is opened, instructors of field-based courses have many insights to offer toward meaningful curricular reform.

Preparing Faculty for Field-Based Courses

Field-based courses have grown in popularity for many reasons, including because they boost a university's reputation and ranking. We want to emphasize here that these courses have also become popular among faculty. On the one hand, putting together a field-based course means solving organizational and logistical problems that can seem formidable, yet on the other hand the prospect of time away from the regular classroom routine can be enticing. Of course, some faculty most decidedly do not want to teach outside the traditional classroom. For others, even the thorny challenges associated with field-based courses can be invigorating. For faculty who relish this kind of course, the experiential approach to learning is a decided plus. Moreover, ensuring that a course is not simply a voyeuristic exercise is just one of the ethical challenges that can motivate an educator; teaching an ethically grounded field-based course can be a form of political practice for a committed instructor, especially when the substance of the course addresses issues close to his or her heart. For instructors and administrators, the challenge of coordinating these courses with traditional curriculum or curriculum delivered electronically can be intellectually challenging too. The chapters in this volume provide many examples of what else we, as faculty, get out of these courses. For instance, they can be opportunities to cultivate intellectual and personal connections with our students that are not possible inside the classroom or through online education. Experiencing the same conditions of conflict together can add a new layer to the intersubjective relationship between student and teacher. When our partners in the field are also considered, the student-teacher relationship takes on new textures, complexities, and value. Through field-based courses, instructors can deepen their own relationships with partners with whom they might pursue constructive and meaningful projects over the course of years.

It is hard to deny that these courses might seem adventurous and that sometimes as faculty we fall into the same trap as our students in wanting an exciting experience outside the routine of classroom lecture and discussion. The instructor who makes it up as he or she goes along might be a motivating image for some. But such a cavalier approach could be a recipe for disaster when students and local partners are involved. Throughout the volume chapters, authors offer many examples that can help faculty prepare for these courses, even for the unanticipated occurrences that will most surely arise. Highlighting best practices that can be distilled into training for faculty or be used to build a knowledge base is imperative. With respect to preparing faculty for field-based courses, best practices include pre-trip trainings that emphasize pedagogy and ethics, staff support for logistical elements, and adequate recognition by university administration of the many forms of support that faculty who engage in these courses might need, including financial.

Many of the chapters emphasize debriefings as integral to the learning process for students. Often we fail to recognize that courses are also learning experience for instructors, especially for new instructors. In our estimation, debriefing is a best practice for faculty, yet the opportunities for debriefing during and after field-based courses might be limited. With the goal of increasing the opportunities for debriefings for faculty, our own view is that most field-based courses should involve coinstructors. There are many good reasons for this position; however, the opportunities for on-the-spot debriefing is chief among them. Relatedly, coteaching can provide the checks needed to be sure that a course is on track ethically and that multiple perspectives can be marshaled to address any ethical challenges that arise. Providing opportunities for more comprehensive debriefing after the field-based portion of a course is also important and can yield new insights into many aspects of this type of teaching. Faculty and staff with experience in field-based learning can play key roles as sounding boards and mentors for faculty who seek to debrief.

Topics on the Horizon

One of the most difficult challenges is creating field-based courses that are sustainable institutionally; sustainability should include the requirement that field-based courses be accessible to the widest possible range of students. Several of our authors have developed approaches to financial sustainability through engaging students in fundraising, identifying donors, securing financial aid for students, or leveraging institutional funds to cover the expenses of those unable to afford a travel-based course. However, more attention to the issue of sustainability is warranted. Perhaps additional evidence of the worth of field-based courses, produced through the types of research mentioned in this section, could be used to convince administrators to build field-based options into basic tuition and fees.

What is likely to be a steady increase in field-based courses offered in conflict zones is already prompting scholarship on a range of topics, and more will be forthcoming. For instance, gaining more nuance and more precision in the assessment of student learning as a result of such courses is an imperative. Not only will more attention to what is learned on these trips answer some questions about the design of these courses, but such scholarship will also put to rest suspicions about the "lightweight" intellectual nature of learning outside the classroom. The emphasis on measuring student learning tracks the growth in "audit culture" across academic institutions, which demands an accounting of the "results" of any educational initiative. Yet assessing the impact of these courses might require expansion and transformation of the approaches taken to measuring that impact. This in turn might contribute to increasing the incorporation of these pedagogical approaches into the curriculum.

For instance, evaluating the quality of teaching as it relates to these courses would be enhanced by using different measures than the standard teaching evaluation forms that students fill out at the end of a course. In the intensity of finishing a field-based course, students and faculty alike usually find it difficult to judge the course's success, including what they learned or taught effectively and what impacts were made. The logistical snafus and personal challenges that are virtually unavoidable during field-based courses make their way into the ratings on conventional evaluation forms perhaps to a greater degree than they might in a conventional course. While some students express extremely positive personal transformation as a result of field-based courses, others experience profoundly destabilizing reactions; both of these are intended, yet their effects on student responses to traditional evaluation questions might fail to capture the extent and value of what they have learned. Offering students a range of ways to evaluate field-based courses is, at a minimum, a strategy to surmount this problem. One option is to convene students after the field-based portion through a focus group or an online discussion of the course. Student might also be encouraged to provide feedback to staff or administrators who have knowledge of field-based learning and/or responsibilities for field-based learning programs. Long-term evaluation of field-based learning experiences is especially important, as the effects of field-based courses may not emerge for years (Lazarus 2011). It can be difficult for faculty to keep in touch with students in the years following a program; thus, a unit- or school-wide approach to surveying the alumni of field-based trips might be best.

From our own experience, peer-to-peer evaluation of teaching, whereby another instructor accompanies the group during a portion of the field-based course, was extremely important in helping us to improve the courses that we created through our Department of Education grant. However, unless funded externally, such an evaluation is not easy to undertake. An on-site evaluator was instrumental in literally seeing instances of student learning, and also elements that detracted from it, that were not apparent to the instructors. Debriefings during the course and afterward yielded many insights into the challenges of field-based courses and how to surmount them. Evaluators might want to be aware that, in our experience, each time an evaluator accompanied a course, dramatic developments repositioned the evaluator, turning her into a coinstructor, a mediator, or a sounding board as a crisis emerged. These experiences only deepened our appreciation of the complexity of field-based courses in conflict zones and generated new approaches, such as a program of pairing experienced instructors with faculty who had not yet run a field-based course.

Another area for research exploration is inquiry into how participation in field-based courses has shifted the ways in which faculty teach. We have both made changes in our own teaching, in particular expanding our use of experiential learning in the traditional classroom, adding opportunities for students to engage in reflection, both through writing assignments and through debriefings following experiential learning activities, and more directly connecting what we do in our classes to cocurricular activities. In one of our courses, for instance, students prepare and then facilitate a dialogue event that tackles a current, controversial topic such as immigration policies and race relations in the United States and then mount that event, which is open to the whole university community. Through such activities, students are provided with additional opportunities to hone the skills they will need when they embark on a field-based course in a conflict zone and when they enter the job market. Our involvement with experiential learning has also changed our graduate teaching, as we encourage graduate students, especially doctoral candidates, to seek out opportunities to learn how to teach experientially and to practice such teaching. One of us mounted a course for graduate students that focused on supporting experiential learning school-wide. An example of experiential learning itself, this course involved students in conducting and assessing ELAs in undergraduate classrooms, organizing an experiential learning workshop for the campus, and creating video debriefings of instructors following field-based courses. Through these experiences of teaching and research about experiential learning, these graduate students gained valuable insight and experience potentially relevant to future employment.

Online learning as a companion to field-based courses is an area ripe for new research. Admittedly, we have not ventured too far into online learning in the courses that we have mounted, yet this ever-increasing option for course delivery cannot be ignored. As a practical matter when traveling, it is easier and more efficient to use an online platform to share course materials. That said, lack of access to the Internet can be a barrier! Delivering part of the course online can circumvent the problem of convening students for pre-trip and post-trip meetings. The possibilities for incorporating online learning into field-based courses are myriad, and we look forward to research that will begin to establish best practices.

Our last topic on the horizon is perhaps the most important. Very little research has been done from the perspective of the individuals and communities whose willingness to work with faculty and students makes possible field-based courses. Throughout this volume we have emphasized the importance of establishing strong, transparent, respectful, and mutually beneficial relationships with local partners. Yet it is still difficult to answer key questions: Do all our efforts to treat partners fairly, ethically, and as full participants in certain activities of the course have the effects we intend? Are we creating experiences that are true partnerships? At a minimum, field-based courses should build in evaluation of the activities that we undertake with partners and analysis of the findings should inform future collaboration. Yet the importance of these partnerships implies the need for more in-depth inquiry beyond routine evaluations. Other questions for research include: How much does our engagement in local contexts matter to our partners? What is their image of a successful collaboration? Ethically, and in order to create sustainable courses, we need good answers to these questions.

Field-based courses, including field-based courses in conflict zones, are increasingly popular at institutions of higher learning. As the chapters in this volume have emphasized, locating field-based courses in conflict zones does not necessarily mean taking students to far away locales. Conflict zones can be found many time zones away but also in communities not far from our universities and colleges. This approach means that students who may not be able to participate in courses that involve long-distance travel can still benefit from the transformative learning that these types of courses offer. Encouraging institutions of higher learning to support the development and teaching of a wide range of field-based courses is therefore essential. By creating more robust assessment tools and identifying best practices, we can be better positioned to show our institutions how students (and faculty) benefit from participating in such courses and their value to students' education. At the same time, we need to recognize that field-based courses in conflict zones are very diverse and even idiosyncratic. It is not easy to quantify the transformative learning generated by the challenges—ethical, emotional, and analytical—that students face and overcome when pushed out of their comfort zones. Yet it is the experience of grappling with these challenges—whether students manage to succeed or fail on any one occasion—that makes field-based courses so valuable for educating students to be more skilled, confident, and self-reflective researchers and practitioners.

REFERENCES

AACU (Association of American Colleges and Universities). "High-Impact Educational Practices: A Brief Overview." Accessed September 2, 2016. http://www.aacu.org/leap/hips.

Aall, Pamela R., Jeffrey W. Helsing, and Alan C. Tidwell. 2007. "Addressing Conflict through Education." In *Peacemaking in International Conflict: Methods and Techniques*, 1st ed., edited by I. William Zartman, 327–53. Washington, DC: United States Institute of Peace.

Abu-Nimer, Mohammed. 1999. *Dialogue, Conflict Resolution, and Change: Arab Jewish Encounters in Israel*. Albany, NY: SUNY Press.

———. 2004. "Education for Coexistence and Arab-Jewish Encounters in Israel: Potential and Challenges." *Journal of Social Issues* 60 (2): 405–22.

Adwan, Sami, and Dan Bar-On. 2000. *The Role of Non-Governmental Organizations in Peacebuilding between Palestinians and Israelis*. Jerusalem: Peace Research Institute in the Middle East.

———, eds. 2006. *Learning Each Other's Historical Narrative: Palestinians and Israelis*. Peace Research Institute in the Middle East. http://vispo.com/PRIME/narrative.pdf.

Allport, Gordon W. 1954. *The Nature of Prejudice*. Reading, MA: Addison-Wesley.

Al Ramiah, Ananthi, and Miles Hewstone. 2013. "Intergroup Contact as a Tool for Reducing Resolving, and Preventing Intergroup Conflict: Evidence, Limitations, and Potential." *American Psychologist* 68 (7): 527–42.

Altbach, Phillip G., and Jane Knight. 2007. "The Internationalization of Higher Education: Motivations and Realities." *Journal of Studies in International Education* 11 (3–4): 290–305.

Amulya, Joy. 2004. *Guide to Integrating Reflection into Field-Based Courses*. Center for Reflective Community Practice. Accessed September 15, 2011. http://bit.ly/20uG2PL.

Anastasakos, Vasiliki. 2013. "Teaching Peace through Short-Term Study Abroad: Long-Term Benefits for Students and Faculty." In *Peacebuilding in Community Colleges*, edited by David J. Smith, 105–18. Washington, DC: United States Institute of Peace Press.

References

Andreasson, Stefan. 2005. "Orientalism and African Development Studies: The 'Reductive Repetition' Motif in Theories of African Underdevelopment." *Third World Quarterly* 26 (6): 971–86.

Andreotti, Vanessa de Oliveira, ed.. 2014. *The Political Economy of Global Citizenship Education*. New York: Routledge.

APSA (American Political Science Association). 2011. *Political Science in the 21st Century*. APSA Task Force Report.

Avruch, Kevin. 2003. "Context and Pretext in Conflict Resolution." *Journal of Dispute Resolution* 2003 (2): 353–65.

Avruch, Kevin, and Peter Black. 1993. "Conflict Resolution in Intercultural Settings: Problems and Prospects." In *Conflict Resolution Theory and Practice: Integration and Application*, edited by Dennis Sandole and Hendrick van der Merwe, 131–45. Manchester: Manchester University Press.

Bahng, Grace. 2015. "Using Community Partnerships to Create Critical Service Learning: The Case of Mar Vista Gardens." *Journal of Public Affairs Education* 21 (1): 55–70.

Balboa, Cristina M., and Maryam Zarnegar Deloffre. 2015. "Policymaking in the Global Context: Training Students to Build Effective Strategic Partnerships with Nongovernmental Organizations." *Journal of Public Affairs Education* 21 (3): 417–34.

Barber, Benjamin R., and Richard Battistoni. 1993. "A Season of Service: Introducing Service Learning into the Liberal Arts Curriculum." *Political Science and Politics* 26 (2): 235–40.

Barnes, Aristotlen J. 1979. *Who Should Know What? Social Science, Privacy and Ethics.* Harmondsworth, UK: Penguin.

Batchelder, Thomas H., and Susan Root. 1994. "Effects of an Undergraduate Program to Integrate Academic Learning and Service: Cognitive, Prosocial Cognitive, and Identity Outcomes." In *Journal of Adolescence* (17): 341–55.

Battistoni, Richard M. 1997. "Service Learning as Civic Learning: Lessons We Can Learn from Our Students." In *Education for Citizenship: Ideas and Innovations in Political Learning*, edited by Grant Reeher and Joseph Cammarano, 31–50. Lanham, MD: Rowman and Littlefield.

———. 2000. "Service-Learning in Political Science: An Introduction." *PS: Political Science and Politics* 33 (3): 614–16.

Bekerman, Zvi. 2007. "Rethinking Intergroup Encounters: Rescuing Praxis from Theory, Activity from Education, and Peace/Co-Existence from Identity and Culture." *Journal of Peace Education* 4 (1): 21–37.

Bennett, Claire, and Daniela Papi. 2014. "From Service Learning to Learning Service." *Stanford Social Innovation Review*. http://ssir.org/articles/entry/from_service_learning_to_learning_service.

Bennett, Janet M. 2008. "On Becoming a Global Soul: A Path to Engagement during Study Abroad." In Savicki, *Developing Intercultural Competence and Transformation*, 13–31.

Better Care Network. 2014. "Better Volunteering, Better Care." http://www.bettercarenetwork.org/bcn-in-action/better-volunteering-better-care.

Biddle, Pippa. 2014. "The Problem with Little White Girls, Boys and Voluntourism." *Huffington Post*. The Blog, April 25. http://www.huffingtonpost.com/pippa-biddle/little-white-girls-voluntourism_b_4834574.html.

Bowman, Kirk S., and Ashley Jennings. 2005. "Pura Vida: Using Study Abroad to Engage Undergraduate Students in Comparative Politics Research." *PS: Political Science and Politics* 38 (1): 77–81.

Branan, Nicole. 2009. "Lending a Helping Hand." *International Educator* 17 (1): 34–41.

Braskamp, Larry, David C. Braskamp, and Kelly C. Merrill. 2009. "Assessing Progress in Global Learning and Development of Students with Education Abroad Experiences." *Frontiers: The Interdisciplinary Journal of Study Abroad* 18 (Fall 2009): 101–18.

Brewer, Elizabeth, and Kiran Cunningham. 2009. "Capturing Study Abroad's Transformative Potential." In *Integrating Study Abroad into the Curriculum: Theory and Practice across the Disciplines*, edited by Elizabeth Brewer and Kiran Cunningham. Sterling, VA: Stylus.

Bringle, Robert G., and Julie A. Hatcher. 1996. "Implementing Service Learning in Higher Education." *Journal of Higher Education* 67 (2): 221–39.

———. 1999. "Reflection in Service Learning: Making Meaning of Experience." *Educational Horizons* 77 (4): 113–19.

———. 2000. "Institutionalization of Service Learning in Higher Education." *Journal of Higher Education* 71 (3): 273–90.

———. 2011. "International Service Learning." In *International Service Learning: Conceptual Frameworks and Research*, edited by Robert G. Bringle, Julie A. Hatcher, and Steven G. Jones, 3–28. Sterling, VA: Stylus.

Brown, Peter C., Henry L. Roediger III, and Mark A. McDaniel. 2014. *Make It Stick: The Science of Successful Learning*. Cambridge, MA: Belknap Press.

Brownell, Jayne Elise, and Lynn Ellen Swaner. 2010. *Five High-Impact Practices: Research on Learning Outcomes, Completion and Quality*. Washington, DC: Association of American Colleges and Universities.

Bruner, Jerome. 1990. *Acts of Meaning*. Cambridge, MA: Harvard University Press.

Bulman, Chris, and Sue Schutz, eds. 2013. *Reflective Practice in Nursing*. 5th ed. Hoboken, NJ: Wiley-Blackwell.

Campus Compact. "Who We Are." Accessed September 1, 2018. https://compact.org.

Cantor, Jeffrey A. 1997. "Experiential Learning in Higher Education: Linking Classroom and Community." ERIC. http://eric.ed.gov/?id=ED404948.

Caplan, Neil, Wendy Perlman, Brent E. Sasley, and Mira Sucharov. 2012. "History, Rationality, Narrative, Imagery: A Four-Way Conversation on Teaching the Arab-Israeli Conflict." *Journal of Political Science Education* 8 (3): 288–302.

Carlson, Jerry S., and Keith F. Widaman. 1988. "The Effects of Study Abroad during College on Attitudes toward Other Cultures." *International Journal of Intercultural Relations* 12 (1): 1–17.

Carstarphen, Nike, Craig Zelizer, Robert Harris, and David J. Smith. 2010. "Graduate Education and Professional Practice in International Peace and Conflict." United States Institute of Peace. Special Report 246, August 2010, 1–12.

Chambers, Robert. 1997. "Whose Reality Counts? Putting the First Last." *Intermediate Technology Publications*.

———. 2012. "Why Don't All Development Organizations Do Immersions?" *From Poverty to Power* (blog), September 6, 2012. http://oxfamblogs.org/fp2p/robert-chambers-why-dont-all-development-organizations-do-immersions/.

References

Che, Megan, Mindy Spearman, and Agida Manizade. 2009. "Constructive Disequilibrium: Cognitive and Emotional Development through Dissonant Experiences in Less Familiar Destinations." In *The Handbook of Practice and Research in Study Abroad: Higher Education and the Quest for Global Citizenship*, edited by Ross Lewin, 99–116. New York: Routledge.

Cheldelin, Sandra, and Wallace Warfield, with January Makamba. 2004. "Reflections on Reflective Practice." In *Research Frontiers in Conflict Analysis and Resolution*, 64–78. Fairfax, VA: Institute for Conflict Analysis and Resolution, George Mason University.

Cobb, Sara. 2013. *Speaking of Violence: The Politics and Poetics of Narrative Dynamics in Conflict Resolution*. New York: Oxford University Press.

Cohen, Jeremy, and Dennis F. Kinsey. 1994. "'Doing Good' and Scholarship: A Service Learning Study." *Journalism Educator* 48 (4): 4–14.

Colvin, Christopher J. 2006. "Trafficking Trauma: Intellectual Property Rights and the Political Economy of Traumatic Storytelling." *Critical Arts: A Journal of South-North Cultural Studies* 20 (1): 171–82.

Contu, Alessia, and Hugh Willmott. 2003. "Re-embedding Situatedness: The Importance of Power Relations in Learning Theory." *Organizational Science* 14 (3): 283–96.

Crabtree, Robin D. 2008. "Theoretical Foundations for International Service-Learning." *Michigan Journal of Community Service Learning* 15 (1): 18–36.

Cromwell, Alexander. N.d. "Building Cultures of Peace: The Long-Term Effects of Field-Based Peace Education with Pakistani Youth." PhD diss., George Mason University.

Darling, Jonathan. 2014. "Emotions, Encounters and Expectations: The Uncertain Ethics of 'The Field.'" *Journal of Human Rights Practice* 6 (2): 201–12.

David, Jane L. 2009. "Service Learning and Civic Participation." *Educational Leadership* 66 (8): 83–84.

Deardorff, Darla K. 2008. "Intercultural Competence: A Definition, Model, and Implications for Education Abroad." In Savicki, *Developing Intercultural Competence and Transformation*, 32–42.

Delli Carpini, Michael, and Scott Keeter. "What Should Be Learned through Service Learning?" *PS: Political Science and Politics* 33 (3): 635–38.

Dewey, John. 1933. *How We Think: A Restatement of the Relation of Reflective Thinking to the Educative Process*. New York: D. C. Heath.

———. 1938. *Experience and Education*. New York: Kappa Delta Pi.

DiMola, Sandi, and Rachel Lunsford. 2007. *Refugee Resettlement: Is Pittsburgh a Model?* Pittsburgh: Mediators Beyond Borders.

Donnelly-Smith, Laura. 2009. "Global Learning through Short-Term Study Abroad." *Peer Review* 11. http://www.aacu.org/peerreview/2009/fall/donnelly-smith.

Dostilio, Lina D., and Sarah M. Brackmann, Katheleen E. Edwards, Barbara Harrison, Brandon W. Kliewer, and Patti H. Clayton. 2012. "Reciprocity: Saying What We Mean and Meaning What We Say." *Michigan Journal of Community Service Learning* 19 (1): 17–32.

Driscoll, Amy. 2006. "The Benchmarking Potential of the New Carnegie Classification: Community Engagement." Carnegie Foundation for the Advancement of Teaching. http://compact.org/resource-posts/the-benchmarking-potential-of-the-new-carnegie-classification-community-engagement/4257/.

Drolet, Julie. 2014. "Getting Prepared for International Experiential Learning: An Ethical Imperative." In *Globetrotting or Global Citizenship? Perils and Potential of International Learning*, edited by Rebecca Tiessen and Robert Huish, 185–97. Toronto: University of Toronto Press.

Egger, John B. 2008. "No Service to Learning: 'Service-Learning' Reappraised." *Academic Questions* 21 (2): 183–94.

Evert, Jessica. 2014. *How Does Global Service-Learning Become a Dis-service in Health Settings? Commentary from Child Family Health International.* http://globalsl.org/cfhi/.

Eyler, Janet, and Dwight E. Giles Jr. 1999. *Where's the Learning in Service-Learning?* San Francisco: Jossey-Bass.

Eyler, Janet, Dwight E. Giles Jr., and Angela Schmiede. 1996. *A Practitioner's Guide to Reflection in Service-Learning.* Nashville, TN: Vanderbilt University Press.

Farmer, Paul, Gustavo Gutiérrez, Michael Griffin, and Jennie B. Weiss. 2013. *In the Company of the Poor: Conversations with Dr. Paul Farmer and Fr. Gustavo Gutiérrez.* Maryknoll, NY: Orbis Books.

Fobes, Catherine. 2005. "Taking a Critical Pedagogical Look at Travel-Study Abroad: 'A Classroom with a View' in Cusco, Peru." *Teaching Sociology* 33 (2): 181–94.

Frank, Arthur W. 2002. "Why Study People's Stories? The Dialogical Ethics of Narrative Analysis." *International Journal of Qualitative Methods* 1 (1): 109–17.

Franklin, Kimberly. 2010. "Long-Term Career Impact of Professional Applicability of the Study Abroad Experience." In *Frontiers: The Interdisciplinary Journal of Study Abroad* 19: 169–90.

Freire, Paulo. 2008. "The 'Banking' Concept of Education." In *Ways of Reading*, 8th ed., edited by David Bartholomae and Anthony Petrosky, 242–54. Boston: Bedford–St. Martin's.

Furco, Andrew. 1996. "Service-Learning: A Balanced Approach to Experiential Education." In *Expanding Boundaries: Serving and Learning*, 2–6. Washington, DC: Corporation for National Service.

Galtung, Johan. 1969. "Violence, Peace, and Peace Research." *Journal of Peace Research* 6 (3): 167–91.

Gershon, Ilana. 2011. "Neoliberal Agency." *Current Anthropology* 52 (4): 537–55.

Giroux, Henry. 2014. *Neoliberalism's War on Higher Education.* Chicago: Haymarket Books.

Global SL Blog. 2016. "Fair Trade Learning: Summary and Key Documents." http://compact.org/resource-posts/ftl/.

Gopin, Marc. 2009. *To Make the Earth Whole: The Art of Citizen Diplomacy in an Age of Religious Militancy.* Lanham, MD: Rowman and Littlefield.

Gorski, Paul C. 2008. "Good Intentions Are Not Enough: A Decolonizing Intercultural Education." *International Education* 19 (6): 515–25.

Hansen, Toran. 2008. "Critical Conflict Resolution Theory and Practice." *Conflict Resolution Quarterly* 25 (4): 403–27.

Harre, Rom, and Nikki Slocum. 2003. "Disputes as Complex Social Events: On the Uses of Positioning Theory." *Common Knowledge* 9 (1): 100–118.

Hart Research Associates. 2015. *Falling Short? College Learning and Career Services: Selected Findings from Online Surveys of Employers and College Students Conducted on Behalf of the*

References

Association of American Colleges and Universities. Washington, DC: Hart Research Associates. http://bit.ly/1ukus51.

Hartman, Eric. 2014. "Educating for Global Citizenship: A Theoretical Account and Quantitative Analysis." *American Democracy Project eJournal of Public Affairs Special Issue on Global Engagement* 3 (1). http://ejopa.missouristate.edu/index.php/ejournal/article/view/25.

———. 2015a. "Fair Trade Learning: A Framework for Ethical Global Partnerships." In Larsen, *International Service Learning*, 215–34.

———. 2015b. "The Utility of Your Students: Community Partners' Critique. In *Service Learning Pedagogy: How Does It Measure Up?*, edited by Virginia M. Jagla, Jean R. Strait, and Andrew Furco, 231–56. Charlotte, NC: Information Age Publishing.

Hartman, Eric, and Richard Kiely. 2014. "A Critical Global Citizenship." In *Crossing Boundaries: Tension and Transformation in International Service Learning*, edited by Patrick M. Green and Mathew Johnson, 215–42. Sterling, VA: Stylus.

Hartman, Eric, Benjamin Y. Lough, Cynthia Toms, and Nora Reynolds. 2015. "The Beauty of Global Citizenship: The Problem of Measurement." In *Going Glocal: The Theory, Practice, Evaluation, and Experience of Education for Global Citizenship*, edited by B. Oomen, E. Park, M. Sklad, and J. Friedman. Amsterdam: Drukkerij Publishing.

Hartman, Eric, and Anthony C. Ogden. 2014. "UK Education Abroad Faculty Toolkit: Fair Trade Learning." Accessed 27 August 2018. http://www.uky.edu/toolkit/fair-trade-learning.

Hartman, Eric, Cody M. Paris, and Brandon Blache-Cohen. 2014. "Fair Trade Learning: Ethical Standards for Community-Engaged International Volunteer Tourism." *Tourism and Hospitality Research* 14 (1–2): 108–16.

Hartman, Hope J. 2010. *A Guide to Reflective Practice for New and Experienced Teachers*. Practical Guide Series. New York: McGraw-Hill Higher Education.

Hébert, Ali, and Petra Hauf. 2015. "Student Learning through Service Learning: Effects on Academic Development, Civic Responsibility, Interpersonal Skills and Practical Skills." *Active Learning in Higher Education* 16 (1): 37–49.

Helman, Sara. 2002. "Monologic Results of Dialogue: Jewish-Palestinian Encounter Groups as Sites of Essentialization." *Identities, Global Studies in Culture and Power* 9 (3): 327–54.

Hepburn, Mary A., Richard G. Niemi, and Chris Chapman. 2000. "Service Learning in College Political Science: Queries and Commentary." *Political Science and Politics* 33 (3): 617–22.

Hettler, Shannon, and Linda M. Johnston. 2009. "Living Peace: An Exploration of Experiential Peace Education, Conflict Resolution and Violence Prevention Programs for Youth." *Journal of Peace Education* 6 (1): 101–18.

Hewstone, Miles, and Rupert Brown, eds. 1986. *Contact and Conflict in Intergroup Encounters*. Oxford: Oxford University Press.

Hill, Marcia, Kristin Glaser, and Judy Harden. 1995. "A Feminist Model for Ethical Decision Making." In *Ethical Decision Making in Therapy: Feminist Perspectives*, edited by Elizabeth. J. Rave and Carolyn C. Larsen, 18–37. New York: Guilford.

Hirsch, Susan F., Ned Lazarus, Andria Wisler, Julie Minde, and Gina Cerasani. 2013. "Pursuing Research through Focus Groups: A Capstone Experience Meets Disciplinary, General Education Goals." *CUR Quarterly* 33 (4): 23–27.

References

Hoffa, William W. 2007. *A History of U.S. Study Abroad: Beginnings to 1965; A Special Publication of* Frontiers: The Interdisciplinary Journal of Study Abroad. Carlisle, PA: Forum on Education Abroad.

Hollander, Elizabeth L., and John Saltmarsh. 2000. "The Engaged University." *Academe* 86 (4): 29–32.

hooks, bell. 1992. *Black Looks: Race and Representation.* Boston: South End Press.

———. 1994. *Teaching to Transgress: Education as the Practice of Freedom.* New York: Routledge.

Hunter, Susan, and Richard A. Brisbin. 2000. "The Impact of Service Learning on Democratic and Civic Values." *Political Science and Politics* 33 (3): 623–26.

IIE (Institute of International Education). 2015a. Andrew Heiskell Awards for Innovation in International Education. Institute for International Education. https://www.iie.org/Why-IIE/Announcements/2015-01-26-Heiskell-Awards-2015.

———. 2015b. *Open Doors.* Institute for International Education. http://www.iie.org/en/Research-and-Publications/Open-Doors.

Illich, Ivan. 1968. "To Hell with Good Intentions." Presentation to the Conference on Inter-American Student Projects (CIASP), Cuernavaca, Mexico, April 1968.

Iram, Yaacov. 2006. "Culture of Peace: Definition, Scope, and Application." In *Educating Toward a Culture of Peace,* edited by Yaacov Iram, 3–12. Greenwich, CT: Information Age Publishing.

Ish-Shalom, Piki. 2011. "Theoreticians' Obligation of Transparency: When Parsimony, Reflexivity, Transparency and Reciprocity Meet." *Review of International Studies* 37 (3): 973–96.

Jacoby, Barbara, ed. 1996. *Service-Learning in Higher Education: Concepts and Practices.* San Francisco: Jossey-Bass.

Jacoby, Barbara, and Nevin C. Brown. 2009. "Preparing Students for Global Civic Engagement." In *Civic Engagement in Higher Education: Concepts and Practices,* edited by Barbara Jacoby and Associates, 213–26. San Francisco: Jossey-Bass.

Jenkins, Shannon. 2010. "Service Learning and Simulations." *PS: Political Science and Politics* 43 (3): 541–45.

Jiang, Xiaoli. 2016. "Effect of Pre-Departure Culture Preparation Course on Student Learning International Fieldwork." *Creative Education* 7: 1237–43.

Jones, Steven. 2011. "Research on International Service-Learning: Implications for Internationalization Strategies." Conference presentation at Forum on Education Abroad.

Juneau, Thomas, and Mira Sucharov. 2010. "Narratives in Pencil: Using Graphic Novels to Teach Israeli-Palestinian Relations." *International Studies Perspectives* 11 (2): 172–83.

Kiely, Richard. 2004. "A Chameleon with a Complex: Searching for Transformation in International Service-Learning." *Michigan Journal of Community Service Learning* 10 (2): 5–20.

———. 2005. "A Transformative Learning Model for Service-Learning: A Longitudinal Case Study." *Michigan Journal of Community Service Learning* 12 (1): 5–22.

King, John C. 2009. "Demistifying Field Research." In *Surviving Field Research: Working in Violent and Difficult Situations,* edited by Chandra L. Sriram, John C. King, Julie A. Mertus, and Olga M. Ortega, 8–18. London: Routledge.

References

Kolb, Alice Y., and David A. Kolb. 2005. "Learning Styles and Learning Spaces: Enhancing Experiential Learning in Higher Education." *Academy of Management Learning and Education* 4 (2): 193–212.

Kolb, David A. 1984. *Experiential Learning: Experience as the Source of Learning and Development.* Englewood Cliffs, NJ: Prentice Hall.

———. 2015. *Experiential Learning: Experience as the Source of Learning and Development.* 2nd ed. Upper Saddle River, NJ: Pearson Education.

Kozak, Jennifer, and Marianne A. Larsen. 2015. "Conclusion: ISL and Host Communities: Relationships and Responsibility." In Larsen, *International Service Learning*, 263–76.

Kuh, George D. 2008. "Excerpt from High-Impact Educational Practices: What They Are, Who Has Access to Them, and Why They Matter." Association of American Colleges and Universities. http://www.cuny.edu/about/administration/offices/ue/cue/KuhHighImpactPractices2008.pdf.

Lakoff, George and Mark Johnson. 1980. *Metaphors We Live By.* Chicago: University of Chicago Press.

Lambright, Kristina T., and Yi Lu. 2009. "What Impacts the Learning in Service Learning? An Examination of Project Structure and Student Characteristics." *Journal of Public Affairs Education* 15 (4): 425–44.

Lang, Michael D., and Alison Taylor. 2000. *The Making of a Mediator: Developing Artistry in Practice.* 1st ed. San Francisco: Jossey-Bass.

Larsen, Marianne A., ed. 2015. *International Service Learning: Engaging Host Communities.* New York: Routledge.

Lasker, Judith. N. 2016. *Hoping to Help: The Promises and Pitfalls of Global Health Volunteering.* Ithaca, NY: Cornell University Press.

Laubscher, Michael R. 1994. *Encounters with Differences: Student Perceptions of the Role of Out-of-Class Experiences in Education Abroad.* Westport, CT: Greenwood.

Laue, James, and Gerald Cormick. 1978. "The Ethics of Intervention in Community Disputes." In *The Ethics of Social Intervention*, edited by Gordon Bermant, Herbert C. Kelman, and Donald P. Warwick, 205–32. Washington, DC: Hemisphere.

Lazarus, Ned. 2011. "Evaluating Peace Education in the Oslo-Intifada Generation: A Long-Term Impact Study of Seeds of Peace 1993–2010." PhD diss., American University.

Lederach, John Paul. 1995. *Preparing for Peace: Conflict Transformation across Cultures.* New York: Syracuse University Press.

———. 1997. *Building Peace: Sustainable Reconciliation in Divided Societies.* Washington, DC: United States Institute of Peace Press.

Legault, Albert. 2000. "NATO Intervention in Kosovo: The Legal Context." *Canadian Military Journal* 1 (1): 63–66. http://www.journal.forces.gc.ca/vo1/no1/doc/63-66-eng.pdf.

Lester, Scott W. 2015. "Melding Service Learning and Leadership Skills Development: Keys to Effective Course Design." *Journal of Experiential Education* 38 (3): 280–95.

Liebkind, Karmela, and Alfred L. McAlister. 1999. "Extended Contact through Peer Modeling to Promote Tolerance in Finland." *European Journal of Social Psychology* 29 (5–6): 765–80.

References

Lough, Benjamin J., and Lenore E. Matthew. 2014. "International Volunteering and Governance." United Nations Volunteers Programme and the International Forum for Volunteering in Development. http://forum-ids.org/2014/10/unv-forum-paper#discussion_paper.

Lowe, Allyson M., and Sandi DiMola. 2012. "The Use of a Service-Learning Model in the Teaching of Conflict Studies: A Case Study of POL 350; The Lawrenceville Dialogue Project." American Political Science Association Teaching and Learning Conference, Washington, DC, February 17–19, 2012.

Mac Ginty, Roger. 2011. *International Peacebuilding and Local Resistance: Hybrid Forms of Peace.* New York: Palgrave Macmillan.

Madar, Chase. 2010. "The People's Priest." *American Conservative* 9 (2) 24–26.

Maoz, Ifat. 2011. "Does Contact Work in Protracted Asymmetrical Conflict? Appraising 20 Years of Reconciliation-Aimed Encounters between Israeli Jews and Palestinians." *Journal of Peace Research* 48 (1): 115–25.

Martin, Emily. 2000. "Mind-Body Problems." *American Ethnologist* 27 (3): 569–90.

Marx, Karl. 1974. "The Eighteenth Brumaire of Louis Bonaparte." In *Karl Marx: Surveys from Exile; Political Writings, Volume II,* edited by David Fernbach, 143–250. New York: Vintage Books.

Maulden, Patricia, and Lisa Shaw. 2012. "Field-Based Experiential Learning: Post-Conflict Peacebuilding in Liberia." Paper presented at the International Studies Association Conference Annual Convention, San Diego, April 2012.

McMillan, Janice, and Timothy K. Stanton. 2014. "Learning Service in International Contexts: Partnership-Based Service Learning and Research in Cape Town, South Africa." *Michigan Journal of Community Service Learning* 20 (1): 64–78.

Mezirow, Jack. 1978. "Perspective Transformation." *Adult Education Quarterly* 28 (2): 100–110.

———. 1997. "Transformative Learning: Theory to Practice." *New Directions for Adult and Continuing Education* 74: 5–12. doi: 10.1002/ace.7401.

———. 2003. "Transformative Learning as Discourse." *Journal of Transformative Education* 1 (1): 58–63.

Mitchell, Audra. 2013. "Escaping the 'Field Trap': Exploitation and the Global Politics of Educational Fieldwork in 'Conflict Zones.'" *Third World Quarterly* 34 (7): 1247–64.

Mohanty, Chandra Talpade. 1992. "Feminist Encounters: Locating the Politics of Experience." In *Destabilizing Theory: Contemporary Feminist Debates,* edited by Michele Brett and Anne Phillips, 74–92. Stanford, CA: Stanford University Press.

Murithi, Tim. 2009. *The Ethics of Peacebuilding.* Edinburgh: Edinburgh University Press.

Nader, Laura. 1980. *No Access to Law: Alternatives to the American Judicial System.* New York: Academic Press.

NAFSA. N.d. "Sample Study Abroad Evaluation Form." Accessed November 16, 2016. https://www.nafsa.org/Resource_Library_Assets/Migs/OPO_SIG/Sample_Study_Abroad_Evaluation_Form/.

Nan, Susan Allen. 2010. *Theories of Change and Indicator Development in Conflict Management and Mitigation.* Washington, DC: United States Agency for International Development. http://pdf.usaid.gov/pdf_docs/PNADS460.pdf.

Nelson, Hilde Lindemann. 2001. *Damaged Identities, Narrative Repair.* Ithaca, NY: Cornell University Press.

References

Nike, Carstarphen, Craig Zelizer, Robert Harris, and David J. Smith. 2010. "Graduate Education and Professional Practice in International Peace and Conflict." Washington, DC: United States Institute of Peace.

Nolting, William, Debbie C. Donohue, Cheryl Matherly, and Martin Tilman. 2012. *Internships, Service Learning, and Volunteering Abroad: Successful Models and Best Practices*. Washington, DC: NAFSA.

NSSE (National Survey of Student Engagement). 2010. *Major Differences: Examining Student Engagement by Field of Study; Annual Results 2010*. Bloomington: Indiana University Center for Postsecondary Research.

———. 2015. *Engagement Insights: Survey Findings on the Quality of Undergraduate Education*. Bloomington: Indiana University Center for Postsecondary Research. http://nsse.indiana.edu/html/findings.cfm;http://nsse.indiana.edu/NSSE_2015_Results/pdf/NSSE_2015_Annual_Results.pdf.

O'Connor, Pat. 2014. *Management and Gender in Higher Education*. Manchester: Manchester University Press.

Ogden, Anthony C. 2006. "Ethnographic Inquiry: Reframing the Learning Core of Education Abroad." *Frontiers: The Interdisciplinary Journal of Study Abroad* 13: 87–112.

———. 2010. *Education Abroad and the Making of Global Citizens: Assessing Learning Outcomes of Course-Embedded, Faculty-Led International Programming*. Saarbruecken, Germany: VDM Publishing.

———. 2015. *Toward a Research Agenda for U.S. Education Abroad*. AIEA Research Agendas for the Internationalization of Higher Education. Washington, DC: Association of International Education Administrators.

Ogden, Anthony C., Heidi M. Soneson, and Paige Weting. 2010. "The Diversification of Geographic Locations." In *A History of U.S. Study Abroad: 1965 to the Present*, edited by William W. Hoffa and Stephen C. DePaul, 161–98. Carlisle, PA: Forum on Education Abroad.

Oksala, Johanna. 2016. *Feminist Experiences: Foucauldian and Phenomenological Investigations*. Evanston, IL: Northwestern University Press.

Paczyńska, Agnieszka. 2015. "Teaching Conflict and Conflict Resolution." In *Handbook on Teaching and Learning in Political Science and International Relations*, edited by John Ishiyama, William J. Miller, and Eszter Simon, 173–84. Northampton, MA: Edward Elger.

Paige, R. Michael, Elizabeth M. Stallman, and Jasmina Josić. 2008. "Study Abroad for Global Engagement: A Preliminary Report on the SAGE Research Project." Presentation at NAFSA: Association of International Educators Region II Conference, Park City, UT, October 21–24, 2008.

Perry, James L. 1996. "Measuring Public Service Motivation: An Assessment of Construct Reliability and Validity." *Journal of Public Administration Research and Theory* 6 (1): 5–22. (We used a modified version of the Public Service Motivation Scale [PSMS] that appears in *The Measure of Service Learning: Research Scales to Assess Student Experiences* by Robert G. Bringle, Mindy A. Phillips, and Michael Hudson, published by the American Psychological Association [Washington, DC] in 2004.)

Peschl, Markus F. 2007. "Triple-Loop Learning as Foundation for Profound Change, Individual Cultivation, and Radical Innovation." *Constructivist Foundations* 2 (2–3): 136–45.

Peterson, Chip, Lilli Engle, Lance Kenney, Kim Kreutzer, William Nolting, and Anthony C. Ogden. 2007. *Education Abroad Glossary*. Carlisle, PA: Forum on Education Abroad.

Pettigrew, Karen. E. 1998. *The Role of Community Health Nurses in Providing Information and Referral to the Elderly: A Study Based on Social Network Theory*. London, ON: University of Western Ontario.

Philpott, Daniel, and Gerard F. Powers, eds. 2010. *Strategies of Peace: Transforming Conflict in a Violent World*. Oxford: Oxford University Press.

Porfilio, Brad J., and Heather Hickman, eds. 2011. *Critical Service-Learning as Revolutionary Pedagogy: A Project of Student Agency in Action*. Charlotte, NC: Information Age.

Prado, Paola, Autumn Quezada-Grant, and Kerri S. Warren. 2014. "From Poverty Tourism to Fair Trade Learning: Best Practices for Ethical and Responsible Global Service Learning Community Engagement in Latin America." Forty-Third National Society for Experiential Education Conference. Baltimore, MD.

Prentice, M. 2007. "Service Learning and Civic Engagement." *Academic Questions* 20: 135–45.

Prilleltensky, Isaac. 2012. "Wellness as Fairness." *American Journal of Community Psychology* 49 (1–2): 1–21.

Prins, Esther, and Nicole Webster. 2010. "Student Identities and the Tourist Gaze in International Service-Learning: A University Project in Belize." *Journal of Higher Education Outreach and Engagement* 14 (1): 5–32.

Program for Deliberative Democracy. 2010. "Local Government at the Crossroads: Critical Choices for Our Communities." http://hss.cmu.edu/pdd/polls/fall10/Local_Government_Booklet.pdf.

Pugh, Jeffrey. 2013. "The Short-Term 'Bridge Model' Study Abroad Program." *PS: Political Science and Politics* 46 (4): 791–96.

Rees, Tony. 1991. "Ethical Issues." In *Handbook for Research Students in the Social Sciences*, edited by Graham Allan and Chris Skinner, 140–51. London: Falmer.

Remen, Rachel N. 1999. "Helping, Fixing or Serving?" *Shambhala Sun*, September 1. https://www.uc.edu/content/dam/uc/honors/docs/communityengagement/HelpingFixingServing.pdf.

Reynolds, Nora P. 2014. "What Counts as Outcomes? Community Perspectives of an Engineering Partnership." *Michigan Journal of Community Service Learning* 20 (1): 79–90.

Richmond, Oliver P. 2011. *A Post-Liberal Peace*. New York: Routledge.

———, ed. 2010. *Palgrave Advances in Peacebuilding: Critical Developments and Approaches*. New York: Palgrave Macmillan.

Rodgers, Carol. 2002. "Defining Reflection: Another Look at John Dewey and Reflective Thinking." *Teachers College Record* 104 (4): 842–66.

Romano, Arthur, Susan F. Hirsch, and Agnieszka Paczyńska. 2016. "Teaching about Global Complexity: Experiential Conflict Resolution Pedagogy in Higher Education Classrooms." *Conflict Resolution Quarterly* 34 (3): 255–79.

Romme, A. Georges, and Arjen van Witteloostuijn. 1999. "Circular Organizing and Triple Loop Learning." *Journal of Organizational Change Management* 12 (5): 439–53.

Rosen, Yigal, and David Perkins. 2013. "Shallow Roots Require Constant Watering: The Challenge of Sustained Impact in Educational Programs." *International Journal of Higher Education* 2 (4): 91–100.

References

Rosenberg, Marshall B. 2003. *Nonviolent Communication: A Language of Life*. 2nd ed. Encinitas, CA: PuddleDancer Press.

Rotberg, Robert I., ed. 2006. *Israeli and Palestinian Narratives of Conflict: History's Double Helix*. Bloomington: Indiana University Press.

Salomon, Gavriel. 2004 "A Narrative Based View of Coexistence Education." *Journal of Social Issues* 60 (2): 273–87.

Savicki, Victor, ed. 2008. *Developing Intercultural Competence and Transformation: Theory, Research, and Application in International Education*. Sterling, VA: Stylus.

Schimmel, Noam. 2009. "Towards a Sustainable and Holistic Model of Peace Education: A Critique of Conventional Modes of Peace Education through Dialogue in Israel." *Journal of Peace Education* 6 (1): 51–68.

Schneider, Andrea K., and Katie Lonze. 2013. "Get on the Plane: Why Understanding the Israeli-Palestinian Conflict Is Best Understood by Traveling There." *Cardozo Journal of Conflict Resolution* 15 (1): 85–104.

Schön, Donald, A. 1984. *The Reflective Practitioner: How Professionals Think in Action*. New York: Basic Books.

———. 1987. *Educating the Reflective Practitioner*. San Francisco: Jossey-Bass.

School of Integrative Studies. N.d. "Experiential Learning." George Mason University. Accessed August 27, 2016. http://integrative.gmu.edu/current-students/experiential-learning.

Scott, Joan W. 1991. "The Evidence of Experience." *Critical Inquiry* 17(4): 773–97.

Sedlak, Carol A., Margaret O. Doheny, Nancy Panthofer, and Ella Anaya. 2003. "Critical Thinking in Students' Service-Learning Experiences." *College Teaching* 51 (3): 99–103.

Selby, Robert. 2008. "Designing Transformation in International Education." In Savicki, *Developing Intercultural Competence and Transformation*, 1–12.

Sellars, Maura. 2014. *Reflective Practice for Teachers*. Los Angeles: SAGE.

Sharpe, Erin K., and Samantha Dear. 2013. "Points of Discomfort: Reflections on Power and Partnerships in International Service-Learning." *Michigan Journal of Community Service Learning* 19 (2): 49–57.

Shore, Cris, and Susan Wright. 1999. "Audit Culture and Anthropology: Neo-Liberalism in British Higher Education." *Journal of the Royal Anthropological Institute* 5 (4): 557–75.

Sigmon, Robert. 1979. "Service-Learning: Three Principles." *Synergist* 8 (1): 9–11.

Singer, Peter. 1993. *Practical Ethics*. Cambridge: Cambridge University Press.

Slimbach, Richard. 2016. "Deschooling International Education: Toward an Alternative Paradigm of Practice." In *International Education's Scholar-Practitioners: Bridging Research and Practice*, edited by Bernhard Streitwieser and Anthony C. Ogden, 195–210. Oxford: Symposium Books.

Snell, Robin Stanley, Maureen Yin Lee Chan, Carol Hok Ka Ma, and Carman Ka Man Chan. 2015. "A Road Map for Empowering Undergraduates to Practice Service Leadership through Service-Learning in Teams." *Journal of Management Education* 39 (3): 372–99.

Sobania, Neal W., ed. 2015. *Putting the Local in Global Education: Models for Transformative Learning through Domestic Off-Campus Programs*. Sterling, VA: Stylus.

Spencer, Sarah E., and Kathy Tuma, eds. 2002. *The Guide to Successful Short-Term Programs Abroad*. Washington, DC: NAFSA.

Sprague, Mary, and Olivia Hu. 2015. "Assessing the Value to Client Organizations of Student Practicum Projects." *Journal of Public Affairs Education* 21 (2): 263–80.

Sprague, Mary, and R. Cameron Percy. 2014. "The Immediate and Long-Term Impact of Practicum Experiences on Students." *Journal of Public Affairs Education* 20 (1): 91–111.

Staywyse. 2012. *Youth Travel: The Next BIG THING at ITB Berlin 2012.* Association of Youth Travel Accommodation. http://staywyse.org/2012/03/09/youth-travel-the-next-big-thing-at-itb-berlin-2012/.

Stearns Center for Teaching and Faculty Excellence. N.d. "Experiential Learning." George Mason University. Accessed September 2, 2016. http://ctfe.gmu.edu/teaching/experiential-learning/.

Stoecker, Randy, and Elizabeth A. Tryon. 2009. *The Unheard Voices: Community Organizations and Service-Learning.* Philadelphia: Temple University Press.

Stone, Douglas, Bruce Patton, and Sheila Heen. 2010. *Difficult Conversations: How to Discuss What Matters Most.* New York: Penguin.

Stowe, Noel J. 2006. "Public History Curriculum: Illustrating Reflective Practice." *Public Historian* 28 (1): 39–65.

Suleiman, Jaber. 1997. "Palestinians in Lebanon and the Role of Non-Governmental Organizations." *Journal of Refugee Studies* 10 (3): 397–410.

Taylor, Beverley Joan. 2010. *Reflective Practice for Healthcare Professionals: A Practical Guide.* 3rd ed. Berkshire, UK: Open University Press.

Taylor, Edward W. 1994. "Intercultural Competency: A Transformative Learning Process." *Adult Education Quarterly* 44 (3): 154–74.

Thomson, Susan M. N.d. "Developing Ethical Guidelines for Researchers Working in Post-Conflict Environments: A Research Report." Program on States and Security, Ralph Bunche Institute for International Studies, Graduate Center, New York. http://conflictfieldresearch.colgate.edu/wp-content/uploads/2015/02/Developing-Ethical-Guidelines.pdf.

Tilghman, Shirley. 2007. "Community Based Learning Initiatives: Reflecting on Ten Years of the CBLI." Address to the faculty, alumni, and students of Princeton University.

Toms, Cynthia. 2013. "The Economy of Global Service-learning and the Problem of Silence." http://globalsl.org/economy-global-service-learning-problem-silence/.

Trilokekar, Roopa Desai, and Polina Kukar. 2011. "Disorienting Experiences during Study Abroad: Reflections of Pre-service Teacher Candidates." *Teaching and Teacher Education* 27 (7): 1141–150.

Tryon, Elizabeth, Carly Hood, and Malika Taalbi. 2013. *Examining Institutional Frameworks for Global Service Learning and Community-Based Research.* Washington, DC: NAFSA.

Vande Berg, Michael, R. Michael Paige, and Kris Hemming Lou, eds. 2012. *Student Learning Abroad: What Our Students Are Learning, What They're Not, and What We Can Do about It.* Sterling, VA: Stylus.

Walker, Tobi. 2000. "The Service/Politics Split: Rethinking Service to Teach Political Engagement." *PS: Political Science and Politics* 33 (3): 646–49.

Warfield, Wallace. 2002. "Is This the Right Thing to Do?" In *A Handbook of International Peacebuilding,* edited by John Paul Lederach and Janice Moomaw Jenner, 213–23. San Francisco: Jossey-Bass.

References

Warfield, Wallace, and Alicia Pfund, eds. 2013. *From Conflict Resolution to Social Justice: The Work and Legacy of Wallace Warfield.* New York: Bloomsbury Academic.

Williams, Robin M., Jr. 1947. *The Reduction of Intergroup Tensions: A Survey of Research on Problems of Ethnic, Racial, and Religious Group Relations.* New York: Social Science Research Council.

Williams, Tracy R. 2005. "Exploring the Impact of Study Abroad on Students' Intercultural Communications Skills: Adaptability and Sensitivity." *Journal of Studies in International Education* 9 (4): 356–71.

Winslade, John. 2009. "Tracing Lines of Flight: Implications of the Work of Gilles Deleuze for Narrative Practice." *Family Process* 48 (3): 332–46.

Wolcott, Harry. F. 1995. *The Art of Fieldwork.* London: Altamira.

Wood, Elizabeth J. 2006. "The Ethical Challenges of Field Research in Conflict Zones." *Qualitative Sociology* 29 (3): 373–86.

Younes, Maha N., and Silvia M. Asay. 2003. "The World as a Classroom: The Impact of International Study Experiences on College Students." *College Teaching* 51 (4): 141–47.

Zemach-Bersin, Talya. 2007. "Global Citizenship and Study Abroad: It's All about U.S." *Critical Literacy: Theories and Practices* 1 (2): 26.

CONTRIBUTORS

Daniel R. Brunstetter is Associate Professor in the Department of Political Science and former Faculty Director of Study Abroad at the University of California, Irvine. His research on the ethics of war and peace has appeared in *Ethics & International Affairs*, *Political Studies*, the *International Journal of Human Rights*, and elsewhere. He is the author of *Tensions of Modernity: Las Casas and His Legacy in the French Enlightenment* and coeditor of *The Ethics of War and Peace Revisited: Moral Challenges in an Era of Contested and Fragmented Sovereignty* as well as *Just War Thinkers: From Cicero to the 21st Century*. In the role of faculty adviser, he has led multiple international experiential learning trips with The Olive Tree Initiative.

Alison Castel is Assistant Professor of Rhetoric and Communication at Regis College. Previously, she was on the faculty at the University of Colorado teaching Peace and Conflict Studies. She holds a PhD from the School for Conflict Analysis and Resolution (S-CAR) at George Mason University, where she was Dean's Fellow for the Center for Narrative and Conflict. Dr. Castel has fifteen years of experience in peace and conflict studies practice and pedagogy, including in Israel/Palestine, Thailand, Indonesia, Cambodia, Rwanda, Colombia, and Northern Ireland. Her current research and practice focuses on peacebuilding and transitional justice with emphasis on rural Colombia, narrative and conflict, and ethics in pedagogy.

Contributors

Gina M. Cerasani, PhD, is a conflict resolution specialist in the US Environmental Protection Agency's Conflict Prevention and Resolution Center and an adjunct faculty member of the School for Conflict Analysis and Resolution at George Mason University. As a conflict resolution practitioner, she advises and trains on approaches to resolving environmental conflicts, particularly within communities. She has taught undergraduate and graduate courses in environmental and community conflict resolution, and she has developed and led service learning projects.

Alexander Cromwell is an Instructor at the School of International Service and the School of Professional and Extended Studies at American University. He is also a doctoral candidate at the School for Conflict Analysis and Resolution at George Mason University, where he conducted his research in Pakistan on the long-term effects of international peace education in conflict contexts. He has been leading study-abroad programs to Indonesia every summer since 2014. Previously he worked with the Center for World Religions, Diplomacy, and Conflict Resolution's overseas education program, bringing students to conflict zones in the Middle East and the Balkans.

Maryam Z. Deloffre is Associate Professor of Political Science in the undergraduate program in Political Science and the graduate program in International Peace and Conflict Resolution at Arcadia University. She is author of several articles on nongovernmental organization (NGO) accountability and legitimacy, global pandemic governance, human security and global health, and pedagogy. Her current research explores inter-NGO governance and accountability. Dr. Deloffre holds a PhD in political science from the George Washington University, an MA in international relations from Institut d'Etudes Politiques-Sciences Po Paris, and a BA in political science from the University of Illinois Urbana-Champaign.

Sandi DiMola is Associate Professor of Political Science at Carlow University and chair of the Departments of Management and Government. She is a founding member of Mediators Beyond Borders, an NGO engaged in capacity building in postconflict societies. Dr. DiMola received graduate degrees from the University of Pittsburgh and the Duquesne University School of Law. Dr. DiMola, a Fulbright Scholar, teaches courses in American politics and public policy.

Leslie Dwyer is Associate Professor and Director of the Center for the Study of Gender and Conflict at the School for Conflict Analysis and Resolution at George Mason University. She is a cultural anthropologist (BA, University of Pennsylvania; MA and PhD, Princeton University) whose academic research focuses on issues of violence, gender, postconflict social life, transitional justice, and the politics of memory and identity. Her most recent project, supported by grants from the MacArthur Foundation, the H. F. Guggenheim Foundation, and the United States Institute of Peace, is an ethnographic study of the aftermath of political violence in Indonesia, where she has worked for over twenty years.

Eric Hartman serves as Executive Director of the Haverford College Center for Peace and Global Citizenship. He is lead author of *Community-Based Global Learning: The Theory and Practice of Ethical Engagement at Home and Abroad*. Dr. Hartman cofounded Globalsl.org and the Global Engagement Survey (GES), initiatives that advance best practices in global learning and cooperative development within community-campus partnerships. He has written and taught widely on issues relating to the pursuit of global citizenship through such partnerships. Dr. Hartman holds a PhD in international development from the University of Pittsburgh Graduate School of Public and International Affairs.

Susan F. Hirsch is a cultural anthropologist (BA, Yale; MA and PhD, Duke) and the Vernon M. and Minnie I. Lynch Chair and Professor in the School for Conflict Analysis and Resolution at George Mason University. Her publications include *Pronouncing and Persevering: Gender and the Discourses of Disputing in an African Islamic Court*, *In the Moment of Greatest Calamity: Terrorism, Grief, and a Victim's Quest for Justice*, and (with E. Franklin Dukes) *Mountaintop Mining in Appalachia: Understanding Stakeholders and Change in Environmental Conflict*. As a two-time Fulbright Fellow, she has taught at the University of Dar es Salaam and the University of Malta.

Contributors

Pushpa Iyer is Associate Professor in the Graduate School of Policy and Management at the Middlebury Institute of International Studies. Dr. Iyer is the founding director of the Center for Conflict Studies, where she plays the role of editor, trainer, researcher, and organizer. As a practitioner with years of experience working on identity conflicts, nonstate armed groups, civil wars, and peacebuilding, Dr. Iyer is a long-term advocate for the poor and marginalized communities in Gujarat State in India. She continues her activism work in the United States through programs designed to fight racial inequity, discrimination, and violence.

Allyson M. Lowe is Vice President of Academic Affairs at Trocaire College in Buffalo, New York, and previously Dean of the College of Leadership and Social Change at Carlow University. A political scientist by training, Dr. Lowe is committed to fostering an engaged citizenry and connecting theory to practice for students and community members alike. Dr. Lowe graduated summa cum laude from Miami University in political science and earned her master's and PhD degrees from Ohio State University, where she specialized in comparative politics and women's studies. Dr. Lowe is a Fulbright Scholar and has taught courses in comparative politics and international relations.

Patricia A. Maulden is Associate Professor of Conflict Resolution and Director of the Dialogue & Difference Project with the School for Conflict Analysis and Resolution at George Mason University, where she received her PhD. Her research interests include generational and gendered dynamics of conflict and peace, social militarization and demilitarization processes, and peacebuilding practices in relation to equity, human rights, reconciliation, and social justice. She has worked in Sierra Leone, Liberia, Burundi, Ethiopia, Turkey, Morocco, Brazil, and Colombia. Dr. Maulden also designs and implements experiential learning programs that bridge theory and practice from the instructor, student, and host community perspectives.

rj nickels is an ABD PhD candidate at the School for Conflict Analysis and Resolution at George Mason University. Their research explores the narrative and intersectional dimensions of conflict between transgender residents and city authorities in Washington, DC, in particular how stories of lived experience may raise moral questions otherwise excluded from public discourse.

Anthony C. Ogden is Associate Vice Provost for Global Engagement and Assistant Professor at the University of Wyoming. Prior to joining Wyoming, he held positions related to international education with Pennsylvania State University, the University of Kentucky, and Michigan State University. A two-time Fulbright recipient, Dr. Ogden has written widely on topics related to education abroad and recently coedited a volume on the issue of scholar-practitioners in international education. Dr. Ogden earned a PhD at Pennsylvania State University in educational theory and policy, with a dual title in comparative and international education.

Agnieszka Paczyńska is Associate Professor at the School for Conflict Analysis and Resolution, George Mason University, and a Nonresident Fellow at the Stimson Center. Her research focuses on the relationship between economic and political change and conflict, globalization and local conflicts, postconflict reconstruction policies, and pedagogy. Her publications include *State, Labor, and the Transition to a Market Economy: Egypt, Poland, Mexico, and the Czech Republic* and the policy brief series Changing Landscape of Assistance to Conflict-Affected States: Emerging and Traditional Donors and Opportunities for Collaboration, which she edited. She holds a PhD in political science from the University of Virginia.

Jennifer M. Ramos is Associate Professor of Political Science and Director of International Relations, and director of Peace and Justice Studies at Loyola Marymount University. Her research explores the evolution of international norms, public opinion, and foreign policy. Professor Ramos's latest work is an edited volume, *Preventive Force: Drones, Targeted Killing and the Transformation of Contemporary Warfare*, with Kerstin Fisk. Her previous books include *Changing Norms through Actions: The Evolution of Sovereignty* and an edited volume, *iPolitics: Citizens, Elections and Governing in the New Media Era*, with Richard L. Fox.

Contributors

Lisa Elaine Shaw is Director of Student Services and Field Experience at the School for Conflict Analysis and Resolution (S-CAR) at George Mason University, where she also is an administrative faculty member. She codeveloped and cofacilitated the Post-Conflict Peace Building Field Experience in Liberia and the Transitional Justice Field Experience in Colombia. Ms. Shaw has twenty years of experience in experiential education and community-based programs at the international, national, and local levels. She has a BA in political science and environmental science (Regis University) and received an MS in conflict analysis and resolution (George Mason University).

Daniel Wehrenfennig, PhD, is Executive Director of The Olive Tree Initiative. He also directs the Certificate Program in Conflict Analysis and Resolution and serves as Vice-Chair of the Chancellor's Advisory Council on Campus Climate, Culture and Inclusion at the University of California, Irvine. He has produced a documentary film for civic education in Malawi. His recent work has been published by *Peace Review*, *Communication Theory*, the University of California Press, Lexington Books, and *Studies in Ethnicity and Nationalism*.

INDEX

A+ Schools, 124
academic projects, 15, 182. *See also* project-based learning
active-learning experiences, 104, 114
activism, 43, 85, 222
American Friends Service Committee (AFSC), 15, 160–61, 163–69, 171–78
applied ethics, 69. *See also* practical ethics
Applied Practice and Theory program (APT), 183, 188, 192–94, 197
appreciative inquiry, 120
Armenia: Olive Tree Initiative program, 91, 94–95, 98, 103; conflict with Turkey, 85, 217
authenticity, 55, 57–59, 61
Avruch, Kevin, 180–81, 186

banking model: Freire's critique of, 50
best practices, 3, 8, 14, 40, 243–45, 250, 254–55; education abroad and, 231, 235, 237; global service learning and, 224–25; reflective practice and, 204; service learning and, 177–78; short-term international immersion and, 114–17; study abroad and, 216; transformation and, 17
Brazil, 138, 165
B'Tselem, 94

Cambodia, 10, 67
Campus Compact, 121, 237–38
capital conscious, 235, 236
caring credibly, 235
Carnegie Community Engagement classification, 237
Center for Peace, Nonviolence and Human Rights, 205

Center for World Religions, Diplomacy, and Conflict (CRDC), 203, 214
Center for Victims of Violence and Crime, 131, 133–34
Challenges to Peacebuilding (course), 67, 70–72
Charleston Job Corps Center (CJCC), 29, 33, 193–95
checklists, 36
citizen engagement, 120, 122–23
citizenship. *See* global citizenship
civic attitudes, 123
civic engagement, 12, 120–124, 130, 160, 172–74, 234, 237
civil society, 64; global, 236
collaboration: faculty and student, 116, 131; local partners and, 45, 131, 254; skills, 172
Colombia: Afro-Colombian community in, 51–54; field-based experiential learning programs, 9, 45, 47, 138; High Mountain Region, 55–57; Service Learning Intensives and, 5, 22, 29, 183
colonialism, 48
colonization, 39
Colvin, Christopher J., 53
comfort zone: faculty, 242; reflective dialogues and, 244; student, 7, 31, 58, 62, 93, 202, 209, 255; transformative learning and, 2–3, 17, 25–26, 63
commercial voyeurism, 116
commodification, 51, 54, 59, 61, 63
Community at Odds, 37, 247
community-engaged learning, 228, 240. *See also* service learning
confidentiality, 21, 36

277

Index

conflict analysis and resolution (CAR), 177; knowledge, skills, and abilities and, 159–60; reflective practice and, 180–83, 186–88, 196–97; shadowing and, 21–22; social justice and, 27–28

conflict assessment, 6, 27, 32, 139–40, 144, 245–47

conflict mapping. *See* conflict assessment

Conflict Resolution Quarterly, 40

conflict resolution training, 27, 191, 194. *See also* conflict analysis and resolution (CAR)

conflict zone: challenges in defining, 7

confrontational behaviors, 153

consciousness: transformative learning and, 201–2

continuously connecting, 235, 236

Council on International Educational Exchange (CIEE), 224

critical inquiry, 232, 239. *See also* critical thinking

critical reflection, 60, 83, 92, 201, 232

critical thinking, 15, 85, 144–49, 152–53, 165, 247; leadership and, 101

Croatia, 16, 201, 203, 205, 210, 215

cross-cultural dialogue, 112

cross-cultural encounters, 48

cross-cultural experience, 62; short-term immersions, 104

cross-cultural understanding, 200

cultural differences, 36, 132

culture: audit, 251; context and, 167, 180, 246; cross-cultural dialogue, 112; cross-cultural encounters, 48; cross-cultural understanding, 200; ethics and, 70, 76, 78; global service learning and, 203–31; Job Corps and, 33, 35; Lawrenceville Dialogue Project and, 133; of peace, 202; organizational, 167, 172; understanding and, 117. *See also* cross-cultural experience

Darling, Jonathan, 26

Day of the African Child, 140

Debating 4 Democracy (D4D), 128

debriefings, 8, 13, 77, 148, 150, 244, 250–51, 252–53

deliberative democracy, 12, 124–25, 128–30

development. *See* international development

Dewey, John, 233

dialogue: facilitated, 11, 31–34, 90, 120, 131–35, 180, 182, 246; intergroup, 87–88. *See also* Lawrenceville Dialogue Project

diaspora, 96, 98

discursive dynamics, 189

discursive frames, 44

disequilibrium, 202. *See also* dissonance

disorienting dilemma, 202

displacement, 39, 51

dissonance, 202, 203, 210, 213

distancing, 100

"do good," 23, 28

"doing well to do good," 50

Don Bosco Homes, 28–30

"do no harm": best practices and, 243, 245; field-based courses and, 8, 25–26, 206; Service Learning Intensives and, 23

ecological model of justice and well-being, 154

education abroad, 224, 228, 230–32, 238–39. *See also* service learning; study abroad

Education Abroad Faculty Toolkit, 238–39

empowerment: academic, 45; caring credibly and, 235; neoliberalism and, 50; social change and, 34; student, 97, 100, 161; women's, 122, 150

ethical challenges: field-based learning and, 7–10, 22–24; pre-trip preparation and, 40, 70, 76–77, 80, 243; reflective practice, 181, 184, 193, 197, 204–6; voyeurism and, 249

ethical commitments, 8, 27, 36, 190, 194

ethical dilemmas: best practices and, 243–44; field-based learning and, 7–9, 32, 66–69, 79–80, 183–84, 206; fundraising and, 23, 28; practical ethics and, 71; pre-trip preparation, 36–38, 75–76, 247–48; Service Learning Intensives and, 21–28; social media and, 77; structural violence and, 195; third-party practice and, 21; transparency and, 211

ethical practice, 22–28, 35–39, 243, 247

ethical service learning, 234–36

ethics: applied, 69; best practices and, 243, 250; conflict analysis and resolution and, 180, 196; field-based learning and, 7–10, 41, 108; global service learning and, 16; neoliberalism and, 57; peacebuilding and, 149; practical, 10, 66, 68–72, 76, 79–81, 197; Service Learning Intensives and, 35–37. *See also* "do no harm"; ethical challenges; ethical commitments; ethical dilemmas

Ethiopia, 17, 231–33, 235–36

experiential learning: classroom-based, 1, 4–5, 9, 24, 37–39, 182, 246; definitions of, 4–5, 42; ethics and, 28, 70–72, 206; growth in, 3; immersion courses and, 46–48, 105, 182–83; intractable conflict and, 86, 92, 96–96, 102; Kolb's approach to, 13, 70–71, 187–188;

Index

pedagogy and, 4–6, 142, 151; reflective practice, 197, 217; school selection and, 4. *See also* Experiential Learning Activities
Experiential Learning Activities (ELAs), 5, 22, 24, 37, 206, 246, 253
experts: banking model and, 50; pre-trip preparation and, 67, 91; students as, 49; use of local, 139, 147, 205. *See also* expertise
expertise: liberal peacebuilding and, 149; reflective practice and, 184–85, 187, 192, 194; students and, 32, 43, 47, 53, 182
exploitation, 39, 57

facilitation, 11, 31–34, 90, 120, 131–35, 180, 182, 246
failure: allowing for, 97, 244; reflective practice and, 23, 47, 167, 192, 244
Fair Trade Learning (FTL), 17, 221, 230, 234–37. *See also* global service learning
female genital mutilation (FGM), 64
feminist scholarship, 42–43, 46, 63, 68
field-based education, 2, 4, 15, 40, 182. *See also* field-based learning
field-based learning: assessment of, 14; benefits of, 4; challenges of, 3; collaborative approaches, 9; conflict analysis and resolution, 182–83; critiques of, 12–13; debriefing and, 8, 13, 77, 148, 150, 244, 250–51, 252–53; ethical challenges and, 7–10, 22–24; ethical dilemmas and, 7–9, 32, 66–69, 79–80, 183–84, 206; ethics and, 7–10, 27, 81, 184; evaluation of, 14, 252; experience and, 59; local partners and, 9, 10–11, 13; pedagogy and, 1, 10–14, 59–63, 138; power and, 43, 48; reflective practice and, 188–93, 193–97; rising interest in, 3–7; student perception of, 14; transformation and, 14–17. *See also* best practices; global service learning; preparation; service learning; study abroad; transformative learning
field-based pedagogy, 1, 10–14, 59–63, 138
field-based practice, 28, 35, 243, 244
field-based research, 8, 24–25
financial aid, 109–10, 251. *See also* student loans
financial transparency, 236
focus groups, 126, 182; Experiential Learning Activities and, 5; Job Corps, 194–96
Forum on Education Abroad, 224, 228, 232
four commitments, 235. *See also* Fair Trade Learning (FTL)
frame of reference, 201–3, 210
frames. *See* frame of reference; narrative

Freire, Paolo, 50
funding: for student participation, 109–10
fundraising, 205, 214, 251; ethical dilemmas and, 23, 28

gender, 43, 46–47, 80, 111, 150
Genocide Memorial, 95
George Mason University, 4, 22, 29, 63, 183, 203, 214
global citizenship, 86, 136, 230, 236, 238
globalization, 4, 27
global service learning (GSL), 16–17, 221, 224–30, 232–36, 238–40. *See also* service learning
GlobalSl.org, 238
Good Friday Peace Agreement, 105–6, 111
good intentions, 8, 16; Illich critique of, 222, 227; global service learning and, 235; overpromising as, 28
group dynamics, 170, 176; learning and, 141, 187
guest speakers, 166, 178, 205

"hands-on" activities, 24, 42, 118, 128, 142
Helping, Fixing, Serving framework, 73–74
Help Save Manassas, 189
Helsinki Committee for Human Rights, 205
"high impact": educational practice, 42, 122; learning and teaching, 3
Homeboy Industries, 114
hooks, bell, 44
human rights, 37, 59, 142, 159, 209

identity: narrative and, 90–91; practical ethics and, 70–74, 76–77, 79–80; transformative learning and, 210–12; traps, 8
Illich, Ivan, 221–24, 226–27, 231, 233, 239–40
immersion, short-term, 15, 104–5, 108–9, 114, 116–18, 183
imperialism, 48, 239
India, 10, 67, 73, 79, 103, 229
Indonesia, 9, 45–48, 58, 60, 63, 201
Institute for International Education (IIE), 228
Institute for the International Education of Students (IES Abroad), 224
institutional review board (IRB), 69, 111, 123, 126
intergroup contact theory, 87
international development, 46, 49, 79, 234
international education, 222–24, 234, 238, 240
International Security (course), 104–10
international service learning (ISL), 49, 226, 230, 239. *See also* global service learning
International Studies Quarterly, 40
internships, 12, 172, 175, 182, 228, 247

Index

intervention: academic projects and, 15; classroom-based, 37–38, 247; conflict, 5–7; do no harm and, 8, 23, 25–26; reflective practice and, 16, 28, 182–84, 187–94; third-party, 21; transformative learning and, 204–5, 211–12
introspection, 99
Irish Republican Army (IRA), 112, 116–17
Israel, 16; Bil'in, 2, 94; Defense Forces (IDF), 94; Jerusalem, 2, 94, 204, 208; Olive Tree Initiative and, 11, 85–88, 91, 94, 103; transformative learning and, 16, 201, 203–9, 214–19

Javeriana University, 29
Jerusalem, 2, 94, 204, 208
Journal of Peace Education, 40
journaling, 13, 15, 27, 113, 204, 244

Kolb, David A.: approach to experiential learning, 13, 70–71, 187–88
Kosovo, 210–11, 215
Khulumani, 53

language skills: global service learning and, 226
Larsen, Marianne A., 226, 230, 239–40
Lawrenceville Dialogue Project (LDP), 131–34
leadership: classroom experiential learning and, 39; development, 86, 88–89, 96–102; service learning and, 15, 162, 164, 172
League of Women Voters, 124
"learning bind," 60
learning objectives. *See* learning outcomes
learning outcomes, 72, 105, 120, 228, 239; best practices and, 115–16, 244, 247; defining, 112–14; service learning and, 123, 162, 178
legibility, 57–58
legitimacy, 58, 152, 213
Lewin, Kurt, 187, 188
liberal peacebuilding, 53, 149
Liberia, 13, 138–43, 146–47, 149–54; Monrovia, 29; Service Learning Intensives and, 5, 22–23, 28–32; Tubmanburg, 2; Undergraduate Experiential Learning Project, 28, 37, 183
Linen Hall Library, 112
"lines of force," 60
Linking Theory to Practice project, 5–6
lodging (for participants), 109–10
logistics, 6, 12, 105, 108–9, 118, 192, 231
loop learning, 71, 146, 181. *See also* multilevel learning; reciprocal-engagement model

marginalization, 53–54
Marx, Karl, 42

master narratives, 43, 53, 91
meaning making, 60. *See also* narrative
mediation: community, 133; peer, 24, 134, 140, 247–48; training, 182, 186
Mediators Beyond Borders, 131, 133–34
mentoring, 97, 103
metaphor, 144
Mezirow, Jack, 201–2
Mitchell, Audra, 26
Monrovia, 29
mountaintop mining, 2
multilevel learning, 143, 145–47, 152, 181. *See also* loop learning; reciprocal-engagement model

NAFSA (National Association for Study Abroad), 62, 224
Nansen Dialogue Center, 205
narrative: commodification and, 51–53, 55; dynamics, 61; experience and, 41, 43–45, 59; identity and, 91, 186; master, 43, 53, 91; reflective practice and, 186
National Survey of Student Engagement (NSSE), 122, 228
neoliberalism, 41, 45, 50, 53, 57; peacebuilding and, 53
Nepal, 10, 67
networks: alumni, 102, 214; events, 178; instructors', 52, 108, 139, 206; professional, 104, 166, 172, 229; support, 97
neutrality, 124, 190, 210
nongovernmental organizations (NGOs), 67, 134, 205, 216, 230; management, 15, 159–61, 163, 171–72, 174–76; partnering with, 22, 28–29, 37
nonviolent communication, 192
North Atlantic Treaty Organization (NATO), 210
Northern Ireland, 11–12, 103–7, 109, 111–17, 217

Olive Tree Initiative (OTI), 11, 86, 102–3; dialogue and, 87–90; leadership development, 96–102; narrative approach, 90–96
online learning, 253–54
Organization for Security and Co-operation in Europe (OSCE), 205
overpromising, 24, 28–30

Pakistan, 103; youth, 201, 213
Pakistan-U.S. Alumni Network, 213
Palestine: Olive Tree Initiative and, 11, 85–88, 91, 94, 103; transformative learning and, 16, 201, 203–9, 214–19

Index

Peace and Change, 40
Peace Corps, 222
pedagogy, 40; academic, 141–42; conflict resolution, 37, 181; experiential learning and, 4–6, 42, 141–42; field-based and, 1, 59–63, 138; immersive, 230; improvement of, 10–14; innovative, 1; practical ethics and, 71, 77; pre-trip training and, 250; traditional, 2
peer mediation, 24, 134, 140, 247–48
Pennsylvania. *See* Philadelphia; Pittsburgh
Philadelphia, 160, 163
Philippines, 10, 67
photography, 54, 58. *See also* selfies
Pittsburgh: Center for Victims of Violence and Crime, 133; Refugee Center, 133–34; Somali community in, 1, 131–35
political engagement, 123
power: differences, 87, 94; dynamics, 10, 32–34, 36, 148, 249; relations, 13, 60, 143, 147–49, 230
practical ethics, 10, 65, 69–72, 76, 80, 197
practice. *See* reflective practice
practitioners: ethics and, 8, 21–22, 28, 37, 131; global service learning and, 230, 238; learning from, 21, 130, 140–41; students as, 5, 15, 180–82, 192–93, 255; reflective practice and, 16, 185–86, 188; transformative learning and, 200, 204, 306, 211, 217–18
preparation: ethical challenges and, 9–10, 80; ethical practice, 23–25, 35; need for, 2; pre-trip, 6, 23–24, 36–39; reflective practice and, 187, 190; student, 11, 13, 32, 92, 97, 246, 248
presentations: by local community members, 142, 166, 171, 214; class, 177–78; to local communities, 100–101
Prilleltensky, Isaac, 154
privilege: authenticity and, 58; commodification and, 52–53, 230; entitlement and, 10, 26; ethics and, 57, 70, 75, 79; experience and, 46, 48–49, 62; narrative and, 90–91; student understanding of, 39
problem solving: skills, 162, 167, 168, 172; small-group, 24
Program for Deliberative Democracy, 124, 129
project-based learning, 3, 15, 159–61, 162
PRONI Centre for Social Education, 205

reciprocal-engagement model, 138–39, 141, 143–47, 148, 150–51
reflective practice, 16, 22, 27, 184–88, 243, 247; critical, 60–61; critical thinking and, 144; global service learning and, 230; service learning projects and, 161, 168, 178; transformative learning and, 113, 199, 204–5, 216–19; Undergraduate Experiential Learning Project and, 39
reflexive engagement, 152
Regev, Mark, 88
Remen, Rachel N., 73–74
resettlement: Somali community and, 132–36
resituated embeddedness, 151, 154
Richmond, Oliver P., 149
role plays, 4, 24, 32, 38–39, 182, 246. *See also* Community at Odds
Rosenberg, Marshall, 192
Rwanda, 45

Said, Edward, 239
Schön, Donald A., 60, 184–85, 188
Second Intifada, 94
security: code of conduct and, 36; complexity of, 113, 117; harm to locals and, 8, 25; measures, 207–10, 215; social media, 76; of students, 65–66, 68, 237
self-assessments, 27
selfies, 51, 54–55, 61. *See also* social media
self-reflection, 2, 13, 80, 92
Serbia, 16, 201, 203, 205, 210–12, 215
service learning courses, 3–4, 119–20; concept of, 7, 227–30; conflict analysis and resolution, 182–83, 197; creation of, 133–37; critiques of, 12; domestic, 12–13; Ethiopia as case study of, 231–34; Fair Trade Learning and, 234–37; field-based, 138, 140–41, 152, 244; NGO management and, 15, 160–63, 171–75, 177–78; Political Science and, 120–25, 126–31; reflection and, 167–68; role plays and, 38; skill development and, 15–16. *See also* global service learning; international service learning; preparation; Service Learning Intensives (SLIs)
Service Learning Intensives (SLIs), 5–6, 22–24, 183; Charleston and, 33–35, 193; community partners and, 22–23; ethical practice and, 27–29; Liberia and, 29–32
short-term international immersion, 12, 49, 104, 114–17; International Security and, 104–5; Olive Tree Initiative and, 86, 89, 93
Sierra Leone, 10, 64–65, 67, 69, 78
simulations, 4–5, 92, 111, 246. *See also* role plays
Singer, Peter, 69
Skype, 15, 166, 170
social justice, 15, 28, 59, 172, 229, 244
social media, 76–77, 214. *See also* selfies
social responsibility, 163, 230, 234, 239
solidarity, 48, 52, 60, 234, 236

Index

South Africa, 53
Stowe, Noel J., 186
structural violence, 7, 106, 195
student loans, 46. *See also* financial aid
study abroad: arranging, 109; authenticity and, 55; best practices, 216, 218; experience and, 41–42, 44–45, 50, 59, 62–63, 201–3; journaling and, 98; local narratives and, 53; power and, 47, 49; short-term, 49, 86, 89 (*see also* short-term international immersion); student demand for, 4. *See also* field-based learning; service learning
"submission of self," 60
Syria, 16, 201, 214, 216

"technologies of self," 50
"theories-in-action," 185–86
Tirza, Danny, 94
training: conflict resolution, 15, 159, 174–75, 177, 182, 191–94, 200; ethical, 68, 108, 243; of local community, 11, 27, 29, 33, 120, 140, 142, 148; pre-trip, 13, 36, 72–79, 86, 250; simulations and, 246
transformative education, 70–72, 203. *See also* transformative learning
transformative learning, 2, 14–17; best practices and, 244–45, 255; experience and, 41–42, 59; frame of reference and, 201–3; meaningful interaction and, 107; perspective and, 212; reflective practice and, 113; Service Learning Intensives and, 6–7; transformative education and, 10, 66
transparency, financial, 236
travel arrangements, 109–10

Troubles, The. *See* Northern Ireland
Turkey, 91, 94–95, 98, 103, 201

Undergraduate Experiential Learning Project (UELP), 22–24, 28, 37, 39, 183
United Kingdom, 106
US Department of Education, 5, 22, 183, 252
US Department of Labor, 193
US Department of Justice, 224
US Federal Trade Commission, 224
US Immigration and Customs Enforcement, 189
US Peace Corps, 222

Virginia: Prince William County, 15, 188–91
voice: community, 107, 226, 230, 234–35; inclusion and, 190; marginalization and, 43–44, 53, 61, 74, 78, 191; Other and, 91; social change and, 34
voyeurism, commercial, 116
vulnerability, 9, 24, 34, 53, 60

Warfield, Wallace, 188
West Virginia 1, 15, 194; Service Learning Intensives and, 5, 22, 29, 45, 138, 183, 193–96
Winslade, John, 60
women: empowerment and, 122, 150; experience of, 46–47, 51–55; practical ethics and, 65, 69
Women in Black, 205, 211
Wood, Elizabeth, 25

Youth Initiative for Human Rights, 205, 211
Youth Peace Group Danube, 205

Zemach-Bersin, Talya, 48